THE PENGU
SOUTH AFRICAN WINE

THE PENGUIN BOOK OF SOUTH AFRICAN WINE

Michael Fridjhon

PENGUIN BOOKS

Published by the Penguin Group
27 Wrights Lane, London W8 5TZ, England
Viking Penguin, a division of Penguin Books USA Inc, 375 Hudson
Street, New York, New York 10014, USA
Penguin Books Australia Ltd, Ringwood, Victoria, Australia
Penguin Books Canada Ltd, 2801 John Street, Markham, Ontario, Canada
LR3 1B4
Penguin Books (NZ) Ltd, 182-190 Wairau Road, Auckland, New Zealand
Penguin Books, Amethyst Street, Theta Ext 1, Johannesburg, South Africa

Penguin Books Ltd, Registered Offices: Harmondsworth, Middlesex,
England

First published by Penguin Books 1992

ISBN 0 140 17075 8

Typeset by Unifoto
Printed and bound by Creda Press
Cover photograph by Paul Gordon
Cover design and artwork by Hadaway Illustration & Design

CONTENTS

❧ ৺ ৯

PREFACE

৶ঌ ঌ৶

In the past two decades South Africa has passed through a period of enormous upheaval. These changes have touched every aspect of the fabric of society, not merely the more obvious political institutions which have been the public playing fields of the process. For many South Africans, the isolation imposed by apartheid crumbled long before the end of sanctions.

The vanguard of the Cape wine industry started shedding archaic structures and archaic practices during this period. An increasing number of producers began to measure their performance against international benchmarks and found themselves wanting. They replanted their vineyards and upgraded their cellars; they entered into self-imposed minimum wage arrangements with farm labourers prohibited by law from forming their own trade unions. In the last years of the 1980s, by which stage political reform was inevitable, their investment in the soil and in human resources was ready to pay a dividend.

It is hardly surprising that the past two years have seen the publication of some half a dozen new books on South African wine. Just as the political landscape of the country has changed unrecognisably in the last five years, so has the viticultural territory. The varietals which today carry the hopes of the premium wine industry were virtually unknown names to wine farmers in the early 1970s. No one practised vinification in new oak. White wines were generally fragrantly sweet; red wines thick and clumsy. Five brands occupied about 90 per cent of the quality wine market, and the estate wine concept was in its infancy.

I was a witness to many of these changes and this book records the process. I am indebted to innumerable people in the wine industry, without whose assistance I would not have been able to compile this account. Wine producers in the Cape are extraordinarily open people and they give freely of their time. They are willing to disclose a great deal about their business, about their past, and about their hopes and aspirations. They expose young wines to often fearful criticism because they are determined to obtain the best from their vineyards. I am grateful to them all for the opportunity to taste countless wines, young and old, and to learn from their expertise and their experience.

It is impossible to thank adequately the many people who have found themselves woven into this project. Sue Brown and Clive Torr generously agreed to wade through the manuscript. But for their kindness, there would have been countless mistakes: those that remain are entirely my responsibility. Meg Laver at Stephan Welz & Company was a treasure trove of information on old Constantia. Sue Sneddon addressed the problems raised by my computer illiteracy. Jennifer Hogben checked reams of queries and, together with Wendy Gardner, held the fort at the office while I invested my efforts in trying not to abuse my publisher's deadline too monstrously. At Penguin Books Alison Lowry, Sigi Weiss and Pam Thornley nursed the book through its various stages with a calmness which verged on the celestial. My friends and family tolerated the withdrawal from social life which is the inevitable consequence of writing a book. Lyndsay Dal Bianco bore the worst of this with the greatest of patience.

INTRODUCTION

.♨ ?♨.

In 1988 Sydney Back, proprietor of Backsberg in Paarl and doyen of South Africa's estate wine producers, celebrated fifty years of winemaking. The commemorative dinner reflected nostalgia and wonderment: the former out of respect to a bygone era; the latter because what has replaced it would have seemed so inconceivable even twenty years ago that those who are living through these changes suffer from a sense of future shock.

Back's father bought the Klein Babylonstoren property in 1916. The family grew up on what was really a mixed agricultural holding in the shadow of the Tower of Babel, a peak below the Simonsberg. Sheep and cattle were as much part of farm life as the fruit trees and the vines. Sydney went to the local high school and, still a teenager, took over the annual crush in the farm's cellar. The wines came from varietals like Pontac, Hermitage (Cinsaut), Groendruif (Sémillon) and Fransdruif (Palomino), and most of the production was sweet and fortified.

Initially there was no KWV to fix the minimum price of the wine. In years of plenty prices dropped to around a few pence per gallon (a cent or two per litre). In vintages with low yields it was easier to sell the wine, but prices never seemed to rise in line with the shortage. Bulk sales constituted an important avenue of stock disposal though wines were also bottled, more or less by hand, for the local trade. Years later, when the Backs had moved into general liquor wholesaling, the range was increased to include brandy and gin. Producers in the same line of business traded bulk with

1

each other, each farmer maximising income by buying in as much liquor as he needed to satisfy local demand. The wine business, in other words, represented just another dimension of the liquor trade: if you claimed to operate a wine cellar what you really meant was that the focus of your business was wine but that any form of alcoholic beverage was available through your licence.

The Klein Babylonstoren wine farm continued to be a source of grapes for the winery, and a home for the family. When Sydney Back sold the liquor business in the 1960s he kept the property, deciding to develop an estate winery. At the time this was an almost revolutionary idea. There was only a handful of independent estates selling their wines, in bottle, directly to the public or to the licensed trade. For the rest, the country's wine farms were simply points of supply for the wholesale producing merchants. The decision to turn the farm into an estate antedated but anticipated the promulgation of estate wine legislation. Until 1973 any wine farm could call itself an estate, whether or not all the grapes in its cellar were grown on the property. Wine from several properties could be sold as 'estate wine'. The 1973 Act created the structure for the Cape wine industry of today. Sydney Back was several years ahead of the field when he turned Klein Babylonstoren into Backsberg, the first estate winery in Paarl.

The first vintage under the new dispensation was 1969, Back's thirty-first as a winemaker. A small quantity of Cabernet and Pinotage was released, as well as some Chenin Blanc and Late Harvest. A bottle of Cabernet retailed at the farm for about 60 cents, less than the price paid today by the winery for a single cork. Demand for sweeter wines far outstripped interest in the dry reds. The Pontacs and Muscadels of Back's youth had been replaced with Cabernet and Chenin Blanc. Cape Riesling was regarded as the country's most upmarket white varietal, and Shiraz and Pinotage were the only rivals to Cabernet. As an early player in the estate wine trade, Backsberg was able to develop a strong retail following, though this took several years. Initial customers were from the Cape: per capita natural wine consumption was much higher there than in the inland areas around Johannesburg. Backsberg soon acquired a little niche for itself. After all, there were few sources of table wine outside the national brands: those consumers who sought a little exclusivity could buy these Paarl wines and have them railed to their homes for much the same price as the more widely distributed products. The tasting room on the farm, and the guided tour through the cellar became something of an attraction to out-of-town visitors.

This very direct relationship with the market, and with the changing pattern of consumer tastes, enabled the Backs to anticipate changes before many of their competitors. They were in the industry well ahead of the estates which blossomed in the 1970s; their clientele remained loyal, partly because the Backs were able to move with the times, partly because many of their start-up costs had been amortised so that the wines were always good value for money.

Backsberg had one of the first Cape Chardonnays, fully five years ahead of the bulk of the industry. Wooded Sauvignon Blanc, Champagne method sparkling wines, Cabernet/Merlot blends, new clone planting material, virus-free vineyards – all these state-of-the-art features reached Backsberg ahead of the pack. By the time Sydney Back celebrated his fifty years in the industry, not only was the farm unrecognisably different from the one on which he had started his career half a century earlier, it was still setting new benchmarks for the estate wine trade.

Nor has change kept still. On the wine farming side, vineyards are becoming ever more premium, yields are being cut back, production is being limited and fruit trees replace unprofitable varietals. On the human side of the business,

Backsberg was one of the country's first wine farms to involve itself in the community life of farm labour. This means more than a salubrious living environment, with proper cottages and established gardens: it extends to family life, regional choral competitions, sport and recreation.

These changes, like several others in which the Backs have been in the vanguard of the industry, reflect the way that lies ahead. Many of the country's premium wineries now provide housing which exceeds anything made available by producers to labour elsewhere in the world. Productivity incentives ease the tedium of much of the work. The farms become better places for those who inhabit them, and they become more profitable businesses for those who own them. As with Backsberg, there will be changes in planting programmes which extend to uprooting vines and replacing them with fruit trees: the more efficient a business becomes, the more the sentimental attraction of wine farming will be replaced by a long-term view, with its commensurate strategic planning.

The Cape wine industry has changed unrecognisably in the last fifty years. The developments of the last two decades, and the prospects offered by growing export markets, suggest that the next ten years may be quite revolutionary. This book has been written at the threshold, with a view over the shoulder and a glimpse down the road ahead. It documents the history and records the memories. It does not pretend to be a shopper's guide, though it does give the form. It is about wine and wine people, where they have come from, where they are now, and where they are likely to go. It is an account of achievement and frailty, of optimism and survival, and it tells the present-day story of Cape wine.

THE POLITICAL HISTORY
OF THE
CAPE WINELANDS
♨ ⸾

The Dutch East India Company established a permanent settlement at the Cape in 1652. Over 150 years had elapsed since Bartholomeu Dias rounded the continent, thus opening up the sea route to India. Ships had anchored in Table Bay, and many had been wrecked along the coasts of the Cape of Storms before the inexorable logic of a permanent base at the end of Africa took hold of the Company's directors, the Lords Seventeen. It was for this reason that Jan van Riebeeck was dispatched towards the end of 1651 to set up a market garden and victualling station in the shadow of Table Mountain.

With Dutch settlement came viticulture: Van Riebeeck's initial attempts at establishing vineyards proved unsuccessful, though by 1659 he was able to record his first crush. The early days of Cape winemaking are happily lost in history. Quality is known to have been appalling, but then the first settlers never had a viticultural tradition and cellar hygiene was largely unknown. Stories of wine being shipped abroad in unclean pig- and goatskin bags abound. In addition to the vineyard and cellar problems, the taint of the old containers and the inevitable oxidation which occurred during a long sea voyage all contributed to the formulation of a product which clearly defied description.

The arrival of Simon van der Stel as Governor in 1679 brought to the settlement a personality with sufficient interest

5

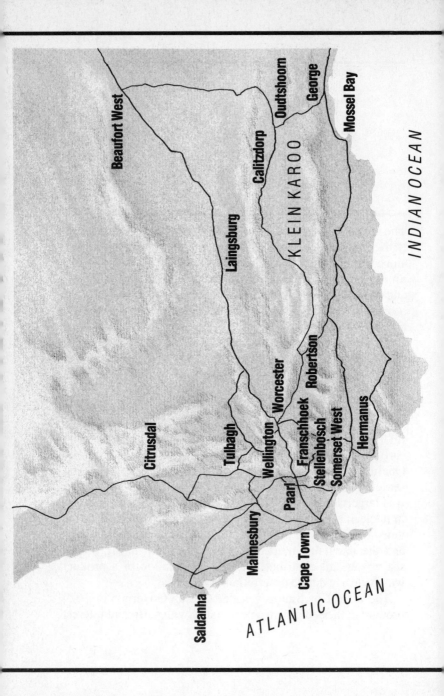

and intelligence to ensure a marked improvement in vineyard and cellar practices. In France, the Revocation of the Edict of Nantes in 1685 brought an end to the religious tolerance accorded to French Huguenots. Suddenly there were innumerable qualified vignerons looking for somewhere to settle. Within a couple of years of the Revocation, hundreds of French Huguenot families came to the Cape. They joined the community of Free Burghers, selling their produce to supplement the Company's victualling requirements.

Their arrival more or less coincided with Van der Stel's grant to himself of several thousand hectares of land in a part of the Peninsula he called Constantia. The combination of luck and good judgement which enabled him to choose as his own property what has come to be regarded as one of the finest blocks of viticultural land in the Cape cannot be overestimated. The farm itself became a model agricultural holding and the quality of his production set a valuable example to the other farmers in the settlement. Company employees and Free Burghers alike profited from the guidelines he laid down as a result of the successful application of more rigorous farming methods. He took instant advantage of Huguenot skills and experience when it came to viticulture and within a few years was producing wine much sought after in the far-flung empire of the Dutch East India Company.

At the same time the settlement at the Cape was expanding. In addition to the French Huguenots, there was also a considerable increase in the Dutch population. These late 17th century arrivals were largely free citizens, compelled to fend for themselves rather than to live off Company salaries. Nevertheless they were obliged to transact most of their business through the Company, particularly in so far as this might relate to the provisioning of ships. To make sufficient land available to the ever-increasing community, Van der Stel opened up the region he called Stellenbosch, some 40 to 50 kilometres away across the Cape Flats. The Huguenots were granted their own valley, a further 20 to 30 kilometres to the north and named, not inappropriately, Franschhoek – meaning literally – the French Corner.

Both regions proved suitable for quality viticulture. While this was not entirely part of the Dutch East India Company's gameplan for the Cape – vegetables and grain were rather higher up the Station Commander's shopping list – the successful coincidence of soil and climate meant that wine farming would always dominate the thinking of the settlers in these communities.

It did not take long for differences between the needs of the Free Burghers and those of the Company to surface. The settlement at the Cape had been established with the sole purpose of victualling ships en route to the Indies. Wine was an integral part of that operation: it helped to improve the drinkability of the ships' water and had some value in medicinal and morale terms. However, the enthusiasm with which the Free Burghers threw themselves into the business of wine farming was in inverse proportion to the quantity of grain and vegetables they delivered for sale to the ships. Van der Stel and his successors importuned, cajoled and finally threatened these free farmers firstly to reduce their involvement in an unnecessary wine trade; secondly, to invest more time and effort in the supply of less romantic and more practical crops which could at least bring the settlement into line with the expectations of the Lords Seventeen.

Over the centuries, little has changed. The Cape still produces more wine than it can possibly consume, whether as wine, brandy, sherry or even neutral alcohol. Struggling wine farmers still elect to try their luck with dubious vineyards, when the same land might more profitably be used for orchards. And the whole business is still overseen by an all-powerful, legally entrenched monopoly, buyers of last resort. The Dutch East India Company no longer exists, however: its role and function in so far as the wine industry is con-

8

cerned has been taken over by the Ko-operatieve Wijnbou-
wers Vereniging – in other words, the KWV.

The KWV has its roots in the endemic problems of the
Cape wine industry. Over-production and under-consump-
tion – the two sides of the same coin – have plagued Cape
wine farmers from the time of Van der Stel. In the 19th century, the political upheavals in Europe had an impact on the
wine trade in Southern Africa on several separate occasions.

Firstly, the Napoleonic Wars brought Britain to the Cape,
initially on a temporary basis but subsequently as the new
master. In time this led to the benefits of Empire – Imperial
Preference and vast markets for low priced, favourably tar-
iffed products, irrespective of their quality. As relations
between France and Britain thawed, however, trade
improved and tariff barriers fell. Suddenly the market for
Cape wine in the United Kingdom collapsed: wine farmers
addicted to easy, undiscriminating sales were unable to
adjust to the new ground rules before firstly oidium and then
phylloxera struck.

These two vineyard diseases decimated the wine production of Western Europe and then the Cape in the second half
of the 19th century. Just as a treatment for oidium was discovered, the second and more deadly phylloxera vastatrix
entered the Continent from America via Britain. Phylloxera
feeds off the roots of the vinifera vine, undermining and
finally destroying its ability to sustain itself. Its spread across
France was as swift as it was frightening: from the mid 1870s
until the late 1880s European vineyards wasted away, income reduced to nothing, debt increased, farmers left the
land, and a crisis of international proportions prevailed. Vineyard material imported from Europe to the Cape brought with
it the same catastrophe of epidemic proportions so that by the
1880s bankruptcies and boundless hardship were widespread.

The French Government offered a substantial prize to
whoever proposed a successful solution to the national prob-

lem. Treatments – which were in several cases more damaging than the malady – were proposed and tested without success. The solution in the end was as obvious as it was elegant: if vineyards in America survived the presence of the endemic phylloxera vastatrix, then American rootstock must be immune to its depredations. The simple expedient of grafting American roots on to European vines brought the vineyards back to life within a few years, though admittedly at a high labour and investment cost.

The recovery of the wine farmers of the Cape followed that of the European producers, but not before estates as famous as Van der Stel's Groot Constantia – for centuries the most renowned of the country's vineyards – had been pushed over the brink of insolvency. The last decades of the 19th century were not easy times in the wine industry in Europe or South Africa. Rebuilding was slow, and whereas the Cape Government had been prepared to take over the Constantia Estate, for the most part lack of capital forced many growers to grub up their devastated vineyards. Marginal areas – usually cooler climate districts and therefore the places more likely to produce delicate wines of great finesse – were the first to go. Regions closest to the major markets survived as new capital came in and replanted, seeking yields that would provide adequate returns.

Inevitably, a glut followed. By the early 20th century overproduction had reached such proportions that wine literally flowed through the streets as tanks were emptied to make way for the next vintage. The wholesale merchants had the growers at their mercy, at times paying as little as a cent or two per litre. The KWV has its origin in successive crises of this kind. By the early 1920s it was a fully fledged producer organisation with legally entrenched powers. Its right to fix (initially distilling wine but later also table or good wine) prices brought a measure of protection to the beleaguered growers. Over time, of course, it insulated them from the reality of the market-place. By the 1970s the KWV, acting for the country's bulk wine producers, fixed annual minimum price increases that exceeded the inflation rate and the market's ability to sustain growth.

A number of important consequences flow from this: wine never achieved the same popularity outside the wine growing areas that it enjoyed in the Western Cape. This situation is as true for South Africa as it is for most countries where wine production is limited to specific geographic regions. In South Africa, the beverage which enjoys the popularity and status of wine outside the wine districts is now beer, though this was not always the case. When distilling wine price increases retained a realistic relationship to the Consumer Price Index, brandy was the drink of choice among an important sector of the population. Over the decades of the 1970s and 1980s beer volumes have increased well ahead of other products. In 1970 beer represented 9 per cent of the total alcoholic beverage market; in 1990 this had risen to 39 per cent. Natural wine, fortified wine, brandy and wine spirits had in the mean time fallen from 33 per cent to 23 per cent.

In the wine drinking areas, the image of the product has always been compromised through cheap bulk wine sales to labourers and blue collar workers. As these people upgraded their quality of life, they put aside not only the cheap wine, but also the taint of wine itself. Beer had always been seen as the more prestigious drink, because it was relatively expensive owing to a higher excise. Wine price increases began to make beer increasingly less expensive to those who had formerly been wine drinkers because of the apparent price advantage. The inroads made by beer in the Western Cape have been largely at the expense of wine.

With the loss of these markets – brandy drinkers to beer for price and health reasons, and wine drinkers to beer for price and image reasons – wine now finds itself less and less able to resist further inflation-related price increases.

11

Economies of scale have been lost at the same time as the brewers obtain further advantage from them. The market has segmented as more boutique producers take their slice from a cake which has not increased in size for years. The major wholesalers are compelled to maintain their infrastructures with fewer profitable products to make up the costs. Even with their considerable domination of the non-beer market, they have not been able to accommodate the changed trading circumstances without loss of margin. Perhaps because of the nature of the ownership of the wine and spirit industry in South Africa today, business efficiency has been lost to structural gameplans.

This is a key factor in understanding how the Cape wine industry works today. When the KWV was formed to represent the interests of the producers in their ongoing battle for margin with the wholesalers, there were thousands of wine farmers and between 50 and 100 wholesalers. So successfully did the KWV maintain the farmers' margins, that it became increasingly difficult for the wholesalers to continue in business. By the 1970s, there were a handful left, and the balance of power between them and the KWV had achieved a reasonable equilibrium. The KWV announced increases in the minimum wine prices, to which the wholesalers voiced their usual objections, and then passed these on to their customers. The wholesalers' cartel was small enough to ensure that the various price-fixing 'codes of conduct' were usually adhered to, and this left the wine and brandy drinkers with little alternative but to drink less, or to change to beer.

In the mid 1970s the beer market was divided between two producers: South African Breweries (SAB) with near enough 90 per cent of the market, and the Rembrandt Group-controlled Intercontinental Breweries (ICB). SAB also owned one of the country's major wine wholesalers, Stellenbosch Farmers Winery (SFW). Dr Anton Rupert's Rembrandt Group owned the other major wine and spirits wholesaler,

Distillers Corporation/Oude Meester. The battle for market share in the beer market had reached carnage proportions, with discounting and dealing focusing the retail industry on beer before any other beverage. The breweries were haemorrhaging but sales were growing as a result of all this activity. In other words, the cosy arrangements in the wine industry may have protected producer and wholesaler margins, but the whole non-beer category suffered as liquor drinkers sought out the most efficient drink and turned to beer.

By 1979 the beer war was costing the Rembrandt Group dearly: SAB was losing margin to maintain its position in the fight, but ICB was running to catastrophic losses. The situation could not continue indefinitely. Towards the end of that year, the late Fred du Plessis, who headed the insurance giant Sanlam, proposed a solution which provided a face-saving way out of the war.

With the consent of government, SAB was offered the opportunity of a total monopoly, with a cost-free takeover of the brewing interests of the Rembrandt Group. In return for this, SAB had to consent to the creation of a wine and spirits company which would incorporate its own wholesaling interests at SFW, as well as those of the Rembrandt Group. This company, which came to be known as Cape Wines and Distillers (CWD), would have three shareholders each holding 30 per cent of the stock, with the remaining 10 per cent available to members of the public. In terms of this arrangement, SAB would acquire 30 per cent of CWD in return for handing over to CWD all its interests in SFW. Rembrandt would get 30 per cent in exchange for its liquor interests. The other 30 per cent block would be held by the KWV, which would have to pay for its equity. The deal was put to bed surprisingly quickly. Few enough people in liquor at the time objected vigorously to the KWV obtaining a meaningful stake in the wholesale sector of an industry over which it already enjoyed prescriptive control. The inevitable conflict of interest of the watchdog of the wine trade enjoying a significant shareholding in a company which would now be handling over 80 per cent of South Africa's wine and spirit sales was all but glossed over in the mad rush to consummate the arrangement.

SAB did not have long to wait before quantifiable reasons for regret would percolate to the surface. Almost as soon as the formation of CWD was announced, Rembrandt and the KWV advised that they would be pooling their shareholdings to create a joint holding company in which they would each have equal shares, and which in turn would therefore be holding 60 per cent (and an absolute voting majority) of all CWD shares. This meant that SAB was condemned to play an emasculated and peripheral role in CWD, having surrendered autonomy of SFW, at that time the country's most successful wine and white spirits wholesaler. No doubt SAB had been aware of this possibility when it undertook to participate in the arrangement. Perhaps the advantage of outright victory in the beer war justified the sell-out. No one, after all, was willing to predict at the time just how long the battle would rage.

From the end of 1979, therefore, the South African wine and spirits industry was effectively controlled by the joint holding company of the KWV and the Rembrandt Group. Its trading arm enjoyed over 80 per cent of the wholesale wine and spirits turnover of the country. It also owned the largest retail chain. The Rembrandt Group separately held 49 per cent of CWD's most effective competitor, Gilbeys Distillers and Vintners (with the remaining 51 per cent held abroad). The KWV's right to determine minimum pricing as well as all its other statutory authorities remained intact. It is difficult to imagine a more entrenched cartel in a so-called free market economy.

Of course, implicit conflicts abounded: how would the KWV fix the annual price increases now that it was not only

14

the farmers' cooperative, but also a co-controlling share-holder of the near monopolistic customer? How could the organisation ensure fair play if an aggrieved party just happened to be one of the few remaining independent wholesalers? How would the KWV's members on the Wine and Spirit Board treat submissions for wine certification if the goods emanated from CWD? How would the KWV exercise its right to examine all producers' invoices (to ensure that minimum pricing regulations were being applied) now that this confidential information could be of enormous value to the trading company in which it shared joint control? The list is endless and the permutations boundless.

Given the opportunities for abuse, it is fair to say that the KWV often walked the tightrope with an unusual amount of equitability. True, there was a disproportionate number of Superior seals awarded to wines produced in cellars controlled by CWD. Some argue that this had nothing to do with the composition of the Wine and Spirit Board with nearly half its members drawn from either the KWV or companies within the CWD stable. They suggest instead that the major producing wholesalers were better able to produce Superior quality wines than independent boutique estates entirely dependent on the premium wine trade for their survival.

Some estates – including one owned by a director of the KWV – alleged that the organisation abused its right to scrutinise export invoices to approach their agents abroad and propose instead the range of wines exported by the KWV. In the midst of all this angry mud-throwing, however, no one pointed out that anyone can find out the name and address of an importer handling a particular brand in a particular country: no abuse of privileged information is required for this. At the heart of this kind of accusation lies the resentment of a statutory body which also enjoys the right to trade in the market it has been charged to oversee.

But the real failure of the KWV to discharge its responsibilities to the industry derives in fact from the cosy minimum pricing arrangements involving the organisation's dual functions of price mediator and major buyer. The easiest way out of this inevitable conflict of interest was for the annual price increases to be acceptable to the farmers and for wholesalers' margins to be fixed at the same time. Farmers' price increases were set at just above, or just below, the Consumer Price Index. Every attempt was made to pass these on to the consumers intact, that is, without the need to absorb them in the wholesalers' margins. The one hand washed the other very elegantly, and the solution worked quite well as long as the economy was buoyant. It would have been an altogether perfect arrangement but for the fact that SAB enjoyed a full beer monopoly. Instead of slipstreaming the rate of annual beer price increases on to wine, Breweries decided to keep beer as competitive as possible and thus to increase market share.

The values of these respective strategies since 1980 are self-evident. The good wine price has been kept just below the increase in the Consumer Price Index and the market for natural wine grew by 40 per cent from 1980 to 1985 and has stagnated since then as the country's economic crisis worsens. Malt beer, on the other hand, has more than doubled in volume in the same decade, and the growth in its consumption has only now started to taper off as the recession of the early 1990s really takes its toll.

It is in this sense that the process begun with the creation of the KWV in 1918 has now reached the limit of its usefulness. The unionisation of wine producers was an inevitable and necessary step in ensuring the survival of the wine industry. As long as supply exceeded demand, and as long as the wholesaling sector was powerful enough to impose its will on the wine farmers, pricing levels remained unacceptably low. This in turn affected the quality of what was produced. The KWV gave the farmers muscle, and created a counterveiling power to pit against the relatively united front presented by the wholesalers. The KWV's power was skewed over time as successive governments appeased the wine farming lobby by entrenching the organisation's statutory authority. This led to the decimation of the wholesale industry. By the 1970s the survivors were able to match the strength and unity presented by the KWV. Uniting the two sectors never increased the efficiency of the system. Doubling the size of a dinosaur does not increase its chances of survival.

The annual wine price increases, insensitively applied especially in the light of how Breweries kept beer price increases well below the rate of inflation, were now an exercise in collaboration between producers and wholesalers. The assumption that the consumer would blithely foot the bill was plainly fallacious. Wine, despite an enormous excise advantage, became an increasingly unattractive and fiscally inefficient beverage. Much of the ground that it has lost to beer has been a direct result of the relationship between the KWV and the wholesalers: a balanced and competitive environment between the two sectors would have done much to ensure that the growth in wine consumption at least kept pace with population increases.

With the ongoing decrease in wine sales, wholesalers attempting to conduct the same business on reducing volumes have felt the attrition on the bottom line. Even among the large national wholesalers business has been so poor that consolidations and retrenchments have become inevitable. There is now only one company of any stature operating outside the ambit of KWV/Rembrandt, and that is Douglas Green Bellingham, and even here it has a 'special relationship' with the KWV inasmuch as it has been dependent in the past on the KWV for its bulk supplies of wine.

Today the major domestic wine wholesalers number four companies: Distillers Corporation/Oude Meester and Stellenbosch Farmers Winery, both controlled by KWV/Rembrandt; Gilbeys Distillers and Vintners, in which Rembrandt has a 49 per cent stake with the remaining shares held by International Distillers and Vintners (IDV); and Douglas Green Bellingham, the recent consolidation of Douglas Green of Paarl (Kersaf Liquor Holdings) with what was formerly Union Wine. Of these, only Douglas Green Bellingham does not operate out of Stellenbosch: Union Wine's cellars were in Wellington near Paarl and Douglas Green was more of a négociant than a producer, so its operations were essentially warehousing and distribution. The other three companies are firmly located in the heart of the winelands, with cellars and production facilities that contribute significantly to the image and wealth of Stellenbosch. The KWV, which owns the greatest expanse of wine cellars in the world, is situated in Paarl. It is technically a wholesaler in its own right, and a significant trader in Cape wines. However, the organisation is constitutionally precluded from selling wine under its own labels in Africa south of the equator.

The four local wholesalers together account for between 90 and 95 per cent of all wine and spirits sales in South Africa. All act as distribution agents for independently managed estates, though by far the major part of their wine business is made up of sales of their own labels. The bulk wines from which these brands are produced are purchased either from growers who deliver grapes to the wholesalers on a more or less annual basis or from the many cooperative wine cellars. In general, the more premium the wine, the more likely it is to have been vinified by the wholesale merchant. The less expensive table wines are usually the result of the careful blending of tankerloads of wine purchased from cooperatives whose entire production is sold either to the wholesale merchants or to the distillers.

In South Africa there are about five thousand grape farmers, the majority of whom are members of these cooperatives. They deliver their grapes to the co-ops at harvest time.

18

Depending on the condition of their grapes, the sophistication of the co-op's accounting system, and the profitability of the crop overall, they are paid for distilling wine or table wine. If their grapes are suitable for the production of quality wines, they may benefit from additional incentives.

Only a hundred or so of the country's five thousand grape growers are actually involved in making wine. Those who have their own cellars fall into two groups – estate wine producers and private producers. The former must farm their grapes and crush them in accordance with very specific regulations governing the production of estate wine. The laws which define the areas of origin and the conditions which apply for estate wine production only came into effect in 1973. Until then, producers were free to make whatever claims they felt might help to sell their wines, including utterly untrue varietal and vintage descriptions and words implying the existence of a farm or an estate.

If a farmer is unable or unwilling to comply with the conditions applicable to estate wine production, he operates as a private producer. This frees him to buy in grapes from vineyards other than his own, and to expand his business so his volume potential is not limited to the size of land on which his cellar is situated. The wholesale merchants are private producers inasmuch as they operate crushing cellars, source grapes from properties other than their own, and expand their sales without the constraints of a single vineyard of origin.

Only one of the wholesale companies is substantially involved in the estate wine business. Distillers Corporation owns a subsidiary called The Bergkelder, which operates in part like a producer cooperative for a group of nineteen estates, several of which it now owns. Some of these estates remain independent, some are half owned by the company. For many of the farmers who have been partners in the scheme, the title deeds have become irrelevant: if The Bergkelder is holding four vintages of your wine, it is not an

19

easy situation from which to extricate yourself. The estates which have entered The Bergkelder partnership have benefited from the immediate access to a national distribution grid. The price they have paid for this has been an increasing loss of independence.

Several of The Bergkelder estates have also invoked the wrath of the Cape Estate Wine Producers' Association because so little of the vinification is done on the estate. By law, all estates must crush their crop in their own cellars, though from that point onwards, the processes of maturation, filtration and bottling can be completed anywhere. With some at least of The Bergkelder estates, compliance with the regulations is limited to the letter of the law alone. Almost as soon as the must has fermented, it is removed from the farm to The Bergkelder to complete its vinification there.

The independent growers have complained that the legal tolerance accorded this operation is inconsistent with the spirit of the wine of origin legislation. They argue that even the issue of non-estate bottling is a dilution of the guarantee of provenance implicit in the concept of a wine estate. As soon as wine is removed from a cellar in which only that estate's grapes may be crushed, there is an increasing risk of cross-blending, confusion or even downright wine fraud. These purists would like to see the estate wine legislation tightened up, forcing farmers to invest in proper cellars and bottling lines. The increased credibility which such rigorous regulations would lend the whole estate wine concept would more than justify the added investment, they believe. Theirs is a moot point. The success of The Bergkelder operation shows that in the mind of the wine-drinking public, the estate wine concept is either ill-defined, or The Bergkelder's arrangements are held to be perfectly satisfactory.

In addition to the wholesale merchants with their branded wines, the estate wine cellars and the private producers, there are a number of cooperatives actively marketing their wines in bottle. The history of the cooperative movement dates back to the early days of the 20th century, and was pretty much a response to the growing economic crisis confronting the farmers.

Although the majority of the co-ops depend entirely on the wholesalers and accordingly sell their wines in bulk, some have cultivated their own wholesale and retail clientele. In part this has been a function of necessity: the wholesale merchants actively discouraged the development of this trade, and threatened to boycott the co-ops if they were to persist in soliciting a parallel trade.

Needless to say, a few of the more adventurous co-ops realised that to yield indefinitely to this kind of pressure would leave them perpetual captives to the system. Those that broke away suddenly had to find a market for the major portion of their production, the part always bought in bulk in the past by the wholesaler. On the other hand, they were able to offer their wines to the licensed trade or even to retail customers at much the same prices that they had been accustomed to receiving from the merchants. In other words, they were able to compete in the market with a considerable price advantage, but now had to deal with hundreds, perhaps thousands, of smaller orders instead of a few big ones.

The tension between these few co-ops and their former customers, the wholesale merchants, has increased over the years. Initially the wholesalers tried to use the threat of withdrawing their purchasing power to stop the rift developing. When this failed, they applied as much political clout as they could muster. The problem posed by the co-ops 'going it alone in the market' was as much a matter of principle as it was of practice. Every litre sold by a co-op to a retailer or private customer is one less sold through the wholesale network; it is also one further step along the path to survival and might inspire the other co-ops to seek independence and control over their marketing destiny. This in turn opens up the very real possibility of the wholesalers losing their traditional role in the market. There would be less reason than ever for the trade to pay them as middlemen, adept at buying bulk at good prices from the primary producers and by astute packaging and blending 'add value' to the product. Taking them out of the equation would save at least some of the cost of this service. In essence the co-ops' policy of self-marketing threatens the future of the merchant wholesalers as far as the table wine business is concerned.

This, then, is the composition of the producer side of the Cape wine industry. Thousands of farmers, around seventy wine cooperatives, about the same number of estates, fewer than half that number of private producers and only four national wine and spirits wholesalers of note. The primary producers therefore number over five thousand, the processors fewer than five. The pure power in the relationship resides with the processors who are more easily unified than the five thousand or so producers against whom they are pitted. In addition the processors enjoy an intimate relationship with the organisation charged with managing the wine industry on behalf of the state.

An overview of the Cape wine industry for the three centuries of its existence shows that while much has changed, a great deal has stayed the same. A Free Burgher from the time of Van der Stel would grasp instantly the nature of the relationship he would have to pursue with the KWV and the wholesale merchants. Carefully managed, his wine farm could produce real wealth. Toeing the line, he would probably avoid impoverishment. But he would always be at the mercy of those through whose hands the bulk of production must pass, an economic serf in a market more medieval than free.

THE MAJOR BRANDS
OF THE
CAPE WINE TRADE

Wine aficionados generally concern themselves with the produce which comes from the rarefied realms of 'boutiques' and estates. Most wine industries around the world depend on the more plebeian trade to survive. In this, South Africa is no exception: in the Cape, as elsewhere, the real literages of the industry are sold as branded wines.

Analysts divide the Cape's production into High-priced (HP), Medium-priced (MP), and Standard-priced (SP) wines. The determination of what fits into each category is based on the selling price of the wine in question. Broadly speaking, most of what is sold with a cork in the bottle is classified as HP wine. The bag-in-the-box wines make up most of the MP sector, and wines sold in returnable bottles and jars account for the SP category.

In Europe this *vin de table* market is largely generic, with different producers selling their wines more for their perceived quality/price relationship than on any added-value attributable to brand. In the Cape, however, the SP market was strongly brand-orientated until quite recently. Even today it is still characterised by the sale of trade mark wines, the bulk of which enjoy their strongest franchise in the Western Cape wine producing region.

Most of the marks which make up this trade are hardly known outside the area, and most of the country's premium wine drinkers have never tasted them. If the names of these millions of litres per year brands are even recognised by the country's wine buffs it does not follow that they speak respectfully of them. Ask in wine circles if anyone has actually tasted Oom Tas, Virginia, Zonnheimer, Paarl Perlé and Lieberstein and the question is more likely to provoke mirth than a positive reply. Many of these self-professed experts might add a further disclaimer in the form of 'I don't generally drink branded wine' as if to assert intense loyalty to the estate wine concept.

Undoubtedly some of these wine amateurs are consistent in their dedication to the boutique wines. If they use the word 'estate' at all, it is meant to describe hand-crafted products, rather than wines whose provenance satisfies the requirements of estate wine certification. In South Africa, the terminology is specifically defined. An estate must actually be registered with the authorities. It may not buy in grapes from any other producer. The wines which acquire estate status must be vinified in the estate's cellars (though not necessarily bottled there) and the label will contain the word 'estate' (or 'landgoed'). The certification seal of the Wine and Spirit Board will confirm this, as well as any other claims as to vintage, varietal and area of origin.

Curiously, South Africa produces a surprising amount of non-estate premium wine, not only from boutique wineries which for one or another reason do not enjoy estate status, but also from the cellars of the wholesale merchants. At least 70 per cent of the HP wine sales are in branded wines, and while this percentage is declining, it still constitutes the heart of South Africa's fine wine business.

With the exception of Nederburg which is in Paarl, and the marks owned and distributed by Douglas Green Bellingham, the domestic HP branded wine trade all comes from the Stellenbosch cellars of the wholesale merchants. Of these, the operation producing the greatest volumes is still Stellenbosch Farmers Winery (SFW). SFW was a subsidiary of

South African Breweries from the 1960s until 1979 when it passed into the control of the syndicate jointly owned by the KWV and the Rembrandt Group. The combination of technologically advanced wine production from the 1950s onwards on the one hand, and the Breweries' understanding of the popular beverage market on the other, gave SFW a remarkable platform from which to launch its wines. While many of these were in the SP wine market – and included products like Lieberstein which was in its time the largest selling branded wine in the world – the expertise also extended to the premium sector. By the time SFW was absorbed into Cape Wines and Distillers in 1979, its list of HP brands revealed an impressive domination of the de luxe wine market.

In its heyday, SFW controlled most of the country's leading marks. Perhaps as corollary, the company has never been much involved with the estate wine business. Only with the introduction of the estate wine legislation in 1973 did SFW make any attempt to own and distribute estate wine, and that was as a boutique exercise, in limited quantities, for sale only through the annual Nederburg Auction.

Together with the many national SP wines which formed the backbone of the company's wine business, SFW's brands were well spread across all sectors of the market. They still include names which have been household words in South African wine for at least a couple of generations: only one brand of note has been developed in the last decade.

Chateau Libertas is in many ways a quintessential SFW brand: created in the 1930s, it has survived the tamperings of several successive marketing departments and still enjoys a reasonable franchise in the mid-price HP market. Despite the implicit claim in the name, there is no château or property from which the grapes derive. The name itself is misleading in terms of current estate legislation for this reason. However, the authorities were pretty much obliged to condone the situation since the rules were only introduced some forty years after the brand entered the market. Except for a brief period in the mid 1970s, the packaging survives the half century virtually unaltered, giving Chateau Libertas an air of permanence, that look of always having been around that finally adds an extra sense of credibility to the product itself.

Over the years the components of this medium-bodied dry red wine have changed: initially a blend dominated by Cinsaut taken off bush vines on unirrigated land (I recall meeting a farmer in Suid-Agter Paarl who showed me the vineyards which he claimed had yielded wine for Chateau Libertas for decades), it has been upgraded over time with increasing quantities of Cabernet. For a time Pinotage was added, though this was limited when it became clear that the other varietals were being overwhelmed by the Pinotage aromas.

The old-style Chateau Libertas wines have shown remarkable longevity. From time to time bottles dating back to the 1940s crop up on auction. SFW still has some wines from these relatively distant (for South Africa) vintages in its cellars and I have been fortunate to taste stocks from ideal storage, as well as from private collections. Most South African red wines would probably have faded away at half the age of some of the bottles I have opened. The 1940 Chateau Libertas is certainly on the way out, though with a graciousness and bearing that does great credit to those who made it. Vintages from the 1950s are still holding their fruit quite well – in many cases a lot better than some of the wines of the 1960s. It is a phenomenon of many of these old-style Cape wines that where the harvest yielded grapes which retained their acidity at optimum ripeness, they have greater staying power and more intensity of flavour than their more scientifically-made modern counterparts.

The 1960s saw a bottle change – from claret to burgundy – and a blend adjustment to a wine of greater accessibility. These wines drank quite well from about five years after the

26

vintage, and while they are often still intact, they do not appear to have gained much complexity from their twenty to thirty years in the bottle. Despite this more 'commercial' style which was in part a response to market demand, as much as to grape availability, Chateau Libertas found itself destined for culling with a marketing shake-up which occurred at SFW in the early 1970s.

The introduction of the wine of origin legislation in 1973 forced a lot of producers to rethink the claims which had often been made – quite casually – on the labels of major brands. In the first years of the new Act wines like Cabernet went into surprisingly short supply once the new regulations demanded that at least 30 per cent of the wine came from the varietal to which the label made claim. In the presence of all this juggling around of limited stocks of Cabernet, and with even less flexibility about vintage disclosure, it made sense to look to wines in the most generic possible framework: if it seemed that wine buyers would just as easily buy a brand without pretensions as to vintage, then it could be commercial suicide to add this constraint to an already stressed problem of grape and wine sourcing. From 1973 to 1976, many of South Africa's best-known wines were in perennially short supply simply because suitable varietals, appropriately certified, turned out to be nearly impossible to find.

Vintage Chateau Libertas became non-vintage Chateau Libertas, with a distinctly different label, different composition and different marketing position. As part of the rebranding exercise it was lumped in a new 'Taskelder' range together with several other products with which it shared nothing in common except the idiosyncrasies of the marketing department. It was not a great success: the traditional Chateau Libertas drinkers despised it, considering it newfangled, tart and evanescent, while its palpable lack of gustatory virtues ensured that it would never really attract new custom.

27

This pointless exercise continued until the late 1970s, when common sense again prevailed and the old-style product, replete in traditional packaging, was relaunched with several other famous SFW brands last seen years before. As part of the hype which accompanied the new old-look Chateau Libertas, SFW invited wine writers to lay down a bottle from the relaunch vintage and keep it for at least five years. The underlying message was clear. Chateau Libertas was back to a blend with reasonable keeping qualities, and the vintages released since then have confirmed this promise.

The most recent vintages combine accessibility with some maturation potential: the wine is a safe drink on a restaurant wine list, and frequently gets included on the South African Airways cabin service for precisely this reason. The current style repays a little cellaring, harmonising and gaining some complexity with bottle maturation. It continues to enjoy a loyal following though its long-term future will depend on its attracting wine drinkers from the new generation.

Its sister wine is called La Gratitude and it, too, dates back to the 1930s. Labelled for packaging identification with Chateau Libertas, La Gratitude is a crisp dry white wine primarily made from Steen (Chenin Blanc) and Cape Riesling, though Chardonnay and Sauvignon Blanc have been added to the blend since 1990. It also vanished in the marketing fiascos of the 1970s and was brought back at much the same time as the red wine. In order to focus attention on yet another dry white blend, SFW invested a fair amount of new wood on the re-release wine. I liked the harmony of wood and fruit, and thought that the new version of La Gratitude (in the old bottle) was a lot better than the wine which had been booted out a decade previously.

Since then the market and the money men have spoken. It seems that the wine was deemed to be 'too woody' and, besides, the cost of barrels could never be recovered in the selling price. What remains is an easy-to-drink white wine of no especial virtue and no real fault, the kind of bottle one might quite easily damn with faint praise. I grant that it won't let you down, though it is just as unlikely to raise you up: once again, a wine for restaurants and aeroplanes.

There is a certain sadness about the fall from grace of La Gratitude. Many people remember it with affection. I know an English Master of Wine who was brought up in Kenya and recalls that La Gratitude was the first wine that he drank. It was shipped to South African servicemen during the war and was offered for sale in many of the traditional export markets in the 1950s and 1960s. Time and fashion have moved on, and wine styles must change with the age. La Gratitude has certainly evolved with the many improvements in the South African white wine industry, but it has not kept pace with the expectations of the increasingly sophisticated wine drinkers. In part this has been a marketing problem: it is difficult to sell an old-fashioned product without cultivar claims to consumers who want to read names like Chardonnay and Sauvignon Blanc on the label. But there may have been a bigger niche for La Gratitude than the position it now occupies in the South African branded white wine market.

Tasheimer Goldtröpfchen is another SFW brand which has an air of having been around for a couple of generations. It, too, went through considerable upheaval with the introduction of the Taskelder range in the early 1970s. Packaging was changed and brand loyalists felt thwarted and disappointed. Reintroduced with its old label at much the same time as SFW's other traditional brands, it appears to have suffered from the decline in the semi-sweet HP wine market.

Nevertheless, several of its re-released vintages have been impressive: South Africa's ubiquitous Chenin Blanc grapes provide SFW with a constant source of quality, fruity fragrant juice from which to make this kind of wine. From 1987 the wine has been certified by the Wine and Spirit Board and admits to vintage variation. Sometimes it is spicier or more honeyed than in other years. It certainly profits from bottle age and has enough sugar, and a good enough structure, to improve for at least five years after the vintage.

From the same generation of SFW brands comes Lanzerac, a brand initially associated with quality red wines, though more recently the company's repository for rosé and white wine. The Lanzerac wines from the 1950s were presented in burgundy bottles and included a Cabernet, a dry red, and the first seriously marketed Pinotage in the Cape. The old Lanzeracs were wines of considerable complexity and longevity. Bottles which today pass through the auction rooms can still provide great drinking pleasure: their fullness of colour combines with a 'jamminess' on the palate to give the impression of an old Cape red that somehow acquired the structure to survive long beyond the expectations of those who made it.

In 1959 a Pinotage from the farms supplying SFW was judged South Africa's champion red wine. Bottled under the Lanzerac label, it has confounded critics of the varietal. Not only does it reveal much greater finesse and harmony than is normally associated with Pinotage, but bottles that are still to be found in a few collections show no signs of fading away. I recall slipping a 1959 Lanzerac Pinotage into a tasting of Burgundies ranging from vintages of the 1950s to those of the 1970s. The panel was a pretty professional lot, with reasonable experience of Pinot Noir and some knowledge of the current styles of South African Pinotage. It took some time before anyone was willing to hazard that the wine was not Burgundy, and then only because it showed all the signs of warm climate vinification. It took even longer before anyone was willing to stake a reputation on its being a Cape Pinotage; no one guessed the vintage with anything like even a 50 per cent accuracy. Relics of this order provide the new generation Cape vignerons and the marketing men who hype their wines with an uncomfortable reminder: South Africa produced superb wines in quite primitive conditions when concerns about quality outweighed the attention invested in yields.

From the 1960s Lanzerac found itself in a skittle-shaped bottle, more appropriate to the rosé which became part of the range than for the Cabernet and Pinotage which represented its red wine selection. Some of the wines of the 1960s were still pretty good, though none deserve the prices they fetch now (largely on account of their rarity) at the annual Neder-burg Auction. The Cabernet certainly lost weight as the 1960s advanced, and the Pinotage became softer and more accessible. Most of the samples available today – whether from SFW's cellars or from private collections – are now drying out. Several of the Pinotages look more impressive than the Cabernets and are holding their fruit much better.

The Lanzerac red wines went out with the brand culling which followed the introduction of South Africa's wine of origin legislation. Despite the later redemption of the range as a whole, the red wines have never been brought back. Old stocks have been sold at the Nederburg Auction since 1975, suggesting that some effort is being made to maintain a little cachet for the mark. The skittle-shaped bottle is still around, and continues to package the Lanzerac Rosé and the newly released Lanzerac Chardonnay.

Few of SFW's popular brands survived unscathed the twin upheavals of the wine of origin legislation and a mad market-ing department. Even the ever-popular Tassenberg, the coun-try's best known (and probably best selling) dry red, had its years of trauma. The fate of Tassenberg over this time is proof that the new regulations alone cannot be blamed for what SFW did to its brands in the early 1970s. Tassenberg was the country's first branded red *vin de table*. It was cre-ated in 1936 and probably did more to bring people to red wine drinking than any other product.

It was always cheap and cheerful, the kind of beverage students used to drink, yet good enough for them to stay with

31

it after graduation. The Cape wine farmers often served Tassenberg as their daily table wine, and on more than one occasion I heard old-timers explain that, notwithstanding the screwtop bottle, the wine really improved with a little 'breathing'. One old Tassenberg purist used to empty his daily bottle into a large, shallow kidney bowl to aerate it for half an hour or so before pouring it back into the bottle to serve.

Old-style Tassenberg was predominantly Cinsaut-based, though over time Shiraz and Pinotage have become an integral part of the wine. As with the old-style Chateau Libertas, this Cinsaut came initially from dry land vineyards which gave the wine concentration and longevity beyond normal expectations. From time to time batches of Tassenberg were bottled with a cork closure, ostensibly for directors of the company. Occasional bottles landed up in private hands, adding more dimension to the already mystical status of this popular red.

When the marketing men laid their hands on Tassenberg in the early 1970s they commissioned a label upgrade, and then added the wine to the nearest range of convenience. Because they considered their Taskelder range too upmarket for Tassenberg, they ignored its social mobility and consigned it to their 'popular' (ie downmarket) Kellerprinz brand. Once again, traditionalists were outraged: they did not see their beloved Tassenberg comfortable in the company of products like Amarosa; they distrusted the new packaging, and they were convinced that what was in the bottle was thinner and less substantial than anything they would have been comfortable to serve.

SFW persisted with the marketing programme for about a decade, and then capitulated at much the same time as Chateau Libertas was restored. Tassenberg was relaunched in 'its original packaging' to more or less universal acclaim; cork-sealed bottles were 'leaked' into the market. There is now also a Reserve version, containing some Cabernet and Merlot, with a cork closure as standard.

The fate of Tassenberg in the 1970s was marketing and not legislation related. The wine has never been certified, nor have claims been made about it which would require the seal of the Wine and Spirit Board. There were no pretensions as to origin, vintage or cultivar and therefore no reason why anything needed to change when the wine of origin legislation was introduced in 1973. The marketing moguls misread the market and the status of the brand in downgrading it to the Kellerprinz range. The fact that Tassenberg today is back to its original packaging, and that the brand has, if anything, shown itself susceptible to upgrading (through the premium, cork-closed version) is proof of the status and vitality of the mark.

One of the SFW brands which has continued to flourish, almost entirely unhampered by the incursions of the marketing department, is Grand Mousseux, South Africa's most popular range of sparkling wines. Although recently its domination of the market has been somewhat usurped by Cinzano Spumante, Grand Mousseux remains an institution at toast time on festive occasions. The brand was created at the end of the 1920s and has enjoyed greater sales over a continuous period than any other South African wine packed in a cork-sealed bottle.

In 1935 South Africa entered into an agreement with France by which the French undertook to import Cape rock lobsters (crayfish) in return for which South Africa agreed not to permit the use of the names of French areas of origin. This so-called 'Crayfish Agreement' has been amended several times; it is actively policed by the South African authorities and it has remained intact, with modifications, until the present day. Its existence on the statute books saves South Africans the possible confusion of trying to understand why Mountain Chablis is sweeter than a French wine of the same

33

name. It also prevents wine companies from referring to their bubblies – whether carbonated or méthode champenoise – as Champagne.

Grand Mousseux has been a brand whose targeting – at the popular end of the market – has freed it from the fickleness of the wine snobs. A reliable party product, its two major flavours – Vin Doux, for those with a very sweet tooth, and the Vin Sec, for those with a medium sweet preference – account for most of the mark's sales. In the 1960s the range included a so-called Ruby Cabernet (which was not for the faint of heart), sweet, red and robust, and taken off the market at about the time that red wines became hard to find. Recently, SFW reintroduced a red to the Grand Mousseux brand, a wine called Grand Rouge, for those who prefer the colour purple when it comes to bubbly. All these wines, including the Extra Brut and the Spumanté, are carbonated, as befits their pricing and their pretensions.

Recently, and perhaps because of the growing interest in South Africa in Champagne method sparkling wines, the Grand Mousseux range has taken aboard the Grande Cuvée, made from Pinot Noir and Chardonnay and matured on the lees for at least two years. Obviously the purpose of this wine is to enhance the image of the brand as a whole, and perhaps also to hold on to some Grand Mousseux drinkers who might otherwise wander off in search of something more prestigious. Like the Grand Rouge, the Grande Cuvée can only have limited appeal in the markets in which the bulk of the brand's sales takes place. Both these rather unusual recent additions to the range show that Grand Mousseux does not take its success complacently and in part explain its continued domination of a market for over sixty years.

At the other extreme, the abject failure of the Oude Libertas range to obtain anything more than a toehold in the market in the 1970s shows that there is no easy formula to brand building in the South African wine market. When the wine of origin legislation was clearly on the cards in the early 1970s, producers had no way of telling if consumers would suddenly insist on wines bearing the full seals of the Wine and Spirit Board. Nearly all the established brands could not retain their traditional styles and meet the requirements of the new Act.

Accordingly SFW launched Oude Libertas as a vehicle for wines that would comply with the Board's requirements. Since it was an entirely new concept, there could be none of the problems associated with lack of continuity; if the country's wine drinkers wanted highly certified varietal wines, SFW reasoned that at least it would own a brand that accommodated this market shift.

As things turned out, South Africa's wine drinkers preferred the brands they knew to new regulations they did not understand. They tolerated considerable abuse from producers who could not maintain adequate lines of supply, who changed, relabelled and then reverted to old packaging. In most cases they stuck with what they knew and felt comfortable with, with the familiar, in other words, before committing themselves to a totally new product.

This partly explains the failure of the Oude Libertas range. It was launched with the new regulations, and contained wines whose vintages predated the legislation. It offered only varietal wines, initially Cabernet, Tinta Barocca, Cinsaut and Dry Steen. With the 20/20 vision of hindsight, it is easy to understand why wine drinkers who had never heard of Oude Libertas, and had no knowledge of what Tinta Barocca was or whether they would like it, steered away from the range and stayed with what was familiar. The more adventurous could always visit the wine estates – which were now growing in number – if they wished to experiment with the more esoteric varietals or with less common proprietors' names.

In retrospect, Oude Libertas never had a chance: the reds were at best adequate but unmemorable; the whites were better, easier, and in the case of the Dry Steen, perfectly creditable. A large export of the Oude Libertas wines to the United States towards the end of the 1970s became symptomatic of the brand's problems. Something went wrong with the transaction and a buyer was sought, either in the States, or back in South Africa. The American market did not respond with any enthusiasm to the brand name: 'Oude' was far too close to 'odour' to conjure up any positive attributes. Talk of the parcel's imminent return to South Africa did nothing for the reputation of the range. When the remnants did get back to South Africa, they were too old and too well travelled to be of much interest except perhaps to eschatologists.

This kind of pall seems to have hung over Oude Libertas since its launch. In time SFW yielded to the obvious, culling the range as such and keeping the brand name for special release wines. There have been a couple of good Cabernet vintages put on to the market since this rethink, as well as some exceptional Pinotages.

More of a mixed success has been the Roodendal brand, made mainly in odd years and initially quite competitively priced. It has its followers although little has been invested in the marketing of the wine. It is the low-key equivalent of Graça, the company's greatest wine success in recent years. Launched as a low-budget Portuguese look-alike (though SFW disputes this), Graça arrived replete with Portuguese name and label, no English or Afrikaans anywhere on the package, a slightly *pétillant* wine in a squat Lancers-type bottle.

Pressure from Portuguese producers achieved a reasonable level of disclosure on the label, but not without generating at least the whiff of a suspicion that the wine was targeted at the community of more than half a million people who had settled in South Africa from the former Portuguese colonies. Curiously, however, it appears that Graça was quickly able to achieve an inverted snob appeal among the new generation of yuppie wine drinkers who were emerging as an important buying force by the early 1980s. In due course the advertising focused on this rather ambiguous positioning, showing scenes depicting the aftermath of what was presumably a dinner for a very extended Portuguese family, with the caption 'Graça was the wine'.

Graça's continued growth gives it a unique position among the many brands produced by SFW: it has become the one wine in the HP market where availability rather than rarity remains a selling point. All other brands have chosen to market on shortage, promising 'limited release' or the equivalent catch-phrase as a means of attracting the consumer. Admittedly Graça's positioning at the bottom end of the HP market leaves little alternative. Just the same, a surprising number of producers overwhelmed by oversupply have chosen the rarity route to hook their bait. Perhaps the continued strength of Graça lies in this frankness: the wine is unpretentious so it can hardly disappoint. The marketing come-on is just as direct. Supply is regular, artificial shortage inconceivable, and all this means that you can treat the wine as an easy-going *vin de table* rather than another Chardonnay or Sauvignon Blanc that changes from one vintage to the next, and is never available when you try to buy it.

Nothing about the taste of Graça suggests a Portuguese vinho verde: it is softer, much less acidic, and rounded off with more than a sprinkling of residual sugar. It therefore appeals to quite a wide range of tastes, and complements most warm climate dishes. It is also quite easy to drink on its own. All these factors have combined to give SFW the kind of brand-building encouragement the company needed after the disasters of the 1970s: the Cape's premier branded wine producer has shown with Graça that it is not living entirely off the reputation of its long-established marks.

An equally significant trend is discernible in the recent performance of SFW's most important ranges in the HP wine market. What has been happening with Zonnebloem and Nederburg confirms an oenological renaissance upon which to build a revised marketing statement for both brands.

The Zonnebloem name at SFW dates back to the 1930s and comes from the Zonnebloem farm in Simondium, on the Franschhoek side of Paarl. Originally a source of red wine and red wine grapes, the Zonnebloem property yielded some quite extraordinary wines. Among these was the legendary 1945, a wine to rival the great growths of Bordeaux of the same vintage. I have tasted this wine on several occasions. Even with the occasional imperfect bottle, I have been astonished by its depth and richness, its balance and its structure.

1945 was a particularly impressive vintage at the Simondium farm. Apparently the harvest from the old bush vines was small, though the quality was excellent. Records are scant: the men were still at war, and the crush was said to have been handled by the women. SFW acquired some 2000 gallons of Cabernet – in other words, about 1000 cases – enough, so it was reckoned, for several years.

Doubtless the bulk of the 1945 Zonnebloem was sold before 1950, and most of it must have been drunk by 1955. The few South Africans in those days who cellared their wines for any length of time must have been very satisfied with what they obtained from an investment of a few shillings per bottle. But for the foresight of the winemakers at SFW – who laid down sufficient stocks for the occasional bottle to be opened into the 1990s – no one would have been any the wiser about this gem.

Nor was the 1945 a one-off masterpiece: the 1953 is almost as impressive, so are several vintages from the second half of the 1950s. It was only in the 1960s that the Zonnebloem Cabernet seems to have lost some of that berry intensity. The 1970s saw a substantial shift in style: by 1976 a new lighter vinification prevailed: soft, and far too easily accessible, the modern Zonnebloems made no enemies and precious few friends.

This shift in style coincided with several important changes in the wine market. Estate wines were beginning to acquire their own following. In doing so they threatened the very target market upon which brands like Zonnebloem had built their franchise. The marketing rationale to leave the premium wine business to the estates and to their yuppie clientele had, as its corollary, the decision to cultivate a broader customer base which was less specialised and perhaps less demanding.

While it is difficult to fault the financial logic which underlies this strategy, it is hard to imagine anything which could have done more long-term damage to the brand. The estates were already eroding Zonnebloem's long-established cachet: by turning out easy, undemanding wines SFW was itself consigning the brand to the bourse of the table wine market. There it competed against good quality products which sold for much less than this relatively high-priced brand. SFW was by this stage milking the value in the mark and was hardly likely to price it at the level of its competitors in quality. By the mid 1980s Zonnebloem seemed like a spent force, the kind of wine which would survive on ever-decreasing sales in the market-place until one day the trade would de-list it and and signal its death.

What changed all this was a viticultural and oenological decision to upgrade the wine ahead of its image. Suddenly there appears to have been a critical insight at SFW that quality speaks long after the marketing message has been silenced. Those farmers contracted to deliver grapes to SFW for Zonnebloem were encouraged to renovate their vineyards. New planting material was made available to them, as well as the equipment needed for the deep ploughing and other soil preparation. Grapes which came from the older, better established (however old-fashioned) vineyards were carefully selected. Finally the winery itself was fitted with

the kind of equipment necessary to compete with those boutiques wealthy enough to equip their cellars with state-of-
the-art presses, tanks and barrels.

In the last vintages of the 1980s Zonnebloem has experienced a renaissance. Some of the replanted vineyards are
now coming into production. The general concern with the
quality of the grape material has enhanced the rigour of the
selection process. Vinification techniques have improved,
and the new wood cellar has made its own contribution.
White wines have been the first to reveal the benefits of the
brand rethink. At worst they used to be bland and industrial;
now they have intensities of fruit and flavour that would
serve to inspire many boutique wine producers. The wooded
whites have proved particularly successful. The Grand Soleil
blend of Sauvignon Blanc, Chenin Blanc and Chardonnay
combines structure and elegance with just enough fatness
from the wood to add dimension. The Chardonnay, from the
release of the 1989 vintage onwards, has the same virtues as
the Grand Soleil and the kind of drinkability that makes it
one of the best restaurant Chardonnays produced in the Cape.

It is still too soon to anticipate how the new red wines will
turn out. It is impossible to hope for Cabernets like the
legendary 1945s. That style of winemaking would be as
anachronistic in South Africa as it would be in Burgundy or
Bordeaux. Bush vines giving such low yields are nowadays
considered too much of a liability to be retained indefinitely.
Most of the Cape's quality Cabernet plantings reflect more
modern technologies.

Alongside the Zonnebloem brand at SFW is its sister and
competitor wine, Nederburg. The Paarl winery came into the
company in the 1960s through the acquisition of Monis;
however it was already recognised as the pre-eminent source
of quality wine in that era. Nederburg was a regular winner
of many of the trophies at the annual national wineshow. Its
domination of the competition from the early 1960s onwards

led to an annual removal of the goal posts – as the organisers tried to structure the show categories to 'give someone else a chance'. Cellarmaster for 30 years – until his retirement in 1989 – Günther Brözel, has also collected an enviable list of international awards, including the Robert Mondavi Trophy for the best winemaker in the world, judged by the International Wine and Spirit Competition in London.

Nederburg's oenological and commercial success is a function of its own strongly formulated sense of self-destiny, the material means to implement this, priority in SFW when it comes to sourcing grapes, and a management team who have avoided many of the compromises that come from coasting on success.

For many South Africans who came to wine in the late 1960s and early 1970s, Nederburg's red wines were the quintessential measure of good drinking. Fashions have moved on, and the estates and boutiques now enjoy a disproportionate share of the consumer's mind. The idea of a branded wine rivalling the handmade creations of the small wineries now seems incredible. Nevertheless, on pure performance, Nederburg's reds, especially the auction selections, rank with the best produced in South Africa.

It is difficult to characterise an operation which sells over 500 000 cases of highly branded wine annually, in a total HP market of just over 3 million cases. A vast percentage of what is traded under the Nederburg label is no more than good quality table wine: the Paarl Riesling (Cape Riesling in other words, also known as Crouchen Blanc) accounts for a significant amount of this production. It is crisp, dry, undemanding and undemonstrative. Nederburg also moves a fair quantity of Stein – semi-sweet, slightly fragrant white wine, the South African equivalent of Liebfraumilch.

Alongside these standard commercial wines are several very acceptable red wines: the Nederburg Paarl Cabernet is a good commercial red wine, perhaps not as complex or as long-lived as the regular Nederburg Cabernets of the 1970s but certainly a wine which repays four to six years of cellaring. The Nederburg Baronne (mainly Cabernet and Shiraz) is an easy-drinking restaurant wine which, in some vintages, matures remarkably. The Edelrood is predominantly Cabernet, with some Shiraz and Merlot, and enjoys a following among those seeking a bigger, yet still accessible red wine.

Beyond the standard cellar stocks, however, are special release wines and products reserved for sale at the annual Nederburg Auction. In many cases these are wines representative of the best production in the Cape. Included here are the first few vintages from Nederburg's vineyards in Elgin.

The Elgin project has been undertaken with Dr Paul Cluver on whose fruit farm 'De Rust' the joint venture has been developed. The area, about midway between Cape Town and Hermanus and between 50 and 100 kilometres from Paarl by road, has a climate which is ideally suited to premium grape growing. Now that the vines are reaching bearing age there is no doubt that Elgin will give Nederburg a range of white wines with more intense fruit flavours than has been possible from the company's regular sources.

The Elgin grapes are chilled immediately after harvesting and trucked into Paarl in refrigerated vehicles. This time delay between picking and crushing appears to have no adverse effect on wine quality and may, in some cases, contribute to the development of grape flavours in the wine. At this stage both the Rhine Riesling and the Gewürztraminer show great promise, though the full benefits of the project can only be measured after varietals like Sauvignon Blanc, Chardonnay and Pinot Noir can be assessed with the vines at full maturity.

The Nederburg Auction wines are special selections put aside because of their suitability for select cuvées of such small quantities that it is only appropriate to offer these at the annual Paarl sale. The Nederburg Auction has been the major event on the South African wine calendar from within a few years of its inception in 1975. Nearly two thousand licensees, trade guests, journalists and socialite gatecrashers attend the sale, which is held every April at the Johan Graue Centre adjacent to the Nederburg homestead.

Initially the Auction produced bargains aplenty for the licensees as supply exceeded demand and buyers 'ringed' the sale. Wines like Nederburg's luscious Noble Late Harvest Edelkeur were picked up for less than a rand a bottle in 1975. In those days the regular trade stocks of Nederburg Cabernet sold at two to three times that price. These advantages were short-lived, however: within a few years of the first auction the sale had become the major publicity garnering event in the country and bidders vied with each other to overpay in front of the TV cameras. A few isolated records – the highest price paid for a bottle of Cognac, the highest price paid for a bottle of South African red wine, the highest price paid for a case of half bottles – started to give the sale a bad name.

It has taken until now, nearly two decades after the Auction's inception, for the event to achieve something of a balance. Unfortunately in this time the concept of Nederburg Auction wine has tarnished a little, not so much because of the contents of the bottles, but because the life cycle of the brand is passing into the sere. Premium wine consumers have moved on: despite the fact that many of the Auction cuvées exceed easily the quality of the fashionable boutique wines, they are considered less desirable because the Nederburg brand name is now too widespread and too well known.

This is all the more the pity inasmuch as some of the best examples of South African wine are sold under the Nederburg Auction label. The Edelkeur is certainly a favourite contender for top spot in the Noble Late Harvest class. Nederburg Auction Cabernet – like the 1974 – is possibly the most concentrated and complex Cape wine made from this varietal. Some of the Auction red wine blends are also lead-

43

ers in their class. The current vintages of Chardonnay are impressive, and several of the other sweet wines compare in quality and intensity with Edelkeur.

The Sale has prolonged the life of Nederburg as a premium brand, supporting a range of Auction products with which to maintain the de luxe image of a wine that is otherwise too widely distributed to lay claim to any exclusivity. The real test for the company's marketing department – now that the farm has passed its bicentenary – is how to maintain the upmarket momentum. There are no meaningful shortages of product, and Auction prices have been sufficiently brittle that rarity is not likely to be a credible claim. But at the heart of this marketing dilemma lies the measure of what has been achieved over the years: a brand which straddles the wine market from the mid-end of the popular priced category all the way to the very top of the premium trade. There is no other winery which can pretend to such versatility, and no producer in South Africa matching these volumes.

Next to the branded wines of SFW, those of the Distillers Corporation and The Bergkelder deserve attention. There are many parallels. Distillers and SFW are former competitors who are now controlled by common shareholders. Both companies had high volume brands in the era before estates and boutiques stole the limelight of the wine trade. Their response to the changing circumstances is so different that it is now possible to discern a significant shift in the balance of power in the wholesale trade. Distillers' big-selling HP brands have declined alongside those of SFW, though several continue to enjoy a reputation in certain communities. The two which come to mind immediately are Grünberger Stein and Kupferberger Auslese, both semi-sweet, both one-time category leaders.

Grünberger Stein dates back to 1941. Presented in a traditional Franken boksbeutel, it was one of the first South African branded wines to use its own trade mark container as part of its marketing strategy. At its peak, Grünberger Stein accounted for millions of litres – an extraordinary volume to be carried by a single wine (not a range) in what was then the top end of the country's HP wine market. Its fruity, slightly fragrant bouquet, and the sweetish, rather than cloying palate, made it an easy drink, the kind of product which gently brought people into the world of wine.

For years the brand's owners maintained that they enjoyed sole rights to the squat bottle. Occasionally they would bottle a limited quantity of Gewürztraminer in the boksbeutel and sell it at a considerable premium to the regular Grünberger wine. As the market started to swing away from the sweeter style of table wine, Distillers moved with the times, launching a highly creditable Blanc de Blanc in the same Grünberger package.

The bottle is obviously a little inappropriate for a crisp dry white South African wine. However, the decision to milk the value in the Grünberger brand obviously required a matching presentation. Grünberger Stein was well off its sales peaks of the 1970s and early 1980s and there was still value in the mark. By the time of the Blanc de Blanc launch, Stein had become something of an unfashionable name. The upper reaches of the HP market were drinking drier and with smarter monikers. The Blanc de Blanc was able to capitalise on the opportunity. A more recent introduction, the Grünberger Spritziger, *pétillant* and off-dry, adds its sales to that of the Blanc de Blanc and Stein to maintain at least a semblance of the historic volumes of the brand.

Kupferberger Auslese's brand life follows Grünberger's. It, too, benefited from the decline in the fortified wine market in the 1950s. Muscadels and Jerepigos were losing consumers to lower alcohol natural wine. Many of these converts still sought the fullness and sweetness to which they had become accustomed. Kupferberger occupied the right place at the right time: sweetish and well balanced, it offered a taste and style that was immediately accessible to well-to-do people entering the natural wine market for the first time.

Inevitably such consumers move on, though a surprisingly high percentage remained brand loyal, particularly if wine was really a special occasion beverage and not an everyday drink. Kupferberger has held on to its market longest in the inland country districts, but it no longer enjoys its erstwhile following in the major urban areas. Both Kupferberger and Grünberger have become the victims of the swing towards drier wine, and away from German to the French derivatives. In the 1950s and 1960s German wine styles, German wine names and German bottles were the key to success in the Cape wine industry. However, by the late 1980s the focus on France had superseded Geisenheim and Weinsberg.

Happily for Distillers, the company's HP brand selection included several names well suited to this trend: the most obvious vehicle from which to exploit this shift was Fleur du Cap, a long-established brand whose major shortcoming was a lack of definition. Like Nederburg, Fleur du Cap can at least lay claim to a homestead, though unlike Nederburg, there is no winery attached to the property. The house itself, situated near the historic Vergelegen farm originally laid out by Willem Adriaan van der Stel at the turn of the 18th century, is about a hundred years old. Its formal gardens and its distinctive candy stick chimneys give it a wonderful old world feel. The valley of the Lourensford River near Somerset West is redolent with history, and the properties established there during the early days of white settlement rival Constantia for their graciousness and quiet splendour.

Fleur du Cap itself provides Distillers with a rootstock nursery for some of the vineyard planting material supplied to the company's growers throughout the Western Cape: the grapes which go into the Fleur du Cap wines derive from contract growers and Bergkelder estates, mainly in the Stellenbosch region. Much of what is bought in by the company

46

is vinified at The Bergkelder, though fermented juice and even wine itself is purchased to make up the final blends.

The Fleur du Cap brand has never been positioned at the top end of the HP market. Instead it is offered as a good value alternative to the more expensive estate wines, above mid-price in the HP sector but never at a level which would make it inaccessible. With the constant improvement in The Bergkelder's red wine quality in the last decade, Fleur du Cap is now, if anything, underpriced in relation to the independent estates.

As far back the 1970 Vintage Shiraz – one of the finest wines produced from this varietal in the Cape – Fleur du Cap's reds began to enjoy more attention than the whites. A good Cape Riesling and a reasonably complex Emerald Stein may have been important contributors to the brand's volumes, but by the early 1980s it was clear that Fleur du Cap's future was invested in red wine.

This was, in part, a function of significant changes taking place at The Bergkelder itself: in 1978 Distillers employed as their chief cellarmaster/oenologist a Hungarian refugee named Dr Julius Laszlo. Laszlo had arrived in the Cape in 1975. After working at the Oenological and Viticultural Research Institute in Stellenbosch, he contemplated a job at Anglo American's Boschendal Estate before moving on to The Bergkelder. To both Anglo and The Bergkelder he carried the same message: South Africa suffered from a paucity of quality planting material. For both companies he arranged illegal shipments of virus-free vines. Some of these importations became the source and basis of the 1986 Chardonnay scandal.

He recognised that this same absence of clonal choice severely hampered the red wine industry. The standard Cabernet material was also virus-infected and even in the warmest of Cape vintages could not be relied upon to ripen properly. Suitable red wine grapes were also included in these shipments. Laszlo also encouraged the planting of legally imported varietals like Merlot, until then virtually unheard of outside two or three Paarl and Stellenbosch vineyards.

In other words, Julius Laszlo brought to the Cape a sense of French rather than German viticulture. To this he added French cellar techniques, in particular vinification in new French oak. In retrospect, it seems extraordinary that it was only in the late 1970s, and only as a result of Laszlo's arrival in the country, that the Cape wine industry began to earn its place in the hierarchy of the New World wine producing nations. The facts speak for themselves. There had been virtually no Chardonnay produced before that date, and the only Chardonnay vineyards were endemically infected with leaf-roll virus. Cape Cabernets were world class, but lacked the extra dimension that comes from wood vinification. They also needed the softening and rounding off that Merlot contributes to a blend. Only in 1979 did the Cape produce its first Cabernet/Merlot blend.

While several of the country's independent estates had already begun focusing on these issues, it is impossible to overestimate the inspirational role played by Laszlo. Billy Hofmeyr at Welgemeend had produced the country's first Cabernet/Merlot blend. Frans Malan at Simonsig and Lourens Jonker at Weltevrede had both experimented with new French oak. But Laszlo embodied the knowledge and confidence that comes from working regularly with this kind of material and crystallised the efforts of the Cape's avant-garde at a critical time. He was also prepared – for better and for worse – to commit himself, and the company for which he worked, to a course of action which lay outside the law. In so doing he cut red tape capable of delaying his efforts by decades, rather than by seasons. Most importantly he was able to convince the management of The Bergkelder to believe in his vision, and to invest millions of rands in doing the job properly. Suddenly there really were vast maturation cellars in Stellenbosch with space to hold hundreds (and ultimately thousands) of French barrels. Different sources of wood, different levels of toasting the staves, even different sizes of barrel were all exhaustively tested. By the early 1980s The Bergkelder led the country in terms of availability of premium varietals for vinification and access to the right equipment to see fermentation and maturation through to bottle-ready product.

In this process, Fleur du Cap was a logical beneficiary. While The Bergkelder had other brands which were destined to be in the forefront of these developments, it became inevitable that the average quality of the Fleur du Cap reds would improve enormously. Equally important for the credibility of the brand, the company's commitment to quality red wine production was manifestly apparent. It was only reasonable to assume that some of the new clonal material would find its way into the Fleur du Cap bottles, having spent at least some of its maturation period in new or nearly new wood. Laszlo's influence enhanced the Fleur du Cap range at a critical time in the brand's life: just as South Africa began to discover that there was more to wine than was evident in German vinification techniques, Fleur du Cap, with its rather more French sounding name, was ready to take on the mantle.

This was in part a matter of coincidence: The Bergkelder had already decided that its new premium brand, the range to carry the best of what was now emerging from its Stellenbosch cellars, was to be the rather more South African sounding Stellenryck label. Stellenryck had been around for many years, a rather imprecisely branded vehicle and therefore more malleable when it came to an image upgrade.

The few bottles of Stellenryck reds from the 1970s seemed comparable in style to the old Fleur du Caps, though the name was used more for special releases and probably carried slightly more cachet. The 1979 Cabernet was the first Stellenryck wine to bear the obvious signs of Laszlo's influence: it was more concentrated than the industry average for the vintage, and had obviously come from selected material. The 1980 combined new wood vinification with the better quality juice that Laszlo was directing into the cellar and set a benchmark for the brand to which subsequent vintages have maintained an honourable succession. By the mid 1980s the Stellenryck was widely regarded as the best quality branded Cabernet in the Cape. In 1987, in anticipation of Laszlo's impending retirement, The Bergkelder granted him the right to select the best barrels of the vintage for release under a special 'Cellarmaster's Choice' label. On several pre-release showings, as well as the New World wine auction in 1990, it has presented itself as one of the finest red wines to emerge from the Cape in the era inspired by Julius Laszlo.

Clearly The Bergkelder is the Cape's single most important source of premium wine. In addition to its own brands, it markets the full range of wines produced on the various estates contracted to the company. Despite the more recent joint shareholding which ultimately links Distillers/The Bergkelder to SFW/Nederburg, the company has never participated in the annual Nederburg Auction. Rather than run a similar event, it has wisely decided to market its collector wines through an annual tender conducted through the licensed liquor trade.

An innovative feature of The Bergkelder Tender is that buyers are only expected to pay the lowest price at which the full quantity of wine on offer is actually taken up. If, for example, there are 1000 cases of a particular wine on the Tender, and the various bidders whose combined offers total 1000 cases have pitched their highest bid at R500 and their lowest bid at R350, then all the successful bids will be executed at R350. This may seem unduly equitable but it is worth remembering that the various tenderers have no idea what anyone else is doing. Everyone knows that he can bid at a higher price level than he is likely to be called upon to pay because he is only going to be asked to pay the lowest price at which the full complement of the wine is taken up.

The catch in all this is that providing enough bidders think that way, they will all tender to pay more than they ever expect to be called upon to deliver. The full quantity of wine will then be taken up at prices vastly higher than anyone anticipated. This has happened on more than one occasion, as licensees blithely submit their bids ignorant of how everyone else is also tendering at inflated prices.

The annual rare wine tender is distinguished from another special release scheme managed by The Bergkelder's Vinoteque, the annual wine Pre-release. Based on the Bordeaux *en primeur* sales concept, the Pre-release offers wine buyers the opportunity of 'buying forward' in order to anticipate wine price inflation. The Pre-release prices are usually lower than the current vintages available in the trade and the buyer is obliged to hold the stocks in The Bergkelder's Vinoteque until the group's cellarmaster announces that the wine in question can be released. This delay can be as long as three years, during which time the buyer must pay nominal storage costs. After the notified release date, the buyer is welcome to continue storing his wine in the Vinoteque, and he receives regular reports on its state of maturation.

Both these special release operations have the virtue of enabling The Bergkelder to manage allocation of stock, and equalise discrepancies in supply and demand. The Pre-release brings in useful cash for a discount which adds up to nothing more than establishing the present value of a future asset in what has been largely an inflationary economy. Like all such schemes, it depends on the intrinsic value of the investment staying ahead of the rate of inflation, a certainty in South Africa until supply outstrips demand. With availability of premium wines increasing every year as new vineyards come into production, the safe calculations of the 1980s seem fraught with uncertainties.

The sale of Pre-release stocks also enables The Bergkelder to manage better the disposal of the remaining production of each of the wines in question. Some might be put aside for further maturation and final sale through the regular tender of rare wines several years down the line. The remainder is ultimately allocated to the wholesale sales force, once the group's cellarmaster has pronounced it fit for release. In the days of wine shortages the Pre-release and the Tender took up much of The Bergkelder Vinoteque's stock, leaving the wholesale reps with nothing to offer those licensees who had not participated in either of the two special sales arrangements. With quality red wines now in more general supply, the real question is whether these sales provide the purchaser with sufficient incentive to buy forward, or to invest, in what may become a bear market of protracted duration.

Most of The Bergkelder's quality wines are offered for sale on one or both of these sales arrangements. The one HP brand which seems never to have qualified for the Tender or the Pre-release is H.C. Collison. Introduced in the 1980s as a competitively priced vehicle for Cabernet and Sauvignon Blanc, the Collison wines provided excellent value. The brand name derives from a 19th-century Cape wine wholesaler whose business was ultimately absorbed into the Rembrandt liquor group. The Collison name was retained in the UK as the retail point of sale for the group's products, and the Collison Cabernet provided a well-priced flagship product.

The Bergkelder is also responsible for marketing several sparkling wines. Some, like the Here XVII – named after the Lords Seventeen who directed the affairs of the Dutch East India Company – have enjoyed a following since the days before techniques like méthode champenoise were even considered by the Cape's winemakers. The standard Cuvée, known as Souverein, succeeded in obtaining something of a premium positioning at least twenty years ago, partly because its unique trade mark bottle gave it a distinctive edge, partly because it was a lot drier than many of its competitors, but was still accessible enough on the palate to satisfy a wide spectrum of bubbly drinkers at more upmarket functions.

Its pole position as one of the country's top brands has been overtaken with the introduction of méthode champenoise (now known as 'Cap Classique') as the universally accepted vinification technique for the country's premium sparkling wines. In time the standard French champagne method, with second fermentation carried out in the bottle in which the wine is ultimately sold, has become so much the accepted norm that Here XVII now has its own méthode champenoise Grande Cuvée. The Here XVII Grande Cuvée is a much yeastier wine than many of the méthode champenoise sparkling wines which now dominate the top end of the South African bubbly market. This extra leesy bouquet ensures that the brand has a strong following among those who seek a Champagne style and character in their sparkling wine.

It is not the only méthode champenoise sparkling wine produced by Distillers: the J.C. Le Roux range is a fairly recent bubbly brand, though the name dates back about thirty years to the old Château Le Roux. Initially, the brand was resurrected to carry a sparkling Sauvignon Blanc made by tank fermentation. After the initial success of this wine, also in a slightly squat bottle like Here XVII, the J.C. Le Roux range was extended to include South Africa's first Blanc de Pinot Noir méthode champenoise. At the time, in the mid 1980s, there were no champagne style bubblies made entirely from Champagne varietals. Chardonnay was simply not available in sufficient quantity to justify blending it away in a méthode champenoise and Distillers became the first producer to look to the obvious alternative, Pinot Noir.

In retrospect, the solution was obvious. The Cape had planted a fair amount of Pinot Noir from the late 1970s onwards. However, the only material available legally was the Swiss clone known as BK5. Since it was virus-free, and a prolific bearer, it was readily accepted. Its one major short-coming is that only with the most rigorous of vineyard practices does it produce anything like an acceptable table wine. Its high yields are not conducive to concentrating flavour and colour. Extensive pruning helps a little but the clone is simply not destined to produce great red wine.

However, exactly these shortcomings can be turned into virtues when it comes to making a méthode champenoise. The lightness of colour, itself a consequence of the Pinot Noir anthocyanin structure, lends itself easily to drawing out only the white juice from the red grapes. In other words, it is technically easier than ever to produce an absolutely white wine from the BK5 red grapes. This base wine can then be handled in exactly the same way as a Champenoise might vinify his still wine. The J.C. Le Roux sparkling Pinot Noir set a new standard for South African bubblies. Initially a little harsh in its youth, the wine has shown a capacity to age in the bottle, softening out and picking up a slight yeasty nuttiness which evinces more than a passing resemblance to Champagne.

It was of course inevitable that Distillers would then want to emulate its achievement of the first méthode champenoise Pinot Noir by releasing the country's first Champagne method Chardonnay. This followed about two years later and was never really the same success. The wine itself was not extraordinary and the price provided little motive for anyone seeking to make a regular drink of it. The Chardonnay was acquired when the varietal was still in such short supply that almost anything vaguely acceptable could be counted upon to yield a lucrative income for no real investment in time or effort in the cellar. Undoubtedly this meant that the base wine never had the complexity which might have brought it closer to a Chardonnay from the Côte des Blancs near Epernay. Probably also in the haste to get the wine to the market, it never had as much time on the lees as it needed to pick up the the biscuity yeastiness which adds dimension to a good méthode champenoise. Whatever the case, the Chardonnay has never really added cachet to the J.C. Le Roux range.

Despite the apparent inconsistency of marketing méthode champenoise in the same range as the tank-fermented Sauvignon Blanc, the J.C. Le Roux range has grown in strength with the bulk of its brands and most of its volumes coming from the lower end of the price and image spectrum. Most recent extensions include the J.C. Le Roux Le Domaine and the La Chanson. The former is Distillers' answer to the growing Spumante market in South Africa, a fragrant Muscat-style sparkling wine with a very creditable balance and a pleasingly low alcohol content. The latter is a red sparkling wine, part of the general attempt by the wholesale producers to exploit the swing to sparkling wine by filling the gap left years ago when the last of the red bubblies was withdrawn from the market. It still seems to be a niche product, however, and is not really identified with the J.C. Le Roux brand as a whole. Overall, the range rests on the Asti-style Le Domaine for its volumes, the tank-fermented Sauvignon for its mid-market positioning, and on the méthode champenoise Pinot Noir for its image and credibility.

Distillers' increasing involvement in the premium wine business has also led to several high profile products coming on to the market, either to establish a marketing high ground, or to test the limits of the premium sector, or simply to undermine categories developed by the competition. Two brands that come to mind in this context are the Pongrácz méthode champenoise sparkling wine and the almost equally unpronounceable Aan de Wagenweg range.

The Pongrácz bubbly was launched at the end of the

1980s, a blend of Chardonnay and Pinot Noir (as both varietals had become fairly easily obtainable) in a Krug Champagne-type bottle labelled in a way that was strongly reminiscent of the premium French bubbly. The wine was an instant success, both because its intrinsic qualities were indisputable and also because its packaging was enormously striking, given its relatively low selling price. It had the effect of establishing a new centre of gravity to the price level of the méthode champenoise market. The first reaction of consumers was that they could not believe that so prestigious a wine could be sold so cheaply. The obvious quality of the product allayed any suspicions as to corners cut in the winery and the brand has never looked back. What this launch also established was that the future pricing levels of those products seeking to enjoy a reasonable share of the méthode champenoise market would be much lower than they had been in the past. It was now no longer possible to justify excessive prices for bottle-fermented bubblies. If the Pongrácz with its top-of-the-market presentation could sell at so competitive a price level, then very ordinary méthodes champenoises, in very ordinary bottles with quite unimaginative labels, could hardly expect to sell at a premium to so desirable a product.

The effect of the Pongrácz launch has been felt throughout the bubbly market: as méthode champenoise sparkling wines come down in price, or simply fail to take annual price increases, then tank-fermented and carbonated beverages are forced to maintain appropriate pricing differentials. Distillers can afford to pursue this strategy not only because the corporation benefits from economies of scale not available to the average small producer, but also because it is in the interests of a big company to frighten boutique competitors out of the business. There is no doubt that from a wine, as much as from a strategic point of view, Pongrácz has worked admirably. Many of the smaller estates which looked enviously at the growth in the bubbly market and hoped to profit from a small run of expensive product have rethought their position. Those that were already in the business have been forced to meet the new price levels. To the extent that this has affected vital cash resources, they are not able to advertise and promote their brands as they might have wanted to do. Distillers has therefore secured a potentially dominant position in the one sector of the market which has shown steady growth throughout most of the 1980s.

The same strategy or success cannot be attributed at this stage to the Aan de Wagenweg brand launched at much the same time. The Aan de Wagenweg name comes from the small street in which Distillers' Stellenbosch head office is situated. It is the last remaining demarcated stretch of the old Cape wagon road which linked the farming areas with the harbour of the mother city. Bits of evocative but unpronounceable history are attractive in theory, and do enjoy the virtue that if they are learnt and absorbed they will be remembered. The truth thus far is that the name has not (yet) caught on, and the two wines on which the brand was launched have done very little to assist.

The Chardonnay was positioned as the most expensive commercially available wine made from this varietal. When even long-established boutique brands ran shy of the R40 per bottle mark, the Aan de Wagenweg waltzed into the top price spot. There it stuck for some time, until retailer discounting and producer price deals came along to help shift the stock. There was little to the wine to warrant the price level selected by the marketing men. Awkward, clumsy and lacking real depth and complexity, all that it established was that the market was sophisticated enough to be able to tell the difference.

The Blanc Fumé was marginally more successful. Firstly, it was basically a better wine, more capable of positioning itself organoleptically in the front rank of the wood-matured Sauvignon Blanc market; secondly, although it was targeted to retail at about 30 per cent more than other Blanc Fumés, it was still relatively acceptable white wine value at around R20 per bottle.

The Aan de Wagenweg range is Distillers' top end of their white wine market, seemingly set as a counterpoint to the Stellenryck Cabernet. So far it has neither established the same kind of following, nor has it provided, in its intrinsics, a justification for its price, or even for its existence.

Three other Distillers' brands deserve special comment: Drostdyhof, Pascali, and Cellar Cask. The Drostdyhof range has followed the rest of the group's products in their gradual but visible upgrade. As a brand that was largely associated with the SP and MP wine markets, the quality improvement enables several of the wines to compete comfortably in the HP sector.

The first Chardonnay release was greeted in the industry with some ironic amusement. It heralded, so said the pundits, all the imminence of the Chardonnay flood. When there was so much juice about from this supposedly rare and shy-bearing varietal, how could anyone preserve the myth of a premium-priced Chardonnay?

The price positioning of Chardonnay is of course another issue. In markets where Chardonnay has always been a short-supplied and highly desirable rarity, producers and consumers alike have come to assume that prices will be high because of some mysterious property associated with the grape itself. The truth is that floor prices and therefore premium add-ons are determined by supply and demand. As Chardonnay becomes no rarer than any other varietal on the wine buyer's shopping list, the floor price falls. The add-on for premium product may well increase, if the features of the wines perceived as best are considered desirable enough to as many consumers as it takes to create a relative shortage in those particular products. Cheap Chardonnay in France is about as inexpensive as Chardonnay anywhere in the world.

Montrachet, or Corton Charlemagne for that matter, may sell for fifty or one hundred times the price of the cheapest wine, because of the relationship between supply and demand in that particularly rarefied market.

Drostdyhof's entry into the Chardonnay trade did no more to herald the collapse of prices in the top end of the sector than the invention of the internal combustion engine brought an end to thoroughbred horse racing. The outrageous Chardonnay prices of the last years of the 1980s had been easing with the increase in supply, but the best wines still fetched very solid prices, secure in their quality and their relative rarity.

What the Drostdyhof wine did establish was an appropriate benchmark for the table Chardonnay market. A few months of light wooding gave the lemony varietal character that extra dimension of butterscotch and forced all the other volume producers, who thought they could bluff their way past the question of a little wood ageing, the opportunity to rethink the issue. Together with the other quite impressive Drostdyhof wine, the Waveren Vin Noir – a Cabernet/Pinotage blend – the Chardonnay has contributed to the overall upgrade of the image of the range. As the low end of the wine market becomes increasingly like a battlefield, Distillers, it seems, has taken the decision to leave the fight to the co-ops and to the few Cape-based wholesalers whose cost infrastructures make it possible for them to compete for a slice of this ever-declining cake.

Pascali is the group's red wine answer to SFW's white wine success with Graça. Like Graça, the packaging is designed to create the impression of a European wine – in this case, from Italy. A trade mark bottle combines with a label informing the consumer that the wine is 'Prodotto della Republica del Sud Africa', and the Italian feel is potentially misleading. The Bergkelder naturally denies that this is their intention in any way, but is hard pressed to explain why

59

salient information is not included on the label in either English or Afrikaans.

Finally, no note on the Distillers' wines would be complete without a comment on the Cellar Cask range of wines. Introduced at the end of the 1970s in foil-lined 5-litre cardboard boxes, it revolutionised wine drinking habits in South Africa and redefined the parameters of the SP and MP wine markets. At the time of the Cellar Cask launch, South Africans bought wine either in cork-closed bottles, or in screwtop returnable glass. The cork wine drinkers tended to think of their purchases as special occasion drinks – for laying down, or for opening only when there were enough people about to ensure that the bottle would be emptied.

An earlier attempt, by Frans Malan of the Simonsig Estate, to introduce bag-in-the-box wines in the mid 1970s had failed hopelessly. Firstly the concept was probably a little before its time; secondly, the bag liner was made of translucent plastic. The wine suffered from stability problems, particularly as temperature changes encouraged a certain amount of 'bleeding' through the tap and seals. Retailers found that the stock attracted rodents whose depredations led to further leaking, swarms of fruit flies and an almost constant stench of acetic acid.

While this earlier failure had not attracted widespread attention, Distillers' decision to launch the Cellar Cask range, together with the investment in new filling equipment and the costs attendant on a new concept in the market-place, can only be counted as courageous. It was immediately successful, possibly because of the rigorous quality control standards maintained at the time, possibly because better than average wines were selected for the launch, possibly because there were quantifiable money benefits to go with the convenience factor.

As soon as competitors could gear up to enter the market, they did so, except that they used existing brand names which already enjoyed a following in the SP wine market. The battle raged, generating its own commercial activity around the packaging as much as around the wines themselves. By the time the dust had settled a few years later, it was clear that the wine market had not really grown in size despite the popularity of the bag-in-the-box concept. Moreover, the wine industry's profits had been severely compromised: packaging costs had increased, and were all in a non-returnable form. Wine price profits stayed low, as the wholesale merchants were forced to buy at minimum price levels maintained by the KWV. This reduced their margins as they paid more to the farmers or to the packaging suppliers, retaining less of the surplus as the cut-throat trade limited any chance of an upward increase in their net margins.

Analysts at the time showed that the volumes which had been gained in bag-in-the-box sales had been lost to the jar wine trade. These wines were packed in 2-litre or 4,5-litre returnable glass, and were counted statistically in the SP wine market, because the net cost of the wine, after taking account of the deposit on the bottle, met with the defined criteria of the category. Wines sold in non-returnable foil bags were counted in the MP wine market because packaging costs were added to the basic wine price for analysis purposes. Hence it was shown that the MP market had actually grown by the volume that had been lost in the SP market, and that the wine industry had surrendered a measurable percentage of its value to the purveyors of non-returnable foil and cardboard packaging material.

The arithmetic is indisputable, but time has shown that other trends were concealed in the broad statistical information. The SP wine market was declining as the core Western Cape consumers were upgrading their choice of beverage, moving from cheap wine to better wine, and as better wine became less price competitive *vis-à-vis* beer, to malt beer itself. Spirits drinkers were moving away from the higher alcohol drinks, willing to give wine a chance on more than the irregular special occasion. So it was that the SP wines lost volumes within the wine market, and also to the beer industry, while wine gained some consumers from other sectors.

In all this flux, bag-in-the-box may have played a key role: it provided non-wine drinkers with a convenient, easy to manage myth-free way of approaching wine. Contrary to the original claim that it produced no real growth, it may well be that bag-in-the-box saved the wine market from a real loss in volume. The continued use of the packaging, and the ongoing demand for the increasingly inferior wines that all the producers are putting into their foil bags, suggest that convenience is worth more than organoleptic merit. The established brands are under constant pressure from the retailer's discount products and the many labels placed in the market by regional wholesalers. Branding has become secondary to price, and quality hardly appears to be a factor at all. This is the measure of how the wine market has changed in the decade since Distillers revolutionised the trade by introducing the Cellar Cask bag-in-the-box range.

The other Stellenbosch-based national wholesaler with something of a tradition in wine is the firm of Gilbeys. Closely associated with the spirits business since the original UK owners created their South African subsidiary after World War Two, Gilbeys now accounts for a widely diversified wholesale and retail liquor trade. The business is 51 per cent foreign-owned, with International Distillers and Vintners (IDV) holding the stake that was once W & A Gilbeys. The remaining 49 per cent is owned by the Rembrandt organisation and is separately accounted from the group's other liquor interests. No one who has seriously studied the wine industry in South Africa believes that the relationship is as arm's length as the cosmetics would suggest. On the ground the sales forces compete vigorously for share of market. But

at a strategic level the companies avoid mutually disadvanta-
geous courses of action. This may be attributable to all-round
sensible management. But since the same management is not
always so far-sighted in its planning, the possibility of a
dovetailed division of the market should not be discounted.

Gilbeys is a highly respected national wholesaler, strongly
liquor rather than wine based, with a complementary range
of local and imported spirits and liqueurs. Included in its
product portfolio are a couple of wine ranges mainly
obtained by the acquisition in 1972 of the business of the
Bertrams winery.

Bertrams dates back to the turn of the century, when
Robert Fuller Bertram developed a wine and spirits enterprise which operated out of Constantia near Cape Town. In
time the vineyards and winery were moved across to Devon
Valley in Stellenbosch and Bertrams wines and sherries
became something of a force in the South African market. By
the 1970s the winery was a regular trophy winner at the
national wineshow. Under head cellarmaster Dr Arnold
Schikkerling some impressive Cabernet and Shiraz found its
way to the market, as well as a proprietary blended wine,
Bertrams Stellenrood.

Lack of attention to vineyard and cellar developments
from about 1978 to 1983 cost the brand a certain amount of
credibility. The wines were vinified in the old style without
any real complexity and staying power. At the same time
competitors were upgrading vineyards and introducing new
French oak in their cellars. Once the brand's shortcomings
were recognised by Gilbeys' management, steps were taken
to renovate the range. From the 1984 vintage onwards some
new wood found its way into the cellar. A Cabernet/Merlot
blend bearing the name of the founder of the winery was
launched and immediately earned acclaim. It benefited from
the very old Cabernet vines on the Devon Valley farm, a
much more careful selection of the grapes coming into the

cellar, rigour in vinification, and new wood in maturation. Gilbeys simultaneously launched an upgraded Cabernet and a more carefully selected Shiraz, both with new packaging.

The new look was much more in keeping with the premium products now being offered and the limited volumes sold well enough to suggest that the Bertrams relaunch had successfully repositioned the brand. The second year of the Bertrams upgrade was 1985, a difficult enough vintage in the Western Cape for any winery to be satisfied just as long as a drinkable wine had been produced. Bertrams' selection of what went into the bottle from that harvest confirmed the serious long-term intentions of Gilbeys' management to the quality wine market. The 1986 vintage yielded one of the Cape's best Shiraz wines and seems to have consolidated the renovation programme. It is important now to wait for the newly planted vineyards to reach sufficient age for the selected clonal material to show what the future holds for the Bertrams brand.

Gilbeys also produces the Alphen range of wines, mainly from grapes grown between the towns of Stellenbosch and Somerset West. The winery is on Kleine Zalze, a small farm just outside Stellenbosch on the Somerset West road. The Alphen name enjoys a distinguished history: the original Alphen farm was owned by the Cloetes in Constantia and the name is still very much associated with the region through the well-known Alphen Hotel. The Cloetes moved their wine farming operations over to Stellenbosch in the 1960s, curiously following the example set half a century earlier by Robert Fuller Bertram. The Alphen wines at the time were sold under separate brands of Château Alphen and Alphen Special Old Vintage and their sales declined as the wine market in South Africa began to demand more sophistication with the introduction of the wine of origin legislation in 1973.

The Alphen brand was tampered with several times in the

1970s and 1980s before a major repositioning was attempted in about 1990. The range now includes a Cabernet, a Blanc de Noir, a Chardonnay, a Sauvignon Blanc and a Rhine Riesling. In what appears to be the same branding tradition as Pongrácz and Aan de Wagenweg – in which an unpronounceable name is chosen so that, once learnt, it is never forgotten – Alphen has put some of these varietal wines on to the market under proprietary names. The Sauvignon Blanc trades under the name of Le Fevre and the Rhine Riesling as De Gruchy; the latter, incidentally, was the name of the London wine merchant importing Alphen many years ago. While this may evoke nostalgic sentiments among those for whom this is meaningful information, for most wine drinkers it adds an additional element of uncertainty to a brand which so far has yet to justify the learning effort it expects of the wine drinker.

Gilbeys produces a few other branded wines. Cantori, for example, is the company's answer to Graça's success. Available in a Rosso and a Bianco, the most memorable feature of the wine is the quasi-Italian packaging. Gilbeys' 5-litre vat range is sold under the Valley label, a brand developed in the heyday of the jug wine market. The original Valley jugs were a Gilbeys marketing innovation which gave the wine a slight competitive edge. The trade mark jug bottle was rather more of a dark green glass carafe, and added distinction to the wine at a time when the bulk trade did very little about presentation. Now that the name has been hijacked for bag-in-the-box sales, even this distinction has been lost.

Gilbeys' great wine branding success in recent years has been the conquest of the number one spot in the popular sparkling wine market with Cinzano Spumante. The brand came into a bubbly trade that was utterly dominated by SFW's Grand Mousseux range. A combination of sensible pricing, excellent Asti-style fruitiness and good marketing has lifted Cinzano Spumante to top-seller position in its category. On account of its place in the popular trade, this spicy, fragrant, sweetish sparkling wine is never taken seriously by many of the country's wine amateurs. Like the J.C. Le Roux Le Domaine, it is not an everyday drink, but it does have a place at the table as an accompaniment to fruit and cheese.

The relatively small number of wine brands in the Gilbeys portfolio is partly a reflection of the company's concentration on spirits, liqueurs and imported products. Douglas Green Bellingham (DGB), by comparison, has a much smaller local spirits range and a much wider spread of Cape wines.

Douglas Green Bellingham is the result of the recent amalgamation of the two surviving independent national wine and spirits wholesalers. Formed by the shareholders of Douglas Green of Paarl and Union Wine, each of whom has a half interest in the new entity, DGB incorporates all the brands of the two wholesalers. Since both companies enjoyed an active profile in the popular end of the HP market, there is a certain amount of duplication, but also a choice of products with which to segment the sector.

Douglas Green of Paarl was a relative newcomer as a player in the national wine industry. Formed in the early 1940s, it was a regional wholesaler until the 1970s when its then owner, 'Cappy' Sinclair, increased its wine turnovers sourcing his product directly from the KWV. The range of wines that he brought to the market included products like St Augustine, a medium to full-bodied blended wine said to come directly from the KWV's Roodeberg tanks. St Augustine has developed a considerable following over the years. It is something of a typical Cape red from the old days, containing Cabernet, Shiraz, Pinotage and Tinta, in proportions which alter depending on what comes into the KWV's cellars. Part of its marketing success derives from the fact that KWV's Roodeberg may not be sold under that label in South Africa. Many of St Augustine's faithful followers believe

66

that they are getting the legendary Roodeberg under its local label, and accord it almost mystical reverence.

Sinclair's other Douglas Green brands from the 1970s include the light-bodied St Raphael and the equally inconsequential St Vincent. Many of the other brands that he launched at the time have either been culled or have changed unrecognisably. When he sold the business to Rennies – which subsequently became Kersaf Liquor Holdings – the company suddenly had access to marketing departments and a national wholesale distribution grid. Rennies also acquired the firms of Avrons in Cape Town, J.D. Bosman & Company in Johannesburg, and an option to buy an imported liquor business called Superior Imports. With all these deals in place at the end of the 1970s, Douglas Green was poised to increase its market share. New brands were launched, like the fruity, off-dry St Morand which became something of a favourite in the supermarket trade.

In the 1980s Douglas Green concentrated its bulk wine buying through the KWV, putting such volumes through the Paarl cellars that the KWV increased its bottling operations. Products like Douglas Green Cabernet, Pinotage and Shiraz were launched, performing adequately if somewhat unmemorably. They were received by followers of the Douglas Green brand as good value varietal wines. Most, if not all of this stock came from the KWV's export programme and never totalled a significant share of the HP market.

The thrust that was put behind the dry white wines in the range produced more gratifying results. Both the Blanc de Blanc and the Premier Grand Crû acquired a real following, mainly through a promotional programme which linked regular TV advertising with sales through supermarkets. Together with St Morand and a selection of the company's red wines, the popular dry whites achieved widespread distribution.

Several varietal wines travelled in this slipstream: those

who sought a Sauvignon Blanc, a Bukettraube, a Chenin Blanc, a Cape Riesling or even a Kerner could always look down the Douglas Green list. Since the source of most of this wine was the KWV, Douglas Green could offer a fairly wide range without a vast holding of stock. This trade in local wine, combined with an impressive array of imported spirits, liqueurs and Champagne, gave Douglas Green an interesting, limited, and somewhat versatile role in the wine industry.

Nevertheless, the company's position was far from secure. For a start, because it did not own its own winery, it had no control over its long-term destiny. It was dependent for product on the KWV. The national wine cooperative may have regarded Douglas Green as a model customer, but doubtless if export orders increased suddenly, the KWV would have given priority to them. Beyond the normal insecurity of wondering whether or not your supplier will remember you in times of shortage, Douglas Green had other grounds for concern. The KWV was its source of wine, but also a co-controlling shareholder in two of the company's three most important competitors. With the best will in the world, it was difficult to believe that the arm's-length bulk supply relationship with the KWV could continue indefinitely. Something would have to give, and the Douglas Green management was intent on ensuring that the media and branding investment that had been put into the range would not be compromised.

From the early 1980s onwards Kersaf sought to acquire an interest in Jan Pickard's Union Wine Ltd. The company was showing visible signs of stress, but it had assets whose value was never fully realised: distribution depots in many of the lesser country districts, regional brands that earned good income on virtually no investment, its own winery and, most important of all, a brand which dominated the cheaper end of the HP market.

Douglas Green could see the value in Union Wine, but Pickard was an unwilling seller. In the end, financial pressures forced the company on to the market and coal magnate Graham Beck was there ahead of Kersaf to make the acquisition. Beck had no liquor trade expertise. He did, however, hold the key to solving all of the insecurities of Douglas Green. He could as little have run the business he bought, as Douglas Green could have continued to source product from the KWV: the inexorability of this logic made the amalgamation possible, with the Kersaf camp assuming management responsibility and Union Wine contributing vitally needed assets.

Of these, the Wellington winery and the Bellingham brand were unquestionably the two most important features of the union. Douglas Green would no longer be dependent on the KWV as a source of varietal or branded wine; and instead of plugging away with its supermarket brands, the company could now trade with a tarnished, but none the less nationally recognised mark, the Bellingham brand from Franschhoek.

Bellingham has been in the South African wine market since 1949. Former owner Bernard Podlashuk introduced several new wine concepts to the South African public over the years: in doing so, he created an enormously successful brand which in its time was probably the biggest selling wine in the HP market.

Podlashuk launched the Bellingham Rosé, the Premier Grand Crû (a crisp, dry and suitably bland sort of wine) and the Johannisberger, fragrant and Stein-like in its soft accessibility. He was also the first producer to make a name for a Shiraz, and the Bellingham wine was, for many years, the only Shiraz known to the general public.

The Bellingham Premier Grand Crû traded off the fact that it was an undemanding but nevertheless elegant wine, the sort of beverage which would appeal to off-dry white wine drinkers looking to give up sweetness in a quest for greater sophistication. It made a positive marketing statement about being dry, even claiming on the back label that it was safe for

69

diabetics. By the early 1970s, as the country's upmarket tastes were moving in the direction of dry white wines, it established a niche which developed until suddenly the brand occupied a sizeable platform.

In its time the Grand Crû was the only dry white wine among the country's top five HP wine brands. It was also not the only Bellingham wine among these front rankers. Also in one of the top berths was the Bellingham Johannisberger, decked out in its unique trade mark bottle designed to look like a Dutch gable.

Fashions change and Bellingham's legendary status has declined with the growth of the estate wine trade and the swing away from traditional wine brands. Union Wine's marketing policy did little to help: as the financial circumstances at Union Wine deteriorated in the 1980s, sales and marketing men came to rely on the brand as some kind of miracle vehicle through which they would somehow manage to achieve their targets. To do this without an advertising budget commensurate with the communication problem meant that product discounting was destined to become a way of life. This in turn undermined the prestige and credibility of the brand. It was not uncommon to find that several major outlets in a town were selling one of the Bellingham wines below listed cost – a sure sign of a sales target being helped along with some careful, but widespread, discounting.

Union Wine's product range also included the Culemborg brand, a successful but also fearfully discounted bag-in-the-box and jar wine mark. An enthusiastic distribution policy, and a willingness to discount the wine before price reductions became endemic in the box wine market ensured a reasonable sales volume until the end of the 1980s. Quality was more than adequate. However discounting and an absence of resources for branding had taken its toll prior to the Union Wine/Douglas Green amalgamation.

Much is likely to change once the merger is properly bedded down. The former Douglas Green brands may suffer initially if their wine source of the KWV is severed immediately. It is obviously not possible to acquire overnight the depth of stocks and the range of product that came to Douglas Green from the KWV's cellars in Paarl. On the other hand, access to your own winery gives your marketing and product development people greater freedom to refine the range. The former Union Wine brands can only profit from a strong and orderly marketing policy, and from adequate funds to ensure that branding is thorough and not compromised by cash flow crises.

In the mean time, the KWV is unlikely to suffer from the reduction in bulk sales to Douglas Green. In the heart of the sanctions era, the organisation may well have profited from the prices at which it was able to trade varietal wines to a strong domestic buyer. Many of South Africa's major export customers were precluded from maintaining their purchases, though the wines destined for those countries may have been laid down before the final imposition of sanctions.

Now that most of these trade links have been restored, it is probable that the KWV is undersupplied in many of those products which it made available to Douglas Green. The new arrangements at DGB may therefore suit all parties admirably.

The KWV for its part is now fully focused on its export business. The national wine cooperative, and buyer of last resort from all local producers, is also of course the country's major wholesale winery. Most South Africans are not even vaguely aware of the size and dimension of the KWV's operations. The Guinness Book of Records notes that the Paarl cellars of the organisation are the world's largest. They cover an area of 10 hectares and have a capacity of 136 million litres.

The KWV's statutes specifically prohibit the company from trading wines under its own labels in Southern Africa.

Although this issue has been hotly disputed recently inasmuch as it touches on sales of the KWV's Laborie Estate wine (the KWV says that Laborie is merely an estate owned by the organisation and as such is excluded from the prohibition), the regulation certainly applies to the company's brands. There are arrangements made for the KWV's members to buy a quota of wines for their own use and quantities from these sales to members often make their way in a contraband market. Nowadays this is not rigorously policed: turnover is turnover after all, and the parallel trade does a great deal for brand credibility.

The KWV's bottled wine exports constitute a tiny percentage of the crop handled by the organisation. Much of the cooperative's business is taken up in producing and maturing pot-distilled brandy and neutral grape alcohol. It also operates processing plants for grape juice concentrate used by fruit juice industries around the world. The KWV does not necessarily crush the grapes it is required to sell. Regional cooperatives and private cellars deliver wine to Paarl. Some of this wine goes into the KWV blends; some is blended, stabilised and immediately on-sold, sometimes even in bulk tankers, to customers abroad; some is destined for disposal in an industrial still, where high quality neutral spirit finds a market with gin or vodka producers.

The KWV also offers its services to several of its supplier farmers as an export organisation. Some of the wines are labelled bearing the estate and the KWV's branding and are sold in this packaging either to KWV members or to various export markets. Several of the farms concerned manage special plantings for wines in the KWV's ranges; long-established relationships justify the investment in new vineyard development.

It is as a result of these arrangements that the KWV has been in a position to launch its premium wine range, destined only for sale in export markets. The Cathedral Cellars brand is the organisation's upmarket answer to the estate and bou-tique exports that are earning international attention in the post-sanctions era.

This new range takes its name from the vast Paarl cellars of the KWV. The high-vaulted winery building does bear a strong resemblance to a medieval cathedral, and the dark carved oak vats enhance the impression of a place of wor-ship. The labels dressing up the range have a New World feel to them, in strong contrast to the more traditional KWV packaging for the organisation's regular range of wine.

The 1990 Chardonnay on which the Cathedral Cellars brand was launched turned out to be one of the best Cape Chardonnays of the vintage: soft and accessible, but not unstructured or soggy, it has all the virtues of malolactic fer-mentation without losing any structure. The new oak vinifi-cation also gives complexity to the young wine, in part beg-ging the question of where the wine will go with time: does the KWV mean to vinify its Cathedral Cellars Chardonnay in the same way every year, or is the first release the real bene-ficiary of new barrels?

The 1990 Pinotage poses the same kind of question about itself: the presence of new wood on this wine is palpable: will the Pinotage fruit always obtain the benefit of enough young wood to ensure that it will be softened and har-monised? The vines are old enough, so the only variables are vintage and how the wine is treated in the cellar.

The KWV's Cathedral Cellar range is creditable enough. Both the Chardonnay and Pinotage show that the organisa-tion is intent on presenting its new product as a competitor to the high profile private producers. The Cabernet is well bal-anced though a little too lacking in intensity for my taste, and the Sauvignon Blanc, too harsh. All in all, however, the range is a considerable upgrade on the wines that have done export service since before the Second World War.

The best known of the old KWV wines is undoubtedly the

Roodeberg. Marketed originally as two separate red wines (Number one and Number two) the blend was standardised in the 1950s into a single wine, the style of which changed with fashion and the times, but always with the same purpose in mind: to offer the drinker a wine of reasonable distinction, sturdy enough to survive international travel, accessible enough to be enjoyed on arrival, structured enough to sustain and improve through at least a decade's maturation.

Roodeberg has probably generated more confusion in the mind of the wine drinker in South Africa and abroad than any other product. South Africans have never been able to buy Roodeberg directly in liquor outlets. The wine is sold on a quota basis to those farmers who supply the KWV and is ostensibly made available to them only for their own use. The contraband market in Roodeberg is usually quite active, and lends a credibility to the brand which the contents of the bottle belie: there is a vast difference between good table wine and one for which you would easily perjure yourself. At the same time internationally, Roodeberg communicates an altogether misleading picture of South Africa's quality red wine market. The early drinkability, the gentle fruit character of the Pinotage and the Shiraz, the absence of a strong Cabernet presence, all convey an impression about the better end of the Cape wine industry which is now somewhat out of date.

The truth, as always, lies somewhere between the two positions: Roodeberg is a decent enough table wine which lives up to the intentions of those who put it together. It is as far removed from the top end of the Cape red wine market as Côte du Rhône is from Côte Rotie. This is not just a question of geographic distance: no one delivering grapes that go into the Roodeberg blend would aim to harvest under 8 tons per hectare. Drinkability usually precludes limitless maturation prospects, and nothing is done which could jeopardise the brand's speedy voyage from Paarl to open-bottle-status on someone's diningroom table.

At the same time, Roodeberg's virtues have been over-shadowed by the new-style wines coming from Paarl, Constantia, and Stellenbosch. The wine does not pretend to elegance and balance – if anything, its bluntness, and alcohols around the 13 per cent mark, are something of what the brand is about.

The regular KWV Cabernet is a lighter and more evanescent wine, not nearly as full, as flavoursome or as concentrated as the Roodeberg. Typical as it may be of a certain rather out-of-date style of winemaking, it is hardly the kind of drink which will bring buyers flocking from around the world. The same is true of the regular bottling of Shiraz. While the wine does have an unmistakably obvious varietal character, it lacks weight on the mid-palate and is surprisingly short of intensity. It is also interesting to note that some of the estate wines sold under the KWV joint marketing arrangement, like the Vergenoegd Cabernet and Shiraz, are no bigger and no more precise.

A couple of the white wines are more impressive. The regular Chenin Blanc is a fine example of the varietal, and rivals anything produced in France at twice the price. The Rhine/Weisser Riesling is consistently intense: perhaps too 'terpeney' for palates more accustomed to the German wines, it is nevertheless an honourable New World Rhine Riesling. The Noble Late Harvest is a superb botrytis wine: rich, spicy and honeyed without being cloying, it must, at its price, be the best value 'noble rot' wine made anywhere in the world.

Most recently the KWV released a low price Cape Country branded varietal, positioned as competitively as South African costings make possible. Purists have argued that attempting to meet the Eastern Europeans in this kind of business will ultimately discredit the image and credibility of South African wines as a whole. There is a basis to this kind of analysis, though it is theoretical in the presence of a single and overwhelming market fact: low-priced varietal wines are where the centre of gravity of the trade resides. The Cape Country Chenin Blanc and Sauvignon Blanc may lack refinement, but they perform more than adequately in the market for which they are intended. They also set quality and pricing benchmarks for South Africa's other export-orientated operators, like the national export fruit co-op, Unifruco. A newcomer to wine exports, Unifruco, through its wine wing Vinfruco, trades a range of varietal wines under the Oak Village brand, blending the produce of five Stellenbosch co-ops and several private producers to achieve the consistency and style the market is believed to seek. It is far too soon to estimate the kind of market that Vinfruco will ultimately reach. But it is clear that those who criticise the KWV for fighting it out in the lower price brackets have neglected to consider the very real prospect that as long as such prices are possible, South African wineries will have goods to offer this kind of trade. In this context the Cape Country range is creditable enough and answers an established need in the market.

The KWV's branding has always been subordinated to quality/price considerations. In a few markets – such as Canada before sanctions, for example – there was real cachet to some of the marks, but always in the price band in which they sold. Cape Country has been positioned to do business in a price, not a brand, sensitive category; the Cathedral Cellars range has been set to trade in the opposite kind of environment and branding will assume far greater importance.

This is a relatively new field for the KWV as far as unfortified wine is concerned, and it will be interesting to see how the national cooperative goes about its business. The KWV, South Africa's largest and most important wine trader, and the co-controlling shareholder in businesses which account for 80 per cent of the domestic trade and at least that percentage of export business, owns virtually no brands.

As Cape wines attempt to compete internationally in a post-sanctions era, it is worth reflecting on the fact that the only South African wine name likely to be familiar to well-informed wine drinkers around the world is over three hundred years old: the name of Constantia was established in Europe before even that of Champagne; it has been all but forgotten today. The task confronting the brand managers of the Cape wine industry is simple enough to identify: they must reverse their domestic losses of the past two decades, and make up about three centuries on the world markets.

CONSTANTIA

The history of the Cape wine industry does not quite begin with the Constantia region, though within thirty years of Van Riebeeck's first harvest, the district had already acquired something of the reputation it enjoys today. No account of South African wine could really choose another starting point: the happy coincidence which brought to the Dutch colony a Governor who loved wine, and French Huguenots who understood viticulture, also ensured that the country's finest quality wine district was close enough to Van Riebeeck's original settlement for subsequent generations to be able to draw on the achievement for inspiration.

Simon van der Stel arrived to take up his post as Commander of the Cape of Good Hope in 1679, a mere quarter of a century after the three ships of the Dutch East India Company brought their settlers into Table Bay. He was a man of restless energy and in little time instilled some vitality in the rather staid community. Shortly after his arrival he founded the town of Stellenbosch, advancing the boundaries of what had been until then little more than a coastal settlement. He chafed under his responsibilities at the Castle, seeking rather to explore the hinterland. More than anything else, however, he was anxious to improve the colony's agriculture and was willing to do so by example. In 1684 the former Governor of the Company's settlement in Ceylon, Rijklof van Goens, came to the Cape to recuperate after an illness. Van Goens was a senior officer of the Company and proved to be a willing ally in Van der Stel's long-term plans. He

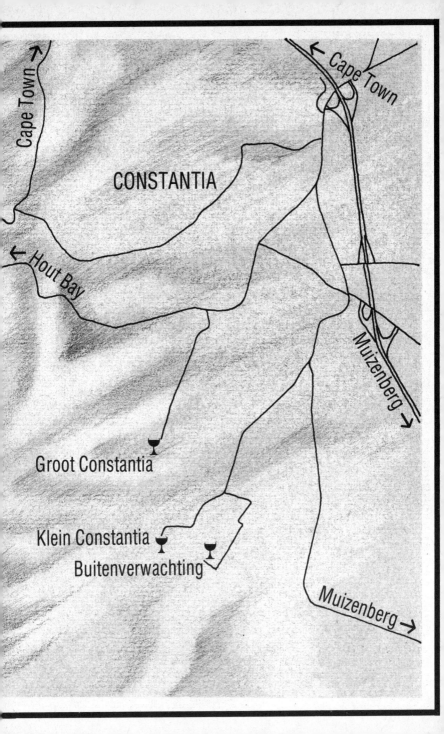

freed the Commander to lead an expedition to Namaqualand and wrote to the Company's directorate, the Here XVII (Lords Seventeen) urging them to accede to Van der Stel's request for a grant of land.

It seems that Van Goens passed a resolution making over to Van der Stel 'heath, vlei, cornland and forest' behind Table Mountain. In 1685 High Commissioner Hendrik Adriaan van Rheede, Lord of Mydrecht, arrived at the Cape empowered to act with authority equal to the Council of Seventeen. Recognising that Van der Stel's skills and aptitude lay more in his practical example than his powers as an administrator, he confirmed Van Goens' resolution, issuing the Commander with a Deed of Grant for the property which lay behind Table Mountain 'at or near the Steenberg, bearing westwards to the said Steenberg, southwards against the land of the free burgher Matthys Michielz, northwards upwards towards the wood named the Hell, and eastwards towards the waste land or Downs; the contents being 891 morgen 300 Roods and 5 feet Rynland measurement'.

This Deed of Grant enjoyed the same force in law as one issued by the Here XVII, an unassailable status which protected Van der Stel's rights. Since other of Van Goens' resolutions were subsequently disallowed by the Council, the Commander's foresight in seeking the High Commissioner's grant cannot be overestimated: his son's unhappy history at Vergelegen in Somerset West also provides proof of the tenuous nature of land ownership under the Lords Seventeen given even slightly irregular circumstances.

Van der Stel named his property Constantia, not after his wife, as was first supposed, nor even necessarily after the Company's ship, but most likely after Van Goens' daughter. He began building the homestead shortly after the Deed of Grant was confirmed and laid out the estate meticulously. Within a short period of time his vineyards were the envy of the colony. His later career in the Company saw him become

Councillor of India. It was only after his retirement that he returned to the Cape as a private citizen, to live and farm at Constantia. By 1705 Valentijn wrote: 'Here alone is found the choice blue grape which produces the lovely red Constantia wine ...'

Van der Stel's empire was considerable. The 891 morgen comprising the original grant covered an area the size of Amsterdam. In addition he acquired several of the adjacent farms, mainly by purchase, and although these reverted to the Company after his death (in 1712), they formed part of a considerable estate during his lifetime. When he died, the property was divided into three portions which became respectively Bergvliet, Klein Constantia (Hoop-op-Constantia) and Groot Constantia. It was on these latter two properties that the worldwide reputation of Constantia wine was founded.

In Van der Stel's time the farm already enjoyed a considerable following for its wines. By and large this was due to the former Commander's disciplined viticulture, which ensured that his wines were better than anything produced in the Cape. However, the real establishment of Constantia as an international producer dates to the period immediately after Van der Stel's death, when the Klein Constantia farm passed – by way of complicated marital arrangements – into the care of Johannes Colijn.

By the 1730s Colijn had developed a considerable export business. To satisfy the demand he needed to increase the literage under production. A partnership arrangement was entered into with the new proprietor of Groot Constantia, Johan Jurgen Wieser. This arrangement continued beyond the deaths of Colijn and Wieser, for the respective heirs were happy to milk the reputation established decades earlier and saw no reason to upset the partnership. Qualities deteriorated, but the wines were still clearly the most desirable of the Cape's crop.

Over a period of time the owners of the vineyards – specifically the Van der Spuys at Groot Constantia – secured from the Company the right to sell a portion of their harvest to the customers of their choice. The increased shipping at the Cape at the time of the Seven Years War no doubt helped to develop this export trade; so did the general tourism: there are innumerable contemporary accounts of visits to Constantia, replete with details of the vineyards and cellars of the two establishments.

In 1776 Groot Constantia passed into the control of Hendrik Cloete. He recognised the extent to which the original name of Constantia had been tarnished by the trade of the 1760s and 1770s and swiftly restored the quality of the wine. It was during the period of his ownership that Groot Constantia's reputation was finally established. The wines made under his stewardship were considered remarkable by his contemporaries. Since enough bottles have survived intact to the present day, it has been possible to ascertain the extent to which this was never a matter of exaggeration.

Cloete fought long and hard to limit the Company's depredations of his precious wine. The Council in Holland had attempted, over a period of many years, to acquire at least one-third of the farm's produce at a fixed price which was much lower than its going commercial value. Cloete had countered this by pointing out that no such claim existed in the farm's title deeds, and that, had he known that the Company might have had an enforceable right, he would never have bought the property.

In 1792 the Company sent out two Commissioners with authority to settle this and other disputes. They immediately acknowledged that the Company enjoyed no entrenched right, and instead requested that Cloete make available to them sufficient stock in Holland to ensure a decent turnout to their sales. All proceeds, less a small handling fee, would be to his account. Cloete appears not to have heard this offer properly. Instead he proposed that he make available to them a fixed quantity of wine at a fixed price, for immediate payment at the Cape.

Commissioner Nederburgh accepted this offer with alacrity and built the ensuing agreement into the title deeds of Groot Constantia. So it was that Cloete threw away an opportunity to use the Company's auctions as a showcase point-of-sale for his world-famous wines. It is interesting to note how accommodating the Commissioners had been in seeking to find an amicable solution for their Constantia requirements. Clearly Cloete's wine was so highly regarded that they could ill afford to be without it. Their wanting to be able to offer it as a marketing and promotional tool for their whole auction programme is a measure of the extent to which the sweet wine of Constantia was a major brand in Europe at the time.

The Cloete era at Constantia consolidated the reputation of the dessert wines produced on what had been Van der Stel's farming empire. Almost all of what was produced landed up in the export markets, partly because demand so far exceeded supply that the captains of passing ships vied with each other in making their purchases, partly because the Company's quota was auctioned abroad. The prices fetched on such sales were well above the going rate for the top Bordeaux estates, and the farm's customer list read like an international Who's Who.

Besides buyers like Frederick the Great of Prussia and Napoleon, there was also the Duke of Northumberland whose investment in two specific vintages, the 1791 and the 1809, was so substantial that we are able today to speak with considerable knowledge about the quality of the wines themselves.

In the late 1970s Sotheby's London offered for sale several bottles of Constantia wine from the cellars of the Duke of Northumberland. The parcel had come from two bins, each

83

marked with the vintage. However, at some stage the two bin lots had been consolidated so that it was impossible to separate out the 1791 from the 1809 with any certainty.

Needless to say, the sale attracted considerable interest in South Africa and a number of bottles found their way back to the southern hemisphere. Several landed up with the KWV and the Oenological and Viticultural Research Institute at Nietvoorbij near Stellenbosch. One was analysed. There has been some dispute as to whether or not the wine could have been fortified. Professor Orffer, who was head of the Department of Viticulture at Stellenbosch University at the time, maintains that all his research reveals that the old Constantia was a natural sweet wine. Professor Diko van Zyl was equally certain on this point: 'Constantia wine varieties consisted of red and white Muscadel, red Pontac, white Frontignac and Steen, they were all natural sweet wines, which means they were not fortified.'

However, the sample analysed after the Northumberland purchase showed an alcohol level at around 15 per cent by volume, too high to have been achieved with natural yeasts, especially allowing for evaporation in shipping and even after bottling. It may well be that the Cloetes made their wine without fortification, but that their buyers – many of whom were responsible for bottling – added some alcohol to strengthen it for the sea voyage and perhaps even to stretch the stock a little.

I have tasted the Northumberland wine on several occasions. Even allowing for the sense of drama which inevitably accompanies such occasions, the wine has always been remarkable. I opened the first bottle within a year of its arrival from the United Kingdom; the hand-blown half pint bottle had a dark and mysterious charm all of its own. Most of the cork was like old cheese, and had to be removed painstakingly from the bottle. The last disc of cork – the part which was actually in contact with the wine – was perfectly intact and I was able to lift it in such a way that no cork fragments fell into the bottle. The wine itself was honeyed and sweet, with the slightly smoky, nutty medicinal character of an old Bual Madeira. It was extraordinarily fresh, and kept its fruit not only for the duration of the tasting. Curiously, it retained its vinous character overnight in the glass and was still lingering there the next morning.

On a subsequent occasion I opened a bottle so badly ullaged – not so much low shoulder as mid waist – that I assumed that the wine would be completely gone. The cork was kept in place with the wax seal – as soon as this was dislodged from the rim, the cork slipped out intact, shrunk like a mummy from years of standing upright and nowhere in contact with the inside neck of the bottle. The wine was quite astonishing: not only was it clearly still alive, it was surprisingly vital and intense, more obviously like an old Madeira but not overwhelmingly medicinal.

Finally, I was once privileged to drink an 1821 French bottling of the legendary Vin de Constance. Opening this bottle proved to be almost as delicate an operation as the first Northumberland wine. The cork was firmly in place, and may even have been renewed once in the lifetime of the wine. Once again, much of it was soggy and falling apart; once again, the disc in contact with the rich sweet wine was perfectly intact, enabling me to complete the operation without fragments falling into the bottle. This Constantia had certainly set out in life as a red wine. The first glassful still had a deep mahogany hue, though this turned to burnt amber literally before my eyes. The wine lost nothing of its fruit and flavour while the colour change was taking place, though within an hour it had started to lose some of its delicacy and finesse, taking on instead the Bual Madeira character which seemed the end-style of the Northumberland bottles.

George Saintsbury, writing his *Notes on a Cellar-Book* in 1912, remarked in the course of his text: 'I wonder if there exists anywhere a bottle of the old original Constantia? I am happy to say that in my youth I once drank it. (I am sorry for anyone who has not, once at least, drunk both real Constantia and real Tokay.) It has not, I believe, been made for many decades, the modern products of the vineyards so called being quite different. But it was of the sort to last.' At the end of a long and distinguished wine drinking career which had its beginnings in the mid 19th century and a reasonable experience of vintages dating back at least to the 1850s, Saintsbury's observation is a measure even then, of its rarity.

Constantia – the region and the eponymous wine – is the logical starting point of an account of South African wine. But for a few happy coincidences, however, this section might have proved as academic as a Mauritian text on the dodo. Constantia suffered a series of natural disasters in the second half of the 19th century – first oidium decimated production from the late 1850s, and then phylloxera destroyed the vineyards themselves. There were no resources left for the replanting programme once it was discovered that grafting vines on to American rootstock would solve the phylloxera problem. The Cape Government bought the Groot Constantia property as an insolvent estate in 1885 for just over £5000. Baron Carl von Babo, son of the director of the Viticultural School at Klosterneuberg in Austria, was given charge of the project.

The Cape Government's decision to buy the historic property probably saved the wine growing region as a whole. Constantia could never hope to compete against the warmer climate areas of Paarl and Stellenbosch, and its land and estates were the more likely victims of township development. The Cloetes' bankruptcy was a reflection on their farming operation, on the declining fashion for sweet wine, and a lack of concern for the quality of what they were producing. New backing might have altered several of these conditions, but it is almost certain that Groot Constantia would have followed the other wine farms in the region into viticultural extinction. Without its continued existence as a wine producer, urban encroachment might, by the 1980s, have left so little land suitable for vineyards that it would not then have been possible to re-establish a real wine estate in Van der Stel's domain.

Groot Constantia's story, from Baron von Babo to the present day, has not been without its own problems. In 1925 a fire destroyed the homestead. Restoration work could not bring back the priceless Cape Dutch furniture engulfed by the blaze. However, the architect Franklin Kendall recreated the building so that it was as it had been 'at its best' – not the gableless house that Simon van der Stel had built, nor the decaying wreck that it had been before the fire, but as it seems to have been in the days when the Cloetes produced its most famous wines.

The farm itself passed through several stages, including, for a period after the fire, a supplier of bulk grapes to Robert Fuller Bertram at High Constantia. Later the vineyard land was leased out, and only reverted to the estate in 1957. Paul Sauer, Minister of Agriculture at the time and himself proprietor of one of the Cape's most famous farms, renewed the idea of a model farm. In time an advisory committee was formed, the old and diseased vineyards replanted, and by 1960 Groot Constantia was again crushing wine in its cellars.

For nearly two decades after the winery began producing, Groot Constantia experienced a boom in demand. Prices admittedly were not high, and the decision to limit purchases to Wednesdays only, with sales restricted to those who actually called at the estate, probably enhanced the sense of rarity.

Constantia wines from the 1960s and early 1970s were very average: delicate and rather uncomplicated, they held together quite well but frequently lacked depth and intensity. A notable exception was the 1974 vintage, which produced –

as with most other regions in the Cape that year – wines of great balance and staying power. All three of the red wine varietals, Pinotage, Shiraz and Cabernet, improved noticeably for the first decade of their lives, and some well-stored bottles look good even now.

The winds of change were blowing through the Cape winelands as the decade of the seventies ended. Groot Constantia was no longer able to sell the kinds of wines which had been acceptable to the relatively unsophisticated buyers who had patronised the establishment since the cellars reopened at the beginning of the 1960s. Vineyards needed upgrading, and the winery needed modernising.

First Neil Ellis (who has since moved on to his own production facility) and then Pieter du Toit have shown that the Government-owned estate can produce high quality wines. The latter's tenure has been all the more remarkable for showing, in addition to several award-winning wines each vintage, a trading profit. This has been, in part, a tribute to the commercial success of the wines themselves, and in part a measure of general manager Danie Appel's firm hand on the helm. The estate's control board has also played a major role in this programme. The previous incumbents do not appear to have been the sort of businessmen able to discern just when their own staff were milking the operation. The story of the estate's deep ploughing and vineyard renewal programme, which yielded sufficient income to the farm manager at the time that he now owns the equipment required for the job, speaks volumes about the financial controls.

The new generation of Groot Constantia wines are heir to the traditions of Van der Stel. While the red wines are less obvious than those of Stellenbosch – and for this reason don't always perform well on blind tastings – they are often refined, beautifully balanced and with mineral flavours – more Margaux than St Estèphe. The Gouverneur's Reserve is

88

the estate's proprietary red, a Cabernet/Merlot blend in which the former predominates. While the wine could profit in its youth from more fleshiness from Merlot, it is probably true of the estate that the region's softer Cabernets are not austere for long and too much Merlot would undermine the ageing potential. The regular Cabernet now shows more berry fruit than in the past, as much a sign of good vinification as more selective harvest methods. Old clone Cabernet in cooler climates tends to yield herbaceous, almost vegetal flavours if it is in the least bit underripe.

Groot Constantia's Shiraz has also benefited from the renaissance: several of the more recent vintages are quite full and aromatic, less intense than Rhône wine, more delicate and accessible. The Heerenrood blend of Cabernet and Shiraz has its followers, though I find that it often shows insufficient fruit for its weight. The Pinotage is a drinkable commercial wine of no great merit.

Among the whites, the Weisser Riesling performs particularly well, year in and year out: it is one of the best wines made from this varietal at the Cape. Likewise the Gewürztraminer, which combines the typical rose petal bouquet of the varietal with a full, sweetish mid-palate and finish. The Chardonnay is on the slightly lean, slightly citrussy side but not harsh, the completed malolactic fermentation rounding it off and leaving a hint of butterscotch on the nose and finish. The Noble Late Harvests are beautifully balanced dessert wines: one, made with Muscat, more intensely fragrant on the nose; the other, a blend of Chenin Blanc and Rhine Riesling, beautifully structured and not overwhelmingly sweet.

Pieter du Toit's Groot Constantia wines have done much to make the estate worthy of its 18th-century reputation. When the Constantia wine route was set up in the mid 1980s several critics wondered whether the most famous of the district's properties would be able to live up to the standards set by the region's other two farms. Today there is no doubt, and this

89

ensures that the wine route nearest to the city centre is also the one guaranteed not to disappoint.

However, the estate which re-established the reputation of the area was Klein Constantia, a farm which for most of its life was bathed only indirectly in the glory of the region's great wines. After Van der Stel's death, when the domain was divided into three separate entities, one of the properties was named Klein Constantia. This estate later came to be called Hoop-op-Constantia and under the ownership of the Colijn family vied with the Groot Constantia of the Cloetes to obtain the best prices for its wines. Most of the land belonging to this farm was reincorporated with Groot Constantia earlier this century.

The estate now known as Klein Constantia, or Little Constantia, comes from a deduction of land made from Groot Constantia in February 1823 by the widow of Hendrik Cloete in favour of her youngest son, Johan Gerhard Cloete. He does not appear to have been much of a wine farmer, and neither he nor his successors seem to have taken a serious interest in the historical role of the Constantia estates. In 1918 the property passed into the hands of Abraham de Villiers, proprietor of a ladies' fashion shop in Paarl. De Villiers married an American heiress and the couple lived on the farm, entertaining lavishly (and farming in a desultory fashion) until his death in 1930. His widow continued to live there until 1955, and her late husband's nephew stayed on until he leased the farm out in 1963 to the Austins, who purchased it outright in 1972.

In 1980 Duggie Jooste bought a very dilapidated Klein Constantia. He immediately brought in the best expertise available to ensure that the historic property would be renovated to yield the optimum from its vineyards. Ernst le Roux, then chief viticulturist at Nederburg, headed a team that conducted extensive soil tests before determining which vines would be planted on which sites. Le Roux also sought out the finest planting material available, including a new Cabernet clone that was virus-free and earlier ripening. He reasoned that since the Constantia climate was already on the somewhat cool side, the generally late ripening Cabernet risked underripeness. Today, with both Cabernet vineyards in full production, it is possible to taste grapes that come from blocks so far apart, in terms of their levels of maturity, that you would assume they came from wholly different climatic regions. Klein Constantia in fact harvests its earliest varietal, Chardonnay, from a late maturing block at the same time as it brings in the first of the Cabernet grapes from an early maturing vineyard.

Duggie Jooste also commissioned a state-of-the-art wine cellar and brought into his team Ross Gower, who had trained under Günter Brözel at Nederburg before working a stint in New Zealand. The first vintage from the new vineyards on this historic farm was in 1986. That year Gower covered himself and the farm in a shower of glory, winning the national trophy for the country's best young white wine, his 1986 Sauvignon Blanc. The next year he repeated the achievement and bettered it: his 1986 Cabernet was adjudged the country's best red wine, and also best wine on the national show. Subsequent vintages have nearly all been trophy winners. In fact, nothing released by the estate is anything less than benchmark wine.

Klein Constantia's Cabernets are considered somewhat controversial in the industry, partly because the new clone tends to yield wines which are fruity and accessible without the depth and tannin normally associated with the varietal in South Africa. They also seem to mature quite quickly, peaking at about five years, to judge from the first releases. This may be a feature of the younger vines, as well as a consequence of the proportions of both old and new clone in the final blend. All the vintages so far reveal a rich berry, almost raspberry, character with just the slightest hint of minty eucalyptus.

The Shiraz has turned out to be one of the finer examples of the rather delicate style yet seen in the Cape. Not very big, but quite smoky with a slight 'bouillon' nose, the Klein Constantia Shiraz is overshadowed by the reputation of the Cabernet.

The estate's Chardonnay shows lovely balance: not too big, nor too wooded, with the right citrus-butterscotch character and the scent of lees on the nose, it has consistently scored well on various blind tastings. The Sauvignon Blanc has an almost Loire-like, or even New Zealand character, the result no doubt of climate and Ross Gower's experience in the Antipodes. The Reserve 1986 which carried off the national championship is still showing well, despite considerable bottle age. Younger vintages are less accessible but seem capable of ageing well.

In 1987 Gower and Duggie Jooste chose to declassify the Sauvignon Blanc of the vintage. The harvest had been difficult enough, and botrytis afflicted many of the grapes at harvest. The wine was blended with some Chenin Blanc and released as a Blanc de Blanc at a much lower price. This has evolved magnificently, and now looks better than the 1988 Sauvignon. A small quantity was left over for the 1992 Nederburg Auction where it occupied the vanguard of the white wine selection. The story of the declassified 1987s deserves to be widely known: it reflects the winemaker and the proprietor's commitment to quality and reputation, willing to undervalue a wine which turned out to be auction material, simply because they believed that it did not live up to the standards that they had set the estate. It also shows that sometimes it is impossible, even for those who should be in the know, to estimate how a wine will evolve.

Klein Constantia also produces a Rhine Riesling, which has a following among those who have not yet abandoned hope with this varietal in the Cape. It is certainly one of the best of the South African Rhine Rieslings, though for all that, nothing exceptional.

Of far greater importance is the Vin de Constance, a look-alike, taste-alike of the famous dessert wines from the 18th and 19th centuries. First produced on the estate in 1986, from a small Muscat de Frontignan vineyard planted expressly for the purpose, its vinification follows as closely as possible the methods believed to have been applied by the Cloetes when they owned the Groot Constantia property. Key elements of this process included reducing the crop by half on the vines, leaving the bunches of grapes to shrivel to almost raisin-like consistency before harvesting, wood vinification, no fortification and, curiously, no botrytis or noble rot.

The second release seems more accessible than the 1986, softer, and more luscious, though no less structured. It is certainly a beautifully made sweet wine, redolent with fruit and yet not cloying. How it will turn out after two hundred years is, of course, impossible to predict. Future generations who may happen across some stocks in their seemingly hand-blown bottles may well be happily surprised, as we who have been fortunate enough to drink some of the original wine of the Cloetes two centuries on.

The third farm in the restored viticultural region of Constantia is Buitenverwachting, also a portion of the original Van der Stel estate, though subdivided from that section of the old Commander's property which came to be known as Bergvliet. It, too, was owned for a time by the Cloetes: Ryk Arnoldus Mauritius Cloete, the son of Hendrik Cloete, acquired the land in 1797 and in time changed its name to Cis-Constantia. Later the property was owned by the Lategan family (through whose hands it passed until it belonged briefly to the Senator who was a member of the Groot Constantia committee). The same family also owned a property which had been divided from the original farm and was known variously as Constantia View and Constantia Uitzig.

Buitenverwachting owner since 1981, Christine Mueller has acquired several blocks from Uitzig in her efforts at reconsolidation, and has also carried on the extensive rebuilding and replanting programme, establishing on the way a model farm, with a model workers' community, organically farmed vineyards, and a restaurant that is consistently rated one of the top three in South Africa.

The cellar itself has been in the care of Jean Daneel since its first crush. His various early releases confirmed that the farm had all the promise of the Constantia region. His later vintages are a considerable graduation, and suggest that Buitenverwachting should be placed among the ten leading viticultural properties in South Africa.

One of the first of the Buitenverwachting wines to garner public attention was the Gamay L'Arrivée, a Beaujolais-style purple-hued red wine that would be the envy of most of the growers in Fleurie. Keatsian in colour, refreshing especially when slightly chilled, it is easily the best Nouveau produced in South Africa.

Now that the more serious red varietal vineyards are coming into production, the L'Arrivée is apt to lose a little of the focus of attention that it enjoyed. For those who eagerly await its release each year, this is no bad thing: there is never that much to go around. The risk, from their point of view, is that the other wines will create more followers for the Buitenverwachting cellar, and this in time may further reduce the availability of South Africa's premier *primeur* wine.

On the other hand, the premium red cultivars present themselves as wholly different wines. The Médoc blend, appropriately branded as Grand Vin in the Bordeaux tradition, is a blend of 70 per cent Cabernet Sauvignon, 10 per cent Cabernet Franc and 20 per cent Merlot, intense, almost cassis-like but also quite chocolatey, a very fine wine that drinks quite well when young, but seems to be structured for considerable ageing.

The Cabernet – to judge from the selection made for the auction of the Cape Independent Winemakers' Guild – is easily in the same league: beautifully oaked, the wine combines fruit and tannin in perfect balance. The auction reserve of Merlot is in much the same class, so rich and packed with flavour that it invites comparison with the average Pomerol. A private tasting held by the members of the Independent Winemakers' Guild rated it the best Merlot in the Cape, an accolade which seems entirely deserved. These wines, together with the L'Arrivée, represent the best reds on the farm at present. There are others, including a disappointing Pinot Noir, and a very acceptable (though completely overshadowed) second claret blend called Buitenkeur.

Among the white wines, the Chardonnay is beautifully structured though perhaps a little austere. The wood and butterscotch flavours are there, but there is perhaps a little too much 'grip' on the palate for drinking comfort. The wooded Sauvignon, sold under the Blanc Fumé label, combines the grassiness of the varietal on the nose with a wonderful use of oak to give it a vanilla richness free of any impression of over-wooding. The Sauvignon character here is quite pungent, and is nowhere more clear than on the unwooded Sauvignon Blanc. This is a very New Zealand style of wine, more so even than that at neighbouring Klein Constantia. Nose and palate combine asparagus and gooseberries, with fruit flavours so strong that first-time drinkers of this style are almost overwhelmed by it.

Of the other wines, there is an acceptable Rhine Riesling, an adequate but unmemorable blended white called Buiten Blanc, a newly released very classical Méthode Champenoise, and a rare, but superbly balanced Noble Late Harvest. This beerenauslese-type dessert wine is sold under the proprietary name of Noblesse, and is certainly one of the best botrytis wines ever produced in the Cape. Different from the Klein Constantia Vin de Constance, it provides further evidence – if this were ever needed – that the region is ideally suited to the production of luscious after-dinner wines.

The renaissance of the Constantia area of origin is a very recent event in South African viticultural history. Only a century ago every wine farm of note in the district was either bankrupt, or given over mainly to residential use. The 20th century saw urban encroachment threaten them all: those who think that Groot Constantia might have escaped the developers should be reminded that after the 1925 fire at the homestead, the disposal of the historic farm was very much an item on the Government's agenda. As recently as 1979 the state-owned wine farm was technically insolvent; Klein Constantia was a ruin, and the description of the farmstead at Buitenverwachting in Jose Burman's *Wines of Constantia* published that year, speaks of the thatched roof supporting 'enough vegetation for a garden'.

The decade of the eighties has come together in the newly formed Constantia wine route. Visitors from Cape Town need travel only 15 minutes to visit the region opened up by Van der Stel, made famous by the Cloetes and the Colijns, and restored today to yield wines that can rightfully take their place at the best tables of the civilised world.

THE WINE CELLARS OF STELLENBOSCH
FROM FALSE BAY TO STELLENBOSCH

The town of Stellenbosch, founded in 1679 by Commander Simon van der Stel, is widely regarded as the centre of the Cape wine trade. The area of origin of which it forms the heart covers a radial distance of 20 kilometres from the town itself. Stellenbosch is one of the most beautiful towns in the Western Cape. Much of its centre has been carefully preserved. Whole streets are lined with buildings which have been declared national monuments: the open squares, the oak trees, the numerous buildings which comprise the various faculties of the university, the gallery of mountains which surround the town all give it a quality and aesthetic grace unequalled in South Africa.

Stellenbosch, like most of the Western Cape wine areas, is classified as Region 3 on Winkler's heat summation table, though it is warmer than Constantia and cooler than Paarl. Its soils vary considerably, from well-drained granitic material on the slopes of the mountains, to wet, rather sandy material on the more level landscape. All of the region suffers from an excess of acidity, necessitating massive lime applications at the time of vineyard preparation. As much as 40 tons per hectare are added in an endeavour to establish appropriate alkalinity.

From a viticultural point of view, the area of origin is usefully divided into several sections: those properties lying between False Bay and the town itself; those farms which lie between Cape Town and Stellenbosch along the line of

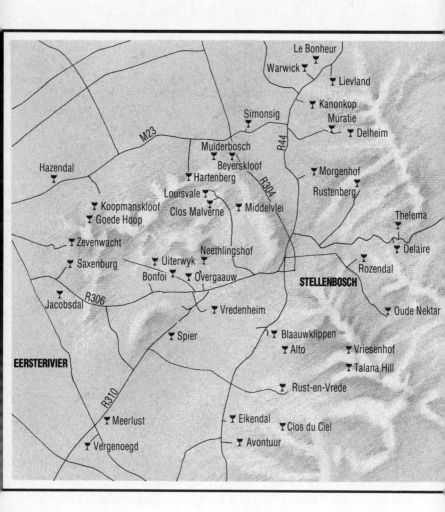

Le Bonheur

Warwick

Lievland

Kanonkop

Simonsig

Muratie

Delheim

M23

Mulderbosch

R44

Beyerskloof

Hazendal

Hartenberg

Morgenhof

R304

Louisvale

Rustenberg

Koopmanskloof

Clos Malverne

Middelvlei

Goede Hoop

Thelema

Zevenwacht

Delaire

Neethlingshof

Saxenburg

Uiterwyk

Rozendal

Bonfoi

Overgaauw

STELLENBOSCH

Jacobsdal

R306

Vredenheim

Oude Nektar

Spier

Blaauwklippen

EERSTERIVIER

Alto

Vriesenhof

Talana Hill

Rust-en-Vrede

R310

Meerlust

Eikendal

Clos du Ciel

Vergenoegd

Avontuur

98

Devon Valley; the cellars between Stellenbosch and Paarl; the wineries between Stellenbosch and Franschhoek, along Helshoogte and the Jonkershoek; and, finally, those producers on the Helderberg road, between Stellenbosch and Somerset West.

This account of the private producing cellars of Stellenbosch will deal with each of these regions in this sequence, partly to facilitate those who, whether by car or with a map, wish to conceptualise the geography, and partly to draw whatever conclusions are possible about the *terroir* of each area.

Each of these regional sections, whether of Stellenbosch or of any other area of origin, deals only with the demarcated estates and the privately owned producing cellars. The chapter on brands covers all the production of the national wholesale merchants, at least to the extent that it touches on the fine wine industry. There is also a separate chapter which deals briefly with the cooperative wine cellars. As far as the estate and boutique wine business is concerned, however, it is this and the following four chapters which detail the Stellenbosch area in the sequence outlined above.

The R310 which links False Bay to Stellenbosch runs from the N2 between Cape Town and Somerset West along the bed of the Eerste River. Just before the western entry to the town it is joined by the R306 (M12) which links Kuils River to Stellenbosch via the Stellenbosch Kloof. The farms on this western flank of the town share a climate that is moderated by the cool breezes blowing in off False Bay.

The first of these estates, coming inland towards Stellenbosch from the sea isVergenoegd, the name meaning literally 'far enough' – a comment no doubt on its historical distance from Cape Town. The property has belonged to the Faure family for several generations. Those who choose to write to the farm will discover that they must address their correspondence to Faure & Faure, P.O. Box 1, Faure, a measure – if this kind of corroboration is sought – of the pre-eminence of the family and farm in the life of the village.

Vergenoegd has been a supplier of grapes and wine to the KWV for many years. Much of what comes off the farm today is sold under KWV labels, including the new prestigious Cathedral Cellars range. Vergenoegd's wines have enjoyed a long association with the quality wine industry in the Cape: vintages from the early 1970s were sought after by aficionados of traditional Cape winemaking. The Cabernets in particular embodied the virtues of the old-fashioned rich berry fruit style without the clumsiness which usually accompanied this harvesting and vinification method. Perhaps because of the proximity to the sea, with the cooling effect of the breezes blowing in off False Bay, the Vergenoegd wines were more delicate and refined than those vintaged closer to the town of Stellenbosch. The Cabernets filled out after about eight years, and in good vintages kept well for at least fifteen. The 1972 was one such wine, as was the 1974. The Vergenoegd Shiraz of the same era was less concentrated than the Cabernet, but often quite perfumed in a smoky, leathery kind of way. The Cinsaut and Tinta Barocca were good value table wines, usually purchased to make up an order for the Cabernet.

From the early 1980s, the Vergenoegd wines seem to lose what little concentration they had, becoming instead too soft and too accessible. Easy and undemanding, they lacked the berry fruit character which had been the real virtue of the traditional wines of the 1970s.

The current vintages are showing a marked improvement on these wines. The Cabernets are starting to pick up a noticeable berry character. The reserve wine has been well oaked, layering fruit and wood vanilla in a way that suggests that great care has gone into the vinification. Clearly Vergenoegd has turned the corner and the next few years could see the restoration of the reputation that the estate enjoyed for most of the 1970s.

The next estate inland is Meerlust, by status as much as by historical claim one of the most important in the Stellenbosch area of origin. It has remained in the Myburgh family for over two hundred years, despite the booms and bankruptcies of the Cape wine trade over this period. At one stage in the early 1980s a wealthy overseas visitor, living in South Africa at the time, offered proprietor Nico Myburgh some R25m to part with the family estate. This was an opening bid, and presumably could have been negotiated upward. Nico turned him down, recognising that ownership of such a property is an act of custodianship not to be discharged in a cavalier fashion. He did however say privately that a point might come when he would feel compelled – if only for the sake of his heirs – to accept an offer that might better secure their future. As it turned out, Nico Myburgh kept the family property, and when he died a few years later, joined those who had managed the responsibility before him in the family graveyard which lies between the homestead and the vineyards.

His son Hannes now runs the property, guided in matters oenological by winemaker Giorgio Dalla Cia. The wines are distributed through The Bergkelder, but the estate and its produce remain firmly part of the Myburgh inheritance. Included in this responsibility is a sense of duty about the quality of what goes into the bottle. A rigorous selection process ensures that anything not worthy of the Meerlust name is sold in bulk. This same care extends to the estate's proprietary wine, one of the first Cabernet/Merlot blends to be marketed in the Cape: from the 1980 vintage, Meerlust's Rubicon has been one of the country's most sought after red wines.

The concern which goes into upholding the name extends at times to real and quantifiable financial investment – such as when Hannes Myburgh and Giorgio Dalla Cia decided to declassify the 1985 Rubicon. The 1985 vintage in the Cape had been a difficult one. Despite careful selection, rigorous vinification and new wood maturation, the blend that year did not live up to the estate's expectations. Accordingly they created a second label Meerlust wine, branded simply as Meerlust Red and offered for sale at about half the price of the regular Rubicon. Those of the estate's customers who had already made *en primeur* purchases of the 1985 were compensated with the superb 1986s. This 1985 Meerlust Red, vinified as a regular Rubicon, has proved enormously successful, partly because of the quality/price relationship, partly because any Cabernet blend from Meerlust will find a ready market. As a wine it was certainly one of the best reds of the 1985 vintage produced at the Cape. Hannes Myburgh believed that he could not compromise the reputation of the Rubicon brand by selling potentially inferior wine under that label.

The Meerlust range is made up at this stage entirely of red wines. The Pinot Noir has started to acquire something of a following, being quite spicy and opening up creditably after six to eight years. For those whose Pinot palates have been schooled on good Burgundy, present bottlings may be a disappointment. However, tank samples of the most recent production show an entirely new style of Pinot emerging: fuller colours, plenty of raspberry fruit, and just the right amount of 'farmyard' on the nose.

The Meerlust Cabernet, now much overshadowed by the Rubicon (and destined in short vintages to be used up in the proprietary wine) can be an excellent Stellenbosch Cabernet, typical of the wines which grow in vineyards closer to the sea. It is usually very finely structured, with delicate berry fruit and a slightly herbaceous roundness. It fills out after about eight years, and keeps well until about fifteen. In lighter vintages the slightly grassy character tends to be stronger on the nose than the fruit, though good oak compensates for any loss of dimension when the wine is young.

The Meerlust Rubicon has suffered from the cult status it enjoyed from the mid 1980s onwards. The wine was overpriced in retail, though quite competitively positioned at wholesale. Shortage is its own kind of marketing device and while it works well when the demand exceeds supply, a change in fashion or an increase in availability is all that it takes to wreck the formula. Both these elements have changed for Rubicon. There is simply more of it being made and there are now many other proprietary Cabernet/Merlot blends on the market. The wine in fact has been getting noticeably better over the years: the Merlot vines have started producing fruit of far greater intensity; the Cabernet vineyards are also gaining real age. The balance of the varietals and Dalla Cia's experience of the wood and the vines increase with every vintage.

The Merlot, which is separately bottled as a special release wine, has also acquired something of a following: it is one of the best examples of the varietal in the Cape, though it was overpriced because of rarity and the positioning statement that was being made. Since it clearly does not live up to the pretensions of the marketing department, the price has been adjusted downwards. This may in time help to create a genuine demand for the wine.

Meerlust will also in time produce a Chardonnay. A small block of vines was planted several years ago to enable winemaker Giorgio Dalla Cia to experiment with different vinification techniques and estimate a suitable maturation cycle for the wine. The samples produced so far suggest that Meerlust's Chardonnay, while very much a latecomer in terms of the South African fashion, will position easily in the front rank of the country. A deep lees character, with enough body and varietal fruit to sustain the heavy oaking in the wine I tasted, are all features that would distinguish this from many of the more commercial wines being churned out by the industry.

No note on Meerlust is complete without an observation about the homestead, one of the Cape's finest and best documented. Hannes Myburgh has recently redecorated the interior in a mixture of Deco, with his own sense of the eclectic: those lucky enough to gain entry will be vastly impressed and amused by the result.

Closer to Stellenbosch on the R310 is the Spier Estate, at one time a leading force in the region's wine route. The property was one of the Cape's earliest producers of estate wine. Long before competitors had made distribution arrangements in the Transvaal, Spier's wines were fully represented in the retail trade. More recently, the farm has been through difficult times. It was one of the largest properties in the Cape and the size of the crop, together with problems of its disposal, almost overwhelmed the operation.

Life seems more manageable now, and the thousands of tourists who visit Spier, dining in one of the two restaurants and perhaps visiting the art gallery, probably leave with the residual impression of the community life of an old Cape Dutch wine farm.

Vinifying a large crop always imposes constraints in terms of quality. In the mid 1970s Spier was able to select out its best varietals from those vineyard blocks which performed well in a particular season. There were, for example, a series of Pinotage vintages which stand up with the finest wines made from this varietal in the Cape. I have a distant recollection of an impressive, almost Burgundian 1969, a very good 1972, a wonderfully complex 1974, and a more than creditable 1976. The Joubert family certainly seemed to understand the varietal and how to vinify it. These wines needed six to eight years to peak, and then seemed to continue along the plateau of maturity for several more years. They confirm that some of Spier's soils are well suited to quality wine production.

Among the white wines, I remember several good Colombard vintages, including one unusual botrytised wine which finished full flavoured and fairly dry. It was sold at a Nederburg Auction amid much interest, not only because of its unusual style, but also because it revealed yet another, little known dimension of the increasingly ubiquitous Cape Colombard.

Current vintages show that Pinotage is still one of the estate's leading varietals, though premium reds like Merlot and Cabernet are in the pipeline. White wines have moved on since the days of the Colombard Auslese 'Trocken'; the Sauvignon Blanc presents quite well, as does the sweetish Chenin Blanc Special Late Harvest. Some of the low-lying vineyards are obviously conducive to 'noble rot' and Spier might profitably develop this aspect of its business.

The last private winery before the R310 meets up with the R306 (which runs through the Stellenbosch Kloof) is Vredenheim, with its two century old manor house and its newly producing cellar in the care of Elzabé Bezuidenhout. The wines are not widely distributed and at this stage some of the releases have done little more than test out the market. Not all the wines are produced in every vintage since the debut 1987 – no Cabernet 1988 was released, nor Blanc de Noir 1990, nor even Special Late Harvest 1991.

The red wines have a curious fragrance and softness which gives them an easy accessibility: both the 1987 and the 1989 Cabernet show a eucalyptus mint character, stronger on the latter than the former and obviously softening with age. The 1990 Pinotage has typical varietal fruit and an easy, almost sweetish finish. There is enough tannin for the wine to have more staying power than its forwardness would suggest, and enough structure on the Cabernets to suggest in time wines worth laying down.

For those whose approach to Stellenbosch from the west

brings them towards the town through the Kloof on the R306, the first three properties encountered are Zevenwacht, Saxenburg and Jacobsdal. Zevenwacht has something of a high profile image, partly because chairman and key shareholder Gilbert Colyn has played the game that way, partly because having actively sought public investors the business of the farm is a matter of public record.

The creation of Zevenwacht is the result of the recent consolidation of two historic farms, Zevenfontein and Langverwacht. The company is not registered as an estate with the Wine and Spirit Board, but it does have a fully equipped cellar and it does bottle at the winery.

Zevenwacht has acquired a special reputation for the quality/price ratio of its wines. The Blanc de Blanc, for example, is sold off the farm at a price which can hardly be matched by the cooperatives, and yet exceeds the quality criteria of many wines which retail for twice the amount. Accordingly, many restaurant chains and private clubs buy it for sale under their own labels, achieving in this arrangement the double advantage of in-house branding with an excellent product.

The Médoc blend is curiously eucalyptus-like on the nose, but full yet easy on the palate. This seems to be a characteristic of the Cabernet, since the regular as well as the Guild Auction Reserve have a strong bluegum nose.

The Shiraz also looks good most of the time: a fairly big wine with a saddle-like bouillon nose, it is both a good example of Cape Shiraz and an excellent blending wine. It is used in conjunction with Cabernet (30 to 70 per cent) to produce a proprietary wine which bears the farm's name and the vintage of production. This is also one of the best-value red wines in the Cape, retailing for less than many blends made from inferior cultivars. It manages to combine enough structure to ensure a reasonable ageing potential, with enough fruit and berry character to be attractive in its youth.

Among the varietal white wines is an excellent Gewürztraminer, easily one of the best in the country. Dry enough to be counted unusual in the Cape, it has the right combination of tropical fruit and rose petals on the nose, with earthy, mineral Alsace-type flavours on the palate. The latest releases of Sauvignon Blanc are also good, full, slightly herbaceous but more gooseberry than asparagus. This is the wine which adds dimension to the Blanc de Blanc, and even to the rather more bulk style Vin Blanc.

Zevenwacht's Chardonnay is still very much in its infancy, the first vintage (1990) having plenty of structure, without, at this stage, all that much depth. This should not necessarily count against it: it had good barrel vinification and some time on the lees, so perhaps these features will show through at the end. At present, the lemony grip on the palate makes it a little difficult to gain access to where the wine might be going.

Finally, Zevenwacht's Rhine Riesling has performed admirably at blind tastings and on the annual auction of the Cape Independent Winemakers' Guild. Like the Gewürztraminer, it seems to combine the virtues of a spicy, fragrant nose with complex mouthfilling flavours.

Zevenwacht's operation has not been without its critics, particularly those who are ill-disposed to key shareholder, architect Gilbert Colyn. Many have argued that those members of the public who are shareholders in the operation have merely funded Colyn's hobby; others observe that the Zevenwacht Farm Village with its two hundred or so cottages effectively alienates the shareholders from the property. Coupled with this is the whole question of the operation's long-term viability: its increased indebtedness to financial institutions is a matter of public record, suggesting mismanagement, underpricing of product, or simply an excessive debt burden. In all these observations there is an element of truth, but Zevenwacht's continued existence should be the concern of the wine industry as a whole. The farm is hampered by debt: the best wines in the world will not free it from its onerous interest payments, especially if they are underpriced in relation to quality. However, raising their selling price may well produce less revenue, and discouraging the private shareholders may alienate custom. There are no quick fixes to its problem, and no more appropriate use for the property or its wine cellar than to continue to produce the fine wines now sold under the Zevenwacht label.

The Saxenburg winery on the Kuils River side of the Stellenbosch Kloof was established on one of the Cape's oldest estates. The land was granted by Willem Adriaan van der Stel, son of the more famous Simon and Commander briefly of the Dutch East India Company colony at the turn of the 18th century. Since then, Saxenburg has passed through the hands of many proprietors, including Anglo Alpha, who had acquired the land for its mineral deposits and then saw the value in it as a quality wine producer.

It is now owned by Adrian and Birgit Bührer from Switzerland: they have continued with the improvements to farm and buildings begun by the previous proprietors and are clearly intent on seeing the farm in the vanguard of the industry's quality producers. Winemaker Nico van der Merwe, formerly with Montpellier in Tulbagh and prior to that at Neethlingshof, surprised the wine fraternity in September 1991 by carrying off the trophy for the country's champion young wine.

Until recently Saxenburg's reputation in the industry rested upon several well-made Pinotages and a couple of impressive Noble Late Harvests. Current releases show very full flavoured reds, especially Cabernet and a Cabernet/Merlot blend, and a further evolution of the Pinotage. Most of these wines have quite a pronounced eucalyptus character, a consequence mainly of the new clone in the Cabernet as well as a feature of red wines from this side of Stellenbosch. The Private Collection Novum – the farm's proprietary wine – offers structure before fruit, whereas the Private Collection Cabernet has softer tannins, with the fruit showing first.

Among the white wines, the Private Collection Sauvignon Blanc reveals a fine marriage of wood and fruit: the vanilla wood character supports the herbaceous fragrance of the varietal, harmonising into one of the Cape's better wood-matured Sauvignons. The Noble Late Harvest continues to impress: high or even very high sugars are held in balance by an appropriate level of acidity, and the botrytis character does not overwhelm the real fruit flavours of the Riesling and Sauvignon Blanc.

Further along the R306 is Jacobsdal Estate with its sandy, gravelly loam soils. It is one of the farms supplying both its grapes and wine for sale through The Bergkelder. Cornelius Dumas, the proprietor, is one of the old school of Cape wine-makers, not given to making pronouncements on the subject of his farm, or the grapes that he harvests. The cellar itself is primitive, but entirely adequate for crushing red grapes: the operations are mechanically sound, the tanks cement rather than stainless steel, the cap of grape skins on the fermenting red wines pushed down and pumped over – there are no roto-tanks anywhere in the low, lean-to looking cellar. Dumas' quiet approach reflects his carefully considered views, rather than an uncertainty about grape farming and red wine making. He assesses change and innovation on the basis of net addition to the finished product. Over the years his Jacobsdal Pinotage has altered in style, though not over-whelmingly. I recall his first vintage, the 1974, and remember that at the time it was less obvious than its co-release through The Bergkelder, the 1974 Meerendal Pinotage. The Jacobsdal was taut and rich, holding on to its fruit and filling the mouth with a rich and highly textured wine. It has lasted well, though its structure was typical of South African red wines at the time and it started to run out of resilience after about a decade.

The newer wines have compensated for this: there is a better acid/tannin balance, which has cost them some weight but obtained the longer lasting structure. Where Dumas has been free to use wood, such as with the 1984 and 1986 vintages, some of the lost volume is made up with this extra density and intensity. Unfortunately, the lighter vintages, which most need the added volume, rarely get the kind of barrels they deserve. This does not necessarily mean new wood, which could easily overwhelm the varietal fruit; but it is necessary to use oak to bring out a dimension which the vintage may have denied the wine.

Jacobsdal is one of the Stellenbosch estates closest to Cape Town, with a view over the Cape Flats to False Bay. Below the line of its vineyards it is witness to urban encroachment as the Peninsula's housing problems spill over from Mitchell's Plain towards Kuils River and then Stellenbosch. This is not a new problem in the Cape, nor is it unique to South Africa. The Graves district of Bordeaux abuts the town itself, so that the region's most famous estate, Château Haut-Brion, is now entirely surrounded by the metropolis. Between the beginning of this century and the 1980s, the number of wine estates in the Graves has reduced by more than a half.

It is not really possible to quantify the effects of urbanisation in the Cape in the same way. South African wine law has a very specific definition of the word 'estate' and prior to 1973 many producing properties would have been deemed estates, but now can no longer make that claim. It is certain that vineyard land is being given over to housing, or to a mixed agriculture more suited to the reduced size of the land. As long as estate wine farming is seen to be less profitable and more risky than real estate development, the problem will continue. Sometimes proprietors will stop 'progress' simply by refusing to budge, perhaps because of some sentimental attachment to the land occupied by their families for several generations.

Farms, like Jacobsdal, which are not part of the Stellenbosch wine route, which have no interface with the public, which are, in effect, the very private property of very private people, possess the balance. Men like Cornelius Dumas go about their business oblivious, almost, of the currents in the industry. They do not seek out overseas investors so that they can make a one-off capital gain on the land; nor do they seek to play with their wines, as if somehow each vintage was a matter of choice. In maintaining a powerful link with the past, in choosing gradual evolution as their means of progress, they stand at the frontier of the future. Others advance the boundaries by breaking with tradition. Cornelius Dumas grounds his world in the achievements of those who have preceded him. He is as important as the revolutionaries, and in the end may prove more intransigent. Jacobsdal Estate seems, very literally, to be the Rorke's Drift of Stellenbosch. In the hands of a lesser personality than Dumas it could as easily be an Isandhlwana.

Once beyond the Stellenbosch Kloof, the region seems safely guarded, for the time being at least, from the incursions of urbanisation. The winding road that passes through the gorge between the mountains forms something of a natural redoubt, and opens up on to a vista of the premier wine town in South Africa. At the bottom of the ravine are several estates and private cellars, beginning with Uiterwyk, which has been the property of the De Waal family since the grant of land was made in 1682.

Uiterwyk is poised at what will unquestionably be a real renaissance for the three hundred year old farm. New plantings of premium varietals, especially Chardonnay, Merlot and additional Cabernet vineyards, will enable the De Waal brothers to add complexity and depth to the existing range. Uiterwyk has been bottling its own wines since 1972, and produced immediately a string of Superior certified Cabernet virtually unequalled by any other producer at the time. I recall that the 1973 had better structure (and yet great suppleness) than most of the other wines of that vintage. The 1974 was quite extraordinary: full, almost black in its youth, the berry intensity of the fruit evolving into a rich velvety red wine, the epitome at the time of the best of the old Cape tradition. The 1975s and the 1976s were also good, though they never equalled the achievement of the 1974. I remember the Cape Riesling produced at Uiterwyk in the wonderful 1974 vintage was also a wine that was spoken of at the time with suitable respect. Harsh and almost without fruit in its early youth, it passed through the various phases of its maturation gaining in stature with every advancement. By the time it reached the 1980s it had achieved the fullness, complexity and golden-green richness of a white Burgundy. On more than one occasion I saw perfectly competent tasters mistake it blind for a Meursault.

The early 1980s were not great years at Uiterwyk, though the problems of the time seem to have been put behind the estate. The grapes which are now crushed in the 18th-century cellar include Cabernet, Pinotage, Merlot, Riesling, Muller-Thurgau, Sauvignon Blanc and Rhine Riesling. The Cabernets are certainly beginning to look more like the industry benchmarks of the 1970s than anything produced in the interim: deep colours, plenty of fruit, grape and wood tannins all in harmony. The Pinotage has an easy balance of fruit and wood, a good varietal wine not overwhelmed by the acetoney character which can be the greatest shortcoming of the varietal, especially in its youth. The Cape Riesling (Crouchen Blanc) is also more or less back to the levels it achieved in the 1970s. The fruit shows well on the young wines, and the structure promises a reasonable ageing potential (for those who like to see a little maturity on this typically Cape style of dry white wine).

Uiterwyk has produced too many good wines in the past

for anyone to doubt its potential. There is every indication that it has turned the corner and will make its own contribution to this unique part of the Stellenbosch Kloof.

The same optimistic assumption could be made of near-neighbour Bonfoi, which delivers grapes to The Bergkelder and also performs its own crush as an estate producer within The Bergkelder range. The Bonfoi Chenin Blanc was one of the better known estate wines made from South Africa's most widely planted varietal. It is now sold as Ouverture, a honeyed, botrytised, beautifully balanced spatlese style of wine, under-appreciated through under-informing the market of its virtues. It is true that this style is hardly in fashion, but many people who would be willing buyers of such wines from Europe, do not appear to know that there is a cellar near Vlottenburg achieving this quality with merit.

Almost next door to Bonfoi is Overgaauw, the Van Veldens' very successful quality wine estate which has been bottling its own harvests since 1970. Visitors to the farm are always struck by the Victorian tasting room, the personal attention with which they are treated, the overall dimension of the wines, and their price/quality ratio.

Braam van Velden has taken over much of the estate's management from his father Dawid, though decision-making is still very much a joint exercise. As a former chairman of the Cape Independent Winemakers' Guild, Braam is also involved in promoting quality wine and working beyond the boundaries of his own farm. Despite this wider industry role, which is both time consuming and sometimes financially onerous, he continues about his business in a modest and unpressured way. Over time he has wrought vast changes but never at an outrageous pace, and always in such a way that the estate's loyal supporters can feel comfortable about the direction he has chosen.

The Tria Corda proprietary wine, a blend of over 60 per cent Cabernet Sauvignon and at least 20 per cent Merlot, with about 15 per cent Cabernet Franc, is one of the Cape's most solid Médoc-style wines, not heavy on the palate so much as well integrated. It is a wine free of any excess: the Cabernet fruit is balanced out with Merlot flesh and the wooding lingers with a hint of vanilla on the nose and a layer of tannin on the finish.

The Cabernet is a wine in a similar vein, not very full, often slightly herbaceous but never mean. Older vintages gained a slightly nutty richness which overlaid the berry fruit; younger wines incorporate a little of the minty character of the new clone Cabernet. The DC Classic – sold only on the Auction of the Cape Independent Winemakers' Guild – is now entirely Merlot, though earlier vintages contained varying blends of Cabernet. Once again, this is not a big wine, though the most current samples have filled out and picked up colour and texture. The regular Merlot follows the same style and has its followers for exactly this reason. I find it a little too lean as a varietal wine, though it is an easy enough drink, taken merely as a well-balanced red.

Overgaauw's Port justly deserves its reputation: a blend of several Portuguese varietals, including Touriga Nacional, Malvasia Rey, Souzão and Tinta Francisca, it takes time to develop but balances out its fullness with a fine bouquet, like dead leaves in a forest. Most of the Cape's so-called Ports are poor excuses, red muscadels and jerepigos dressed up for the more premium market. Overgaauw's has a real claim to be judged like a wine from the Douro, and in good vintages it will not be found wanting.

Two of Overgaauw's white wines warrant a mention. The estate's Sylvaner – for years the only commercially available wine made from this cultivar – has an easy approachability, a delicate fragrance and a fine, taut balance. The Chardonnay is quite steely by comparison, with strong lemony overtones softened slightly by the vanilla butterscotch of the oak. It is a wine with all the keeping qualities sought after by those who like their Chardonnays with some bottle age. A little inaccessible when young, the Overgaauw Chardonnay tends not to perform well at club tastings where most of the samples come from current vintages. Some years, like the 1989 for example, may yet turn out to be more interesting in time than the highly praised young wines of that vintage.

Almost next door to Overgaauw is the much publicised, much vaunted estate of former German banker, Hans Schreiber. He acquired Neethlingshof from Jan Momberg (known as 'Grootbek' – 'big mouth' – as opposed to 'Stiljan' – 'silent John' – his cousin at Middelvlei) in 1985 and has since ploughed countless millions into revamping the historical old farm. Some of this investment has been well spent, and at least 70 per cent of the vineyards are so young that they are only now coming into production. Prior to undertaking this replanting programme extensive soil analyses were conducted and new vines went into properly prepared land. This suggests that when they are mature, and in full production, the fruit they will yield can only make the winemaker's life a real pleasure.

Since Hans Schreiber bought the property, however, life in the cellar has not been easy. Four different cellarmasters were responsible for the first six vintages, a measure perhaps of their difficulties.

In addition, Neethlingshof has been no stranger to the legal fraternity. There was the highly publicised dispute over the meaning of the term 'noble cultivar white wine' when the Drop Inn Group successfully refused to accept delivery of most of the 1985 and 1986 white wine crop on the basis that it did not comply with this description.

It is fair to say that Schreiber has spent far more than the average intelligent investor would have deemed necessary in his upgrade of the Neethlingshof farm. In doing so he may have deprived the winery – in the short term – of the kind of grapes necessary to make substantial and complex dry wines.

Undoubtedly, however, the renewed vineyards will produce grapes of a quality never before seen in the Stellenbosch Kloof and, providing there is a winemaker in his employ who can maximise this advantage, Neethlingshof's wines will vindicate at least some of his investment.

Already there are signs, from the few remaining older vines as much as from some of the younger vineyards, of the potential of the farm: at the 1990 Young Wineshow Neethlingshof produced the champion and reserve champion noble late harvests – wines of great richness and balance – and repeated this success in the same category the following year.

Neethlingshof's self-promotion included the renovation of the old Manor House and its conversion into a restaurant which specialises in oriental food. Part of this decision was undoubtedly motivated by Schreiber's Singaporean connection: he seems to enjoy a close relationship with the East. The Lord Neethling Restaurant has certainly established a marketing niche for itself as a result of this unusual culinary choice. Those who frequent it, especially aficionados of the Szechwan dishes which can sometimes be ordered, commend the combination of the estate's wines with the hot spicy food.

The old Verdun estate lies between Neethlingshof and the remaining cellars which occupy vineyards to the immediate west of the town. In the 1970s Verdun had the distinction of being South Africa's only producer of Gamay and Sauvignon Blanc. I remember tasting the wines on several occasions, as well as a Cabernet of no great merit. The Gamay would certainly not have won the approval of any grower in the Beaujolais: it was a medium-bodied wine, with some fruit and a surprising ability to survive in bottle. However, it never even vaguely resembled any of the European wines made with the varietal, or for that matter, any South African ones produced subsequently.

The Sauvignon Blanc was harsh, crude and clumsy: once

again there was no passing similarity between the Verdun wine and the varietal wines produced in the Cape nowadays. In fairness, the clonal material was considered suspect even then and it is merely a matter of curiosity that a Sauvignon Blanc was ostensibly available in South Africa years before the official first release of the cultivar at the end of the 1970s. It is also a matter of some amusement that both these Verdun wines obtained varietal certification from the Wine and Spirit Board when clearly neither satisfied even the minimum organoleptical features that would have been expected by an experienced taster.

Onwards into the Devon Valley westerly axis of Stellenbosch lie four more cellars before the town itself is reached. Louisvale, a relative newcomer with only three vintages to its credit and only Chardonnay to offer, makes a greater impression than its youth and its limited range would suggest. Ever since Hans Froehling and Leon Stemmet persuaded Neil Ellis to vinify their 1989 vintage for them, Louisvale has been bathed in publicity. The wine was a strikingly good first release, toasty, packed with butterscotch/vanilla and finished with just the right amount of lemon and tropical fruit.

The 1990 was a little disappointing – the same elements, but somehow the balance was different. The 1991 picks up the style of the 1989. Louisvale's Chardonnay, coming as it does from young vines, and showing as well as it does in its youth, is not at this stage a wine for long keeping. The forward fruit and the beautifully balanced oak platform seem at their best quite soon after the wine has been released. There may be another bottle maturation character which will emerge, especially once the vineyards establish themselves better: Neil Ellis' style of winemaking is not generally intended for those who do not like the idea of laying down their wines. No doubt in time he will accommodate the older vineyards, making Louisvale well worth following over the years.

This is probably a suitable point at which to discuss Neil Ellis' own wines. One of the Cape's most innovative winemakers, Neil Ellis went from Groot Constantia to Zevenwacht before branching out as an independent cellar consultant and contract winemaker. It is on this basis, for example, that he produces the Louisvale wines. However, his major ambition has been to make a select range of quality wines, for sale under his own label, from vineyards whose potential he has recognised.

In the few years that his wines have been in the market it has become clear that this very New World approach to wine production pays his followers handsome dividends. There have been several good vintages of Cabernet, intense, well structured, not overly flamboyant but dry, elegant and slightly restrained. The Chardonnays have also been excellent, taut and more citrussy than many, but always with a whiff of butterscotch, a hint of lees coming through the palate, and wonderful finesse.

His Sauvignon Blanc from the Whitehall Vineyard in Elgin has been something of a benchmark wine. It was the first Elgin release and it confirmed immediately the extraordinary potential of the area. The range of flavours, from gooseberries and grass to figs and tropical fruits, surprised even the most ardent of cool climate supporters. Clearly Neil Ellis' skills begin with the correct selection of vineyards for his range; however, the quality of what he has brought into the market confirms that in his own idiosyncratic way, he is a real force in the Cape's fine wine industry.

Up the road from Louisvale is Clos Malverne, yet another tiny boutique winery on the doorstep of Stellenbosch. Its initial releases, made by Jeremy Walker for proprietor Seymour Pritchard, showed remarkable colour and fruit. I had reservations about some of these 1988s: the layers of pigment and grapey bouquet seemed to conceal some instability and I have been a little equivocal about them as a result.

The 1989 Bordeaux blend, sold under the proprietary name of Auret, seemed an altogether different bottle of wine, softened as it was by nearly 20 per cent Merlot from young vines. I am still not entirely happy about the bouquet, but hasten to add that this is a small cavil, given the overall structure of the wine. I have the same views about the Cabernet: the 1988 left me anxious about a wine which I did not think could live up to its promise and its hype; the 1989 is clearly much better.

On the other hand, the Pinotage has been singularly impressive: it shows all the fruit and berry flavours of the varietal and is packed with fullness and depth. Easily one of the best ten Pinotages being made in South Africa at present, it leaves me in little doubt about Clos Malverne's potential as a significant player in the red wine game.

Finally, a note on Les Monts Malverne, a lightish red wine made all the more accessible by the addition of a small percentage of Sauvignon Blanc. I have tasted – or rather, drunk – this wine on several occasions and find it one of the easiest drinking and most approachable of the Cape reds. It is offered somewhat irreverently and yet there is no reason to treat it disrespectfully as a result.

From midway through 1991 Guy Webber took over in the cellar from Jeremy Walker. Only with the release of the 1992 vintage will it be possible to see the extent to which Clos Malverne dominates the wines it releases, and to what measure they bear the personality of the winemaker. With grapes coming from several vineyards, this is not always easy to determine. Walker's 1990 Special Release Clos Malverne was the SA Young Wineshow champion wood-matured red, a single tank containing a mere 120 cases. This kind of flagship wine is wonderfully exciting for collectors, but should not be the only basis for judging a winery's production. The general quality of the present releases speaks more eloquently for Clos Malverne's potential. The future wines of the new man in the cellar will say the rest.

In the same part of the valley is the Bertrams Devonvale winery, dealt with in the chapter covering the country's major brands. To the extent that the Bertrams wines draw their grapes from this little corner of Stellenbosch with its own special reputation and style of wine, it is worth noting that the success of near-neighbours like Clos Malverne bodes well for the Bertrams range once its new vineyards in the same part of the world are back into full production.

The Middelvlei red wine estate owned by 'Stiljan' Momberg is also situated in the valley, almost on the boundary of the town itself. Momberg's grapes and wine are delivered to The Bergkelder, which presently offers two varietal wines under the Middelvlei label.

Both the Pinotage – which has been estate bottled since the early 1970s – and the Cabernet – with the 1981 vintage as the first release – share a certain understated elegance. I recall finding the 1973 Pinotage a little light, and wondered at its ageing potential: however it turned out to be well structured and with great staying power, lasting into the 1980s even if it ceased to improve much after a while. More recent vintages have filled out a little, though they still do not have the depth and corpulence which I think is such a virtue in this otherwise rather forgettable varietal.

The Cabernet follows in many ways the pattern of the Pinotage: never overwhelmingly big, and certainly not in the style of the recent vintages from Bertrams or Clos Malverne, it nevertheless shows great balance and finesse, the effect no doubt of Stiljan's own inordinately quiet temperament. Current vintages have also gained a little in dimension, filling out into a very attractive harmony of fruit and tannin.

Middelvlei is really the last private producing winery on this west side of Stellenbosch: eastwards from here are the vineyards of Oude Libertas and the cellars of SFW, together with the historic Oude Moulen premises of Gilbeys. There are other cellars and estates to the west of the town, but they can only be approached from the north and west, on the other side of the Devon Valley ridge rolling downwards to the N1, the national road linking Cape Town and Paarl.

THE WINE CELLARS OF STELLENBOSCH
THE NORTHERN SIDE OF THE
BOTTELARY HILLS

❦ ❧

Those who approach Stellenbosch from Cape Town along the north-western side of the town encounter their first estate of the region on the M23. Hazendal has been in the Bosman family for five generations. Though it is part of The Bergkelder and distributes its wines through the company, Hazendal is beginning to acquire its own interface with the public. There is talk of a restaurant on the farm, and even of selling some wine through an estate shop. This would all be innovation in the context of Bergkelder wine estates, where farms are not really open to the public.

These changes in part reflect the style of Michael and Carita Bosman, whose easy, disarming manner and infectious enthusiasm make anything seem possible. The two hundred year old manor house is very much a home. The potential austerity of the historic building has been softened by the obvious homeliness of the interior; outside the gables and the line of buildings from the house to the cellar convey a sense of tranquillity which is only disrupted at harvest time.

While Hazendal delivers grapes and bulk wine to The Bergkelder, it also sells two wines under its own label. The Blanc Fumé is particularly striking: full and very intense, it still has all the structure it needs to hold the fruit together while the wine develops bottle age. This style of Sauvignon Blanc is unusual in Stellenbosch, an indication of slower ripening grapes, as well as extra care in the cellar in selecting them.

The other Hazendal wine sold under the estate label is the proprietary brand called Freudenlese, a late harvested Chenin Blanc with sometimes a hint of botrytis. This is a wine too easily quaffed in its youth to have acquired any reputation for how it matures in the bottle. However, its sugar and acid levels permit it a generous ageing and those who have happened across older bottles have been pleasantly surprised by its depth and complexity.

Michael Bosman has also experimented with noble late harvest wines. Although nothing has been released, there is every indication that should he choose to add one to his range, it will be fit to compete with the best in the industry.

A little closer to Stellenbosch is the Goede Hoop Estate of the Bestbiers. Situated quite high up on the Bottelary hills, it faces north and westwards towards Cape Town and the Atlantic. The farm also delivers its entire production to The Bergkelder, vinifying only its red blend – the Vintage Rouge – and, more recently, its Cabernet for sale under its own label.

Goede Hoop's winery is as traditional as can be found in that part of Stellenbosch: once again open cement tanks and time-tested methods of grape handling characterise Johan Bestbier's cellar techniques. His son Pieter, who has recently come back to Goede Hoop, takes over the winemaking and may soon impose his own style on the wines. In the mean time, followers of the farm's blended red still have several vintages made the Johan Bestbier way lying in The Bergkelder's Vinoteque for release over the next few years.

The Goede Hoop Vintage Rouge has changed since its first release, a wine from the 1974 vintage. That was very much an old-style South African red, medium-bodied, quite tannic but with a curiously rich fruit bouquet which developed over the years. The more current releases are no less hard, but they seem to develop sooner. There is more Cabernet in the wine now to give it a little extra backbone, while the Carignan provides some early drinking fruit for the less patient.

The Cabernets released to date are very much in the same style: not very big on the nose, and not very easy on the palate. Wood has been well used to add dimension and time may help to bring out berry aromas and a little more concentration.

Further along the M23, and noteworthy from the road because of the gateposts, is Koopmanskloof, another estate supplying through The Bergkelder. Like many of the properties on this side of Stellenbosch, Koopmanskloof can trace ownership back at least two hundred years. Stevie Smit and his son Stefan run the vineyards and cellar respectively and seem committed to redirecting the farm from white wine production back to pot-distilled brandy, as well as Port, and perhaps even some red wine.

Koopmanskloof is a large property, with northern, eastern and southern slopes spread out over the Bottelary hills. Much of its harvest is never sold as estate wine. However, whatever is marketed under the Koopmanskloof name has been carefully selected. The Smits entered The Bergkelder arrangement in the early 1970s. Previously they vinified, bottled and sold the wines themselves. I remember an impressive Roode Droog blend and a richly robust 1972 Pinotage which needed at least a decade before beginning to open up.

After The Bergkelder took over the bottling and distribution, the focus was on white wine. Blanc de Marbonne was launched, a dry white wine blend initially high in Chenin Blanc, later with more of a concentration of Sauvignon and Sémillon. Current vintages are now entirely Sauvignon Blanc, with more of a tropical fruit/gooseberry nose, altogether very accessible and so changed from earlier releases that the name has been amended as a result: the wine is now sold simply as 'Marbonne' and is clearly upgrading with the times.

Koopmanskloof also bottles a Rhine Riesling, finer than many in the Cape, with enough fruit and acidity to ensure that it does not cloy. Accordingly it ages quite well, the spicy nose giving way to the typically terpene character associated with most Stellenbosch Rhine Rieslings and considered desirable by many, though not by me.

Stevie Smit is a committed environmentalist: this means that treatment of the vineyards is as natural as possible. He has however gone much further with the establishment of a Cape flora reserve on the property, and an active interest in promoting regional walks.

Near Koopmanskloof along the same road towards the town is Kaapzicht, one of the lesser known of the Cape's boutique estates. Winemaker Danie Steytler seems to have mastered the art of retaining fruit flavours on his wines: his limited range of Weisser Riesling, Sauvignon Blanc, Pinotage and Cinsaut share a forwardness on the nose and an ease of drinkability uncommon in the wines of many of the country's upmarket producers.

The Sauvignon Blanc, to judge from limited tasting experience, has typical varietal aromas, well balanced and without the harshness that normally accompanies the Sauvignon fruit when harvested too early: clearly the difficult business of timing the moment of picking was well handled. This same gentle fruit characterises the Weisser Riesling, keeping the terpenes in balance, at least for the time being.

The red wines are as elegant, and what they lack in volume they make up in colour and palate. The Pinotage, in particular, has mouthfilling berry flavours yet remains free of the harsh acetone nose to which the varietal is sometimes given.

Almost at the end of the M23, near where it joins the R304 linking the N1 with Stellenbosch, is Hartenberg, formerly known as Montagne. The estate has belonged to Natal businessman Ken Mackenzie for most of the past decade, and he has invested considerable time and money into upgrading the property. New vineyards are now coming into production, adding more up-to-date clonal material to the blends ageing in the newly constructed barrel cellar. The estate's tasting room is a popular call in the season, as is the lunch facility which manages to attract custom through the winter months as well.

Winemaker Danie Truter has been with Hartenberg since prior to Mackenzie's acquisition of the farm. He is now not only familiar with the vineyards and the cellar, but has also overseen the changes and knows more or less what to expect from the new vines. Truter's stint at Hartenberg is now quite substantial and the experience he adds to the equation becomes an important factor in the farm's future.

Hartenberg enjoyed a considerable reputation in its own right for Cabernet and Shiraz, producing a string of Superior certified wines from 1978 through to 1984. Previously, under its Montagne name, it yielded equally impressive wines from old vineyards established by the Finlaysons who had acquired the property just after the Second World War. Montagne was the training ground for both sons – Walter (who went on to Blaauwklippen and then his Glen Carlou farm) and Peter (Hamilton Russell Vineyards and Bouchard Finlayson).

In the late 1970s Gilbeys acquired the farm and began the renewal programme taken up and completed by Ken Mackenzie. New packaging and new brand names were introduced, and the Montagne Estate reverted to its original name of Hartenberg. Gilbeys' sale of Hartenberg was something of a disappointment to the brand managers who had been working on the project. They recognised the intrinsic merits of the property and saw in its growth and evolution an opportunity to place Gilbeys firmly back in the realms of the premium wine industry.

Ken Mackenzie profited from their work. The redesigned labels were considered strikingly original at the time, and while this may have been a liability with several of the white wines, it did help their branding. The red wines already in the cellar gave Hartenberg a wonderful entrée into the market. The Cabernet and Shiraz of the 1978 vintage were industry benchmarks at the time. The 1979s were also good, and well ahead of the average in this lightweight but eminently drinkable year. The 1980s were also in the same league, so were the 1982s. Ken Mackenzie could go to the market with red wines which were the envy of most cellars and use them to slipstream in the sale of the more prolific white wines.

To this end he established a very sensible marketing policy for his Cabernet, namely, that it would not be released for sale until it was six years old. This created 'demand in anticipation' enabling the farm to allocate stock, rather than having to go out and actually sell the wine. Unfortunately, this sort of strategy works only as long as there is genuine demand: it is of little use in disposing of the more plentiful white wines, several of which were perfectly drinkable.

The world did not beat a path to Hartenberg's cellar door for the Weisser Riesling, the blended dry white Chatillon or the slightly botrytised L'Estreux. In so far as the Weisser Riesling and the Chatillon are concerned, this was hardly surprising: both wines were average, and possibly a little overpriced. The L'Estreux, however, has turned out to be a consummately well-made fruit salad of a wine, with excellent concentration and a lovely balance on the palate. The later vintages have already benefited from the new plantings, and include Morio-muscat, Schönberger and Gewürztraminer.

The Hartenberg red wines appear to have dipped a little in the mid 1980s, though in reality they simply ceased to live up to their pretensions and their pricing. Old-style Cabernet was everywhere being usurped by state-of-the-art clonal selection and new wood vinification, while Hartenberg was still offering 1970s styles at 1990s prices. There were always enough buyers around to take up what was on offer, but the talk in wine circles was not good. The turnaround, however, was imminent and just as these observations percolated through to the market, some serious new wines have emerged.

All this has been a matter of timing. The new wood maturation cellar at Hartenberg has been built, and the Cabernets are now getting the kind of oak treatment commensurate with the estate's status. The Shiraz is still made in a more traditional Cape way, where large old vats contribute as much to the style of wine as new barriques do to Cabernet. Several comparative tastings of Cape, Australian and French Shiraz (Syrah) wines confirm that the good vintages from Hartenberg rank well internationally.

Hartenberg is one of the few Cape estates which still maintains commercial plantings of Pontac, a varietal which was, in its time, pretty much the backbone of the red wine industry. As recently as 1970 Montagne actually certified and sold a Pontac Noir of surprising depth and dimension. Nowadays the estate's plantings are blended into two wines sold mainly on the farm, Paragon and Bin 9. Other varietals unusual for the Cape include Zinfandel and Auxerrois – the latter being the grape mistakenly imported in the late 1970s in the midst of the industry-wide Chardonnay smuggling. Most vineyards were subsequently grubbed up by hundreds of irate farmers who thought they had planted Chardonnay. Danie Truter, like many others, had been the innocent recipient of some Auxerrois. He decided that he liked the wine that it produced and now blends his harvest into the Chatillon. Somewhat mischievously, he speaks of doing a limited bottling only of Auxerrois – perhaps to show those who destroyed their vineyards impetuously, or in pique, that they might have done better to maintain them in preference to replanting with newly imported Chardonnay in time for the glut.

Between Hartenberg and the R304 are two tiny properties, neither really fully in production. Beyerskloof is at least crushing grapes bought in from a neighbour, and has several vintages in the trade. Mulderbosch has produced a little Sauvignon Blanc and Blanc Fumé, but is still waiting for its plantings to establish themselves.

Beyerskloof is a joint venture involving several Johannesburg investors and Kanonkop's winemaker, Beyers Truter. The project is small enough for Kanonkop to tolerate with comfort Truter's involvement; the backers, including Diners Club SA's managing director Hugh Peatling, are keen enough about wine, and well enough connected, to limit the marketing risk inherent in such a project.

At this stage there is little more to Beyerskloof than a few hectares of young vineyard, a rudimentary cellar, and a winemaker whose ability and reputation are sufficiently established that each year hundreds of cases of intensely juicy young red wine are sold to buyers willing to take everything on trust.

Beyers Truter is no ordinary winemaker, and his quiet, seemingly self-deprecating manner belies a profoundly sensible view of red wine making. Truter is one of the new generation of Cape cellarmasters who want to see plenty of colour and flavour without excessive tannin. This may sound typically New World, but it is distinguished in its approach by two factors. Firstly, Cape red wines used to be strong, solid and sometimes overwhelmingly clumsy. Avoiding the pitfalls of that route without falling into the trap of light, personality-free wines has not been easily achieved, given the Cape's climate. Secondly, the Cabernet clonal material available in the past tended to problems of underripeness: extraction of flavour without enhancing the green herbaceous character of the grapes was not easily accomplished.

At Beyerskloof Truter is presently dependent on bought-in grapes from old clonal material which can suffer from ripening problems in very warm, or very cool vintages. What he has achieved is, by South African standards, a very promising balance. His wines show deep colours, with plenty of fruit intensity, lots of cassis and raspberry on the nose and an easy soft finish. Twenty years ago, from the same vines, good vintages would have balanced almost porty berry flavours with tannins to outlast the first decade. If the acid levels had been carefully adjusted, or if (rather more miraculously) they had been naturally more or less correct, the wines would have followed a full, almost Rhône-like course through a lengthy maturation. For every success, there would have been innumerable failures, but in those days most of the wine would have been consumed before five years were out.

There is no saying that Truter's approach is guaranteed to make wines which will outlast the achievements of his prede-cessors. The greatest mistake aficionados of Beyerskloof can make is to assume that what they taste in the youth of the wine is a fraction of what it will become. There is no way of knowing at this stage whether, or what kind of, bottle-aged character will emerge. But this is no reason not to go out and buy Beyerskloof for the kind of wine it is right now.

Mulderbosch will be even more difficult to predict. All that can be said now with any certainty is that Mike Dobrovic, the winemaking half of the partnership, is an inspired cellarmaster with a very real feeling about how to get the most complex wine from the grapes coming into his cellar. His stint at Delaire, Storm Quinan's Helshoogte farm, yielded some excellent wines including a Chardonnay which seemed as breathtakingly perfect as anything that had been made at the Cape to date. Whether he can extend his intu-itions and drive from the domain of the cellar to that of the vineyard, and whether he can establish a farm literally from the bare earth to produce the kind of grapes that he seeks, remains to be seen.

Judging from the 1991 Blanc Fumé, made from purchased grapes and beautifully wooded, as well as from the 1992 Sauvignon Blanc coming off newly acquired vineyards, Mulderbosch has enormous potential. The Blanc Fumé will age well, and the young Sauvignon is drinking remarkably well, given its youth.

Once you cross over the R304 there is only one winery of note before the R44, and that is Simonsig. The estate almost warrants a chapter on its own. With over 250 hectares under vine it is one of the top three volume producers, and achieves its sales results entirely independently of any of the major wholesale firms.

The Malan family runs Simonsig entirely as a hands-on business venture. Much of what was achieved over the years to position the estate in its present place of importance in the local industry was achieved by Frans, father of Pieter (marketing), Johan (winemaking), and Francois (vineyards). An early light in the Stellenbosch Wine Route, he has been a ceaseless publicist not only for Simonsig, but also for the region, and, more recently, for the Cape as a whole.

In the course of a long and distinguished career, during which time he was also KWV director for Stellenbosch, Frans Malan has ruffled his fair share of feathers. The Cape wine industry offers more prima donnas per square metre than La Scala. Much of what he said and did earned more calumny than praise. There is no doubt that his intentions were sometimes laced with expediency and self-interest, but what is of importance is that, in the end, he achieved results that were of benefit to more than his own family estate. Despite his being a member of the Board of the KWV, he consistently opposed the organisation's apparent disregard of the interests of estate wine producers.

The Simonsig wines of the 1970s lacked the elegance and subtlety of what Johan Malan is making today. But they were frank and direct, and several looked good then, and continue to do the farm great credit even today. In particular, the Simonsig Pinotages deserve a mention. The 1970 vintage was sold in a Burgundy bottle with a bright red label so awful

131

it would have discouraged any impulse purchase.

Happily for Simonsig, wine drinkers at the time seemed to know that the contents of the bottle deserved the real focus of attention: these old-style Pinotages were full and robust, with quite a lot of the acetone character in their youth, softening out after five to eight years. The 1972 had an almost Burgundian perfume wrapped into the structure and weight of a wine from the Northern Rhône. One bottling from that vintage was marked '100% Pinotage', earning for Malan one of his many disputes with the authorities about disclosure on wine labels.

Firebrand notwithstanding, Frans Malan has waged his various campaigns over a wider range of territory than the immediate concerns of the Simonsig Estate. He has steadfastly opposed the cosy relationship which exists between the KWV and the major players in the industry. His son Pieter has taken this a step further, leading a group of estate wine producers in a programme aimed at forcing government to reduce the KWV's statutory powers as long as the organisation is commercially involved with the industry. Their rallying cry has been 'You can't be player and referee in the same game', a claim which, while it is logically indisputable, seems not to have moved the authorities to more than a cosmetic show of paying attention.

Simonsig sells an important part of its production under various house brand names, mainly in the restaurant and hotel trade. The success of this side of the estate's business is a reflection of the price/quality value of the wine range, particularly among the more traditional Cape varietals. The Adelberg, for example, is a medium-bodied dry red, briefly wooded and sold young but accessible. A high Pinotage content distinguishes it from many other table wines in the same price bracket: it would not be uncommon to find Cinsaut from irrigated vineyards, soft and almost too sweet, selling from other wineries at a premium to the Adelberg.

The same sense of good value characterises a couple of the

132

less expensive white wines. The Chenin Blanc is often undervalued, especially when it is softened with a little residual sugar; the Colombard performed much the same function; the Franciskaner Special Late Harvest offers more complexity and balance than its price would suggest, and the Vin Fumé is one of the country's best-value wooded Sauvignon Blancs.

The more premium varietals also show well in relation to their price. Several of Johan Malan's Chardonnays have positioned themselves comfortably in the forefront of the industry. The 1988 Reserve may have been a little too accessible in ideal terms, but it was made at a time when Chardonnay was desperately short and it was bound to be drunk rather than cellared. Both the regular bottling, as well as the Reserve (prepared for special releases and various prestige auctions) reveal an enormous competence with the varietal, and an understanding of how to fine-tune the wine. Also among the premium white wines are several versions of Weisser Riesling and Gewürztraminer. All show a wonderful sense of fruit and balance, whether as dry wines or as botrytised dessert wines.

The Simonsig Cabernets have definitely improved since the mid 1980s, taking on more complexity from the grapes, as well as from the wood. The Reserve wines in particular are worth looking out for: vinified in Bordeaux Châteaux barrels, there is a fuller and better integrated oak character from the outset. Wood seems in fact to be the reason for the overall improvement of several of the Simonsig reds: the Shiraz, for example, combines the smoky saddle-leather scent of the varietal fruit with an almost sweet vanilla wood, giving it an easy drinkability. This is even more evident in the Pinotage Reserve, a wine of great depth and flavour. Easily one of the best of the current 'new generation' Pinotages, the basic wine is free of the coarse fruit of young wine and the oak maturation gives roundness and finish.

A final note on Simonsig: the estate was the first South African producer of a méthode champenoise sparkling wine, under its Kaapse Vonkel brand name. The original releases were undistinguished and certainly never justified their purchase price. Since the late 1980s traditional varietals have been used and the wine is certainly clearing the rungs of the ladder to approach the levels of the best bubblies in the industry.

THE WINE CELLARS OF STELLENBOSCH
THE WINERIES ON THE SIMONSBERG
SIDE OF STELLENBOSCH

The approach to Stellenbosch from the north on the R44 from Paarl reveals a select group of wineries representing the best of the region's red wine producers. There are not many cellars, but almost all of them enjoy a considerable reputation for their Cabernets and their Cabernet blends. The climate here is warmer and the region better protected from the devastating south-easter. It is hardly surprising that the later ripening Cabernet profits from this environment whereas the more delicate white varietals risk losing some of their finesse. Chardonnay, that most versatile of the premium white cultivars, still performs here though by and large this is territory for red grapes.

Coming in on the R44 towards Stellenbosch, you will find the Lievland Estate close enough to several Paarl farms almost to suggest inclusion in that area of origin. Yet Paul Benade's prize-winning estate is clearly part of Stellenbosch, for its red wines more obviously resemble those of its neighbours to the south, than those to the north and east. It has a couple of creditable white wines, including a Chardonnay that looks as if it could become in time an important player in the South African context, and a spectacular Noble Late Harvest.

The original vintages of this dessert wine were very much in the German style, rich, strongly botrytised, balanced out with commensurate acidity. The 1989 obtained the highest score of any wine in the 1991 International Wine and Spirit Competition in London and should keep well into the 21st century. A recent change in the winemaking has seen the introduction of Sauvignon Blanc to the blend and a softening out of the sugar and the acid. There will be those who lament the change from the German to the French style, though there is no reason why cellarmaster Abe Beukes cannot make two separate cuvées: Lievland seems to be perfect territory for 'stickies' of quality.

However, notwithstanding the success of the Noble Late Harvest, the farm is ideally suited to red wine production – at least to judge from the Cabernet and the Shiraz. The former, softened with a little Merlot, has an almost spicy berry fruit in good vintages. In less than perfect years it seems a little underripe, and suffers from a slight herbaceousness and absence of substance.

The Shiraz vinification contributes to its regular position in the top flight of Cape wines made from this varietal. The grapes are brought into the cellar at lower than conventional sugars and are handled altogether more delicately. Wooding is substantial, but also finely tuned, resulting in a wine that offers plenty of bouquet from the outset, enough flavour on the palate, and a structure that will keep it this way for many years.

Paul Benade, Lievland's proprietor, is a tireless campaigner for the amendment or abolition of much of the bureaucratic red tape which makes up the control mechanism of the Wine and Spirit Board. This is not a policy designed to attract friends in high places, and the estate has had its fair share of difficulties, though whether or not on this account it is obviously impossible to say. A lesser man, or a lesser estate, would never have kept up the pressure. The truth is that Benade refuses to be intimidated, and Lievland is too good to be restricted to the point that its chances of doing business are actually jeopardised. It will, however, take many more producers than Paul Benade before the seemingly arbitrary powers of the Board are brought under control. Fighting the fight, as far as he is concerned, is not a matter of self-interest, but a commitment to the principle that if something is wrong, it behoves those who know better to go out and campaign for change. Abe Beukes' achievements and the overall performance of the estate may have earned the grudging respect of the Board: otherwise the folk at Lievland live a charmed life, and those who openly side with them should walk on tiptoe and look behind doors before entering and leaving a room.

Up the road from Lievland, though still very much on the northern side of Stellenbosch is Le Bonheur, a Bergkelder estate which has gained much deserved attention for its superb Cabernets and a very useful Blanc Fumé. Mike Woodhead laboured many years to bring this property to its present state of perfection, preparing the soils before planting vineyards with up to 40 tons of lime per hectare. Naturally self-effacing and genuinely modest, he is diffident about the praise constantly heaped on his achievements. When things go wrong due to incompetence beyond his control, he has been known to express himself strongly, very colourfully and, relative to his normal manner, quite volubly.

Le Bonheur came to the market more than ten years ago with one of the country's first Blanc Fumés. It was a wine which, at the time, took even the more sophisticated of the local palates by surprise. Those who knew the wines of the Loire recognised the similarity, felt comfortable with the familiarity and tolerated the differences. As South African winemakers became more adept at vinifying the Sauvignon Blanc grape, the reputation of the Le Bonheur wine suffered by comparison with several of the newcomers: it did not have the depth of fruit, its acidities seemed unduly harsh, it lacked dimension on the nose and palate. Then, towards the end of the 1980s it regained much of this lost ground and current vintages rival the best of the Stellenbosch Sauvignons for the wildness and the pungency of their bouquets.

The Le Bonheur Cabernets deserve the international recognition they have gained, included among which is the Warren Winiarski Trophy at the International Wine and Spirit Competition for the best Cabernet on show. Earlier vintages promised more than they ultimately delivered, a fault more of structure than of *terroir*: the 1982 softened too soon, a fate that is unlikely to befall the 1984 or 1986, whose grip and austerity suggest great keeping qualities at no long-term expense to the fruit.

Le Bonheur belongs to an élite group of farms in the vicinity of Klapmutskop: here Cabernet grapes seem capable of great concentration and longevity. The estate's neighbours have all collected medals and prizes for young red wines, and seen those same bottles years later still in the vanguard of the competition. This northern zone of Stellenbosch may be the region's *route des grands crûs*. Its performance over many years suggests that climate and soil, *terroir* in the traditional French sense of the word, is ideally suited to the production of great red wines.

Almost next door to Le Bonheur, on the same side of the R44 and just a little closer to Stellenbosch is Warwick Estate, another of the Cape's premium red wine producers. Since the release of its first Cabernet – from the otherwise undistinguished 1985 vintage – wine critics and wine drinkers alike have sought out Warwick's releases. Proprietor Stan Ratcliffe keeps an eye on the vineyards, while his wife Norma runs the cellar 'with a woman's intuition', as she explains.

Stan acquired Warwick in the mid 1960s and planted many of the Cabernet vineyards with the best material available at the time. This was of course the virus-infected old clone, a liability in cool vintages where there are always problems of ripening. However, in good years and from the best vineyard blocks, it still produces complex and beautifully structured

red wines.

For years the Warwick grapes were delivered to one of the Stellenbosch wholesalers. Then, in the early 1980s, Norma decided that she would like to become a winemaker. A stint in Bordeaux and a lot of help from her friends was hardly the kind of formal preparation that most people would be happy with before taking on a grape crush, but Norma seems to have managed well enough. The 1984 vintage provided her with a trial run, and the occasional bottles of a wine called 'Femme Bleu' that crop up on auction and in the cellars of people well connected to the estate are the result of this exercise.

The 1985s earned Warwick the kind of attention that ensured that the wine was securely launched. All around Paarl and Stellenbosch winemakers had struggled to get some depth and complexity to their Cabernets; most had to make do with light, underripe wines. The Warwick was one of the stars of the vintage, earlier maturing and without real berry fruit, but creditable enough for the wine fraternity to take note of the newcomer.

The 1986s confirmed all the promise of the 1985s, and then set new standards which even Warwick finds difficulty in equalling easily. A perfect vintage, established Cabernet vines, new Merlot vineyards coming into production and plenty of new wood in the cellar all combined to yield wines which have become benchmarks for the farm. The Cabernet is taut and concentrated, with plenty of power and fruit laced with tannin. It is a wine which needs at least ten years in bottle before it will start showing well. Despite its obvious richness, it is counterbalanced with enough austerity and structure to convince everyone that it is not one of those easy-drinking lightweights which will be overwhelmed with a little bottle maturity.

The tiny quantity of 1986 Trilogy, the estate's proprietary wine, also set an enviably high standard for the Warwick

Médoc blend. Very little was made and most was sold at the New World Wine Auction in 1990 and the Nederburg Auction in 1992. Later vintages have confirmed this promise even though harvest variation has played a role: the 1987 Trilogy is much more accessible than the 1986, largely a function of the forwardness of the Cabernet, since the separately released Merlot showed remarkable concentration.

Warwick now produces several red wines, all of which are related through the Trilogy blend. Cabernet Sauvignon is still very much the estate's regular red wine. More recent vintages have confirmed the style of the 1986s, to the extent that the weather permits any one year to be like any other. The Merlot is often sold as a separate varietal wine. It has a depth and richness unlike many of the lighter, and admittedly more quaffable wines readily available from other farms. The Cabernet Franc is something of a rising star, even in the well-illuminated firmament of Warwick: it is more forward than the Cabernet Sauvignon, yet not overly plump, easy-drinking in quite an austere sort of way. The Trilogy presents itself exactly as a Bordeaux blend: finer and more complex than any of the single varietals, it balances intensity with length, fruit with structure, acid with tannin.

Warwick has also started producing a small quantity of Chardonnay, the work mainly of Norma's assistant, Lola Hunting. Early indications are that this will be a serious first league contender: plenty of varietal fruit, coupled with a strong, but not overwhelming lees character, well finished off with mainly new oak. Since the real business of Warwick is red wines, it seems certain that the Chardonnay, however good, will always defer to the Cabernets and Merlots of the estate.

A little closer to Stellenbosch, and just across the R44 is the Kanonkop Estate, named after the low hill to the back of the farm on which used to be positioned a cannon which signalled to the 18th-century Stellenbosch farmers the arrival of ships seeking victualling in Table Bay. No one disputes the reputation of this estate, one of the country's best known and most admired producers of red wine. The quality of the farm's grapes has been a matter of record for most of this century, though its history of viticulture indeed dates back to the early settlement of the Dutch colony. For most of this century the wholesale merchants have sought out the grapes from Kanonkop precisely because they could be counted upon to upgrade any blend.

In 1973 the estate began bottling a small percentage of its production for sale under its own label. The occasional un-labelled earlier bottlings dating back to the 1960s, usually from the proprietor's cellar, confirm the quality and longev-ity of the farm's wines. I recall a 1972 Pinotage, tasted later in the 1970s, still black in colour and with such intense cassis fruit, that my first impression was of Côte Rotie, somehow transformed with blackcurrant juice.

Kanonkop's public reputation goes back to the first official bottling of the wine, the 1973 vintage made by cellarmaster of the time, rugby Springbok Jan 'Boland' Coetzee. From the release of this first Cabernet, demand for the farm's wines has always exceeded the quantity the estate's owners have set aside for sale under their own label.

The 1973 Cabernet was one of the best red wines of that otherwise unremarkable vintage, and bottles still about – either from auctions or from private collections – substanti-ate its quality as much as its longevity. Several other vintages from the 1970s were curiously disappointing, though their relative under-performance seems not to have dampened the enthusiasm of the estate's committed followers. The 1978 Cabernet vintage vindicated their loyalty and once again focused the South African red wine drinker on Kanonkop's vast potential.

Winemaker 'Boland' Coetzee's departure from the farm to begin his own cellar at Vriesenhof gave Beyers Truter a once-in-a-lifetime opportunity to run a winery that was already something of a national institution. He took his chance with both hands, producing the region's champion young red wine in his first vintage. In fairness, he was not only the obvious successor by virtue of his being there, but he also inherited Frikkie Elias who, as cellar assistant to his predecessor, really did know how to work the winery. He was also the beneficiary of Coetzee's considerable vineyard upgrade programme which had been running for most of the 1970s (and which may in part explain some of the patchy wines from what should otherwise have been a distinguished decade). Whatever the case, within a few years it was clear that Truter's successes were no mere matter of happenstance, of being in the right place at the right time, but reflected a profound understanding of the farm on which he was working, and a real philosophy of red wine making.

It was on his insistence that the estate abandoned its paltry white wines and its frightening Pinot Noir, freeing him to concentrate on the real business at hand: the robust, full-coloured, large-boned red wines which are what Kanonkop is all about. In the last few years he has repeatedly produced wines of such substance and structure that no one today doubts his competence, or the value of the estate's *terroir*.

Kanonkop's Cabernet is one of the Cape's most voluminous wines made from the varietal. Chewy, intense and alcoholic, it is not for the faint of heart: the grape tannins as well as the distinctive oaking pretty much define it as a wine for the long haul. The Paul Sauer blend, named after the late proprietor of the estate, a former Cabinet Minister whose interest in wine was at least as much organoleptical as it was political, is really a Médoc blend with a teaspoonful of Souzão for the colour it hardly needs. Cabernet Sauvignon predominates: the Cabernet Franc is there only to add extra breadth and the 10 per cent Merlot to give it texture. Most years Truter prepares an Auction Reserve, for sale through

142

the Cape Independent Winemakers' Guild. This wine tends to get the best of the wooding and is guaranteed to last longer and give more life at the end.

Perhaps Truter's great distinction at Kanonkop, and the role for which in the end the industry will come to remember him, has been his single-minded battle to obtain recognition for Pinotage as a serious varietal. In this he is very much the heir to Paul Sauer, who gave the cultivar place in his vineyards even before it had a proven track record. Beyers Truter has systematically set out to show that Pinotage, if vinified as a premium red varietal, delivers those qualities expected of a great red wine.

On the way, he has also collected his share of acknowledgement for what has been achieved. He won the Diners Club Winemaker of the Year Award when the Pinotage category came to be judged; his 1989 Pinotage Reserve romped home in the 1991 International Wine and Spirit Competition, bringing not only the satisfaction of that achievement, but also, with his other wines, the crowning glory of the Robert Mondavi Trophy for the International Winemaker of the Year. It is clear now from the 1989 Reserve wine, the 1990 regular and Reserve wines, and from his overall grasp of Pinotage vinification from 1985 onwards, that Truter has fulfilled his aim: if other Cape wineries follow his example, Pinotage can provide the Cape wine industry with the export value equivalent of Australian Shiraz. Needless to say, in this event Kanonkop's would be the South African equivalent of Penfold's Grange.

In the same superb red wine territory, and in fact once the original property from which Kanonkop was divided, is the Uitkyk Estate, formerly owned by Baron von Carlowitz and now controlled by The Bergkelder. With over 150 hectares of vineyard it is no small enterprise. The highest slopes are a four-wheel drive journey into the Simonsberg, but they combine the virtues of the red wine basin extending out towards

Le Bonheur and back towards Stellenbosch itself with some exposure to the sea breezes which crest the ridge of the mountain.

The Uitkyk homestead is unique to the winelands, a late 18th-century Cape Georgian townhouse designed by the famous French architect, Louis Thibault. In Von Carlowitz's time – in other words, from the late 1940s to the early 1960s – Uitkyk produced one of the country's finest reds, a Cabernet of cherry-like colour intensity and lingering berry flavours. For ten years from 1963 to 1973 Uitkyk bottled no wines. Then, through The Bergkelder it began releasing wines which immediately earned the attention of the wine fraternity.

Looking back on the 1973 Uitkyk Carlonet, the estate's proprietary Cabernet Sauvignon, it is easy to see why it attracted so much interest even then. Well structured though not too full, it showed good balance and like the Cabernet from nearby Kanonkop, comfortably exceeded all expectations for that vintage. Winemaker at the time, Dr Harvey Illing, continued to produce impressive wines through most of the decade of the 1970s. The 1974 was widely recognised as one of the estate's best-ever wines, overshadowing not only the more average vintage of 1975 but also the highly reputed 1976. By the early 1980s The Bergkelder was already changing the wine's style prior to bottling. Structure was being gained at the expense of fruit, finesse at the cost of flesh on the palate. With The Bergkelder already halfway towards owning the historic property, it was only a matter of time before the company took control and began a massive renovation programme on the vineyards and cellar.

The wines which are now emerging from Uitkyk are more representative of this new generation. The very young Cabernets already have more volume and flavour than some of the wines from the late 1970s and early 1980s. This is in part because The Bergkelder itself has changed some of its handling methods but also because the new man in charge of the cellar, Jan du Preez, has vinified the wines to concentrate the fruit.

Uitkyk also produces the Carlsheim Sauvignon Blanc, a wine that is perhaps too taut on the palate for those who like their Sauvignons with more gooseberry, grassy fruit. The Carlsheim is a wine which has evolved over the years, taking into its blend the increasing quantities of Sauvignon from the plantings of the late 1970s onwards. Now offered for sale as a Sauvignon Blanc, it has managed to keep many of its loyal drinkers while attracting others to the catch-name of a premium varietal.

Uitkyk's other red wine is its Shiraz, released in very limited quantities from the 1973 vintage, and then not again until the 1981 came to the market. The relaunch of the Shiraz provoked more than a little interest in the trade, not only because the 1973 had never been given a chance to become an important seller, but also because it followed a most curious event at auction. Sotheby's were conducting a sale in Pretoria involving the disposal of an important cellar from what was unquestionably the city's best-known de luxe restaurant. Among the wines on offer was some 1973 Shiraz, an unusual item, though by no stretch of the imagination an oenological gem. The wine was estimated at R20 per bottle and the parcel contained three dozen bottles. There was widespread bidding to about top estimate, after which only two buyers were left chasing the first lot. When it was clear that neither would yield the advantage, and the bid on the first case was hovering around the R7 000 mark, Stephan Welz, the auctioneer, spoke to both parties. Shortly thereafter one dropped out and the successful buyer exercised his right to buy the two remaining cases at the price he had just paid for the first of the three dozen.

Since this was a public, commercial auction without any real publicity garnering prospects, this sale of three cases of

Cape wine for nearly R22 000 was a newsworthy event. At about the same time in London an astute buyer might have picked up a case each of all the First Growths from the 1961 vintage and still had some change for his cab fare home. What would possess anyone, no matter how sentimental, to spend so much for the admittedly rare, though not hugely memorable, Uitkyk Shiraz 1973?

The story which emerged provided one of those salutary lessons about bidding at an auction. Both interested parties were acting as agents for people who could not attend the sale. The buyer who finally dropped out of the bidding had been told by a wealthy, but not fanatical collector, to buy the Uitkyk 1973 'at any price' because the vintage was the birth year of his son. The agent, who knew nothing about the wine, took his instructions quite literally, and only when the auctioneer took the unprecedented step of stopping the sale to discuss the matter between both bidders did he realise that he was probably already exceeding his brief. The other agent had been given an almost identical instruction on behalf of a party with an interest in the Uitkyk Estate. He knew that his principal had virtually unlimited resources and assumed that 'any price' meant exactly that: he would have bid the wines to R100 000 per case had the need arisen. Since he had been further instructed to secure the parcel, he was perfectly happy to exercise his option and take the remaining two at their auction record price.

This misunderstanding doubtless had nothing to do with the release, some months later, of the first Uitkyk Shiraz in nearly a decade. However, the investment in the 1973 was not entirely wasted: it generated such publicity and attached such prestige to the wine that the new release came to a suitably receptive market. More recently the wine has started to look worthy of all the launch attention. The latest vintage is somewhat reminiscent of the 1973 at the time of its release, plenty of Shiraz fruit on the nose and not particularly hard on the palate. Current vintages have also profited from the extra dimension of oak maturation, suggesting that in time they will rival on the palate the pretension of the 1973 in the auction room.

Two other famous cellars are situated nearby: Muratie and Delheim. Muratie lies between the R44 and Delheim, so visitors to the latter must actually pass through Muratie before they reach their destination. Muratie's history as a wine farm has been, like most Cape estates, a chequered account of feast or famine. The land grant dates back to 1685, about as old as any Stellenbosch property, and rivalling even Van der Stel's Constantia. For most of this century the farm belonged to the Canitz family, firstly to Paul and more recently to his daughter Annemarie who was born at the turn of the century and died only in 1991. Shortly before her death the estate was acquired by Ronnie Melck, formerly managing director of Stellenbosch Farmers Winery, from the era prior to the company's takeover by the KWV/Rembrandt partnership. Miss Canitz ended her days gracefully at the farm she had lived on all her life. Meanwhile Melck, his viticulturist Hennie van der Westhuizen and winemaker Christo Herrer got on with the business of renovating the vineyards.

Their work was long overdue. Neither Miss Canitz nor her cellarmaster Ben Prince were wine drinkers and over a long period of time Muratie had not only fallen behind the rest of the industry, it had sunk into itself. Its famous wines from the 1960s had been variable enough, but nevertheless enjoyed a following. Among the so-called varietal wines which used to be offered (prior to the 1973 Act which imposed some control on cultivar descriptions) were Muratie Pinot Noir and a Muratie Pinot Noir-Gamay. Any resemblance to Burgundy or Bourgogne *Passe-toutes-grains* respectively was purely coincidental. This does not mean that these old Muratie wines were of dubious quality: on the contrary, nearly all were drinkable, several were very good, and a surprising number have aged rather well.

The Melcks seem to be doing the right things in the right order: vineyards before cellar, cellar before homestead, and so on. And the first releases show that while they have managed to keep a couple of Miss Canitz's brands, they are also moving forward in a direction more appropriate to the late 20th century. The Canitz survivors, at this stage at any rate, are the Port and the Muratie Amber. The former is much more of a Cape than a Portuguese Port, despite the presence of several Port varietals in the predominantly Shiraz blend. The latter is a fortified Muscat, plenty of fruit upfront and enough sugar and alcohol to have a momentum all of its own. Over the years the Amber has acquired the most eclectic following: cabinet ministers and stevedores have found themselves paying homage to the winemaker with the last glass of Amber in the bottle.

Where the new direction at Muratie will ultimately take the Cabernet, Pinot Noir and Shiraz remains to be seen. Early indications are that the wines are being made to show sooner, rather than later, but not at the expense of the flavour constituents. The first releases are quite forward, free of aggressive tannins though with ageing potential.

Further up the hill is Delheim, one of the region's most successful private cellars. The winery draws its grapes from a couple of farms, some spectacular Cabernets off the Vera Cruz vineyard down the road towards Klapmutskop, and a remarkable array of varietals on the main property.

Delheim has been associated with Spatz Sperling for so long that his longtime co-shareholder H.O. Hoheisen, after whose wife Del the farm was named, appears to have been forgotten. More interestingly, Sperling's very firm hand on the business ensures that it handles the passage of winemakers with the greatest of apparent ease. When Kevin Arnold, who was by then almost a legend, left Delheim to take up a position at Rust-en-Vrede, the industry tut-tutted, assuming that the commercial demise of Delheim was imminent. Arnold's assistant stepped into his shoes with aplomb: he knew his job, he was familiar with the vineyards and he wanted to impose his own personality on the wine.

Philip Costandius has done a vast amount for Delheim in the four or five vintages that he has taken through the winery himself. While Kevin Arnold's great strength was champion quality red wines, Costandius has managed to upgrade the overall standard of the range, and still produce some superb Cabernets and Cabernet blends. As with Arnold's reds, the best wines have come, almost invariably, from grapes grown on the Vera Cruz vineyard. A regular Delheim Cabernet upgraded with Vera Cruz grapes becomes altogether more intense, a concentration of berry flavours with plenty of structure and grip on the palate.

Vera Cruz provides the grapes for the Delheim Grand Reserve, a wine launched in 1982 amid much excitement, initially as a premium Cabernet, but since 1984 increasingly blended with Merlot. The property has now been planted with newer Cabernet clones, giving the recent Grand Reserves a more minty, spicy, berry character than previously. Costandius has maintained the position of the Grand Reserve in the first division of Cape claret blends. He has also managed to produce an excellent value Cabernet, a very drinkable Shiraz, a Merlot of great distinction and several creditable white wines.

Chief among these have been the off-dry and sweeter wines ranging from an overwhelmingly fragrant Gewürztraminer, a spicy – and, for this reason alone, surprisingly interesting – Rhine Riesling, and a trio of honeyed late harvests: regular, special, and noble, all with increasing levels of sugar and botrytis, all with increasingly concentrated aromas and palates.

Delheim's wines owe their popularity to their high quality at competitive prices. They also profit from the auction-style cuvées, flagship wines which garner publicity and measure out performance. In his ability to walk the minefield of the wine industry's politics, Sperling is without peer. A local wag once observed that Sperling has managed to insinuate his wines on to every auction and special release programme operating out of the winelands. 'Spatz,' he added, 'uses a national trade distributor, but also sells directly to several retailers. He also actively encourages retail business off the farm, notwithstanding the complaints from the trade that he parallels against them. Sperling dances at every wedding.'

Of course this is true, but it is a tribute to Sperling's competence and political acumen that, forty years on, he is still running one of the most successful cellars in the winelands, giving value for money for those who seek table wine and ensuring that there are enough premium wines about for Delheim's reputation to rest secure.

Closer to the town, located on a beautiful site with views out towards the Bottelary hills, is Morgenhof, a three hundred year old property on which an upgrade programme has only recently been undertaken. The farm was bought by Rhine Ruhr Holdings in 1981. Ex-KWV cellarmaster Pietie Theron was brought in as a consultant and the early results seem very promising. Theron's strength lies in fortified wines. His first Morgenhof release of note is a 1988 ruby Port, rich, slightly honeyed on the nose but finishing quite dry. More wines like this, but in quantities that at least will make them accessible to the general buying public, will do a great deal for the farm's reputation.

Until now Morgenhof has been dependent on a couple of good Cabernet vintages – the 1984 showing quite well in its youth and the 1988 looking pretty good now – and an acceptable but unremarkable Sauvignon Blanc and Rhine Riesling. Denzel van Vuuren is both general manager as well as hands-on winemaker under the direction of Pietie Theron. Between the two of them they need to optimise the grapes at their dis-

150

An eagle's eye view of the Klein Constantia vineyards (Reproduced by permission of Klein Constantia Estate)

The Klein Constantia underground barrel maturation cellar (Reproduced by permission of Klein Constantia Estate)

The Manor House, Groot Constantia (Reproduced by permission of Groot Constantia Estate)

The fermentation cellar at Vergelegen, Somerset West (Reproduced by permission of Vergelegen)

Aerial view of new winery at Vergelegen. Photographer: Colin Elliot of Studio 7 (Reproduced by permission of Vergelegen)

Winemaker Norma Ratcliffe of Warwick (Reproduced by permission of Warwick Farm)

Jan 'Boland' Coetzee, winemaker at Vriesenhof and Talana Hill

Bottles containing the legendary Constantia wines of the early 19th century (Reproduced by permission of Sotheby's, Johannesburg)

Neil Ellis, Neil Ellis Wines and Louisvale Estate

Winetasting room at La Motte Estate in Franschhoek. Photographer: Dirk Visser (Reproduced by permission of La Motte Landgoed)

Patrick Grubb who has conducted the Nederburg Auction since its inception in 1975
(Reproduced by permission of Jenny McQueen & Associates)

The red wine cellar
at Nederburg in
Paarl (Reproduced
by permission of
Jenny McQueen &
Associates)

Giorgio Dalla Cia, winemaker at the Meerlust Estate in Stellenbosch (Reproduced by permission of Distillers Corporation)

Sydney Back of Backsberg Estate in Paarl (Reproduced by permission of Backsberg Estate)

posal to produce wines which are as striking as the property on which they are made.

The restoration work that has been done at Morgenhof is extensive and involves bringing the buildings painstakingly to original condition. This quality of investment extends to the vineyards, over 40 hectares of which have been planted. With its conference and catering facilities, the property is now very much on the wine map. It needs its new generation of wines to complete its story.

THE WINE CELLARS OF STELLENBOSCH
HELSHOOGTE, IDA'S VALLEY,
AND JONKERSHOEK

There are not many private cellars on the north-eastern (Helshoogte) side of Stellenbosch, but those there are can all be numbered among the region's best producers. On Helshoogte (Hell Heights) itself, the steep mountain pass separating Franschhoek from Stellenbosch, there are two relatively new properties, Thelema and Delaire. Down the pass towards the town are three other wineries of merit: Rustenberg, nestling in the historic Ida's Valley on the very boundaries of the town; Oude Nektar, almost on the edge of the Jonkershoek nature reserve; and Rozendal, a little closer to Stellenbosch next to the historic Lanzerac farm.

Thelema is unquestionably the most striking of all the new wineries in the Stellenbosch area of origin. Located on the northernmost rise of the Helshoogte pass, its vineyards attain an altitude of 550 metres. From that vantage point at the top of the pass, Cape Town itself is visible. It is hardly surprising that Gyles Webb, the winemaker and co-proprietor of the farm, chose this place to settle down. Not that settling down is a term to be used lightly around the Caliban-like Webb. A qualified chartered accountant, he wilfully exchanged vineyards for ledgers, requalified at Stellenbosch University, worked a stint at SFW, did the same for Joe Heitz in California, and then set up Thelema with his wife Barbara and the assistance of family.

For those who know about such things, this has been no

easy path to follow. It is difficult to imagine a less certain existence: there were no vineyards to speak of, so land had to be cleared and its real potential assessed; plantings followed and then a winery. Vines can flourish without any guarantee as to the quality of the fruit. There is no alternative but to carry on, hoping that in the end the grapes which come into the cellar will have the right flavour components. Only from this point onwards can the winemaker really exercise skills that separate the spectacular from the merely sound.

Gyles Webb has run this obstacle course without signs of stumbling. His vineyards are among the finest in the district. His Sauvignon Blanc block, for example, has carried off the Stellenbosch vineyard prize. His cellar is practical, without extravagance, and yet one of the most aesthetically pleasing in the Cape. His wines are sensibly priced and sell out ahead of the release date of the next vintage. Most importantly, each year brings bigger and more complex wines through barrel to bottle, a sure sign that as the vineyards establish themselves, Thelema is destined to become one of the great wineries of the New World.

The farm's most regular seller is its Sauvignon Blanc, one of the better wines in the region, though considered by some to be a little hard, especially in its youth: the grass and asparagus flavours are there, but so is a structure which demands a little bottle maturity. The enormous popularity of the wine ensures that little enough outlasts the year of vintage so its full maturation potential remains to be discovered.

The Chardonnay is one of the Cape's best, a blend of fruit and grip, of oak vanilla and elegance that sets new standards for the industry. Gyles Webb's own sparse style pretty much ensures that his wines, no matter how flamboyant, are never really excessive and the Chardonnay epitomises this. All of the right elements are there, everything is in balance, nothing needs to be sought out, and yet none of the statement has been wasted.

This same style describes the achievement of the Cabernet, as well as the barrel samples I have tasted of his Merlot. The wines are almost overburdened with fruit and juicy texture and yet they are neither flabby nor overly exuberant. New clone Cabernet, as well as *terroir*, are responsible for the spicy, minty character which is woven into the blackcurrant fruit. Webb's use of wood is masterly, giving the wines that extra bit of structure to carry them through and add vanilla to the fruit salad of flavours. The curious feature about these Thelema reds is that though they sound a little too technicolour for serious red wine drinkers, they are so well knitted together, and so obviously fine-tuned by the winemaker, that you know they will evolve past the fermentation fruit stage into something more conventional without actually fading into obscurity.

There is a temptation to label Webb as the quintessential New World winemaker, bringing new vineyards to life, and then magnifying the colours and flavours of his wines. However, the disciplines of the chartered accountant prevail: the well thought out economies are never signs of meanness, but rather of balance, of intensities reined in, rather than unrestrained flood. This in the end positions him closer in style to the winemakers of Europe. Also, these are still early days: the vineyards have produced exceptional fruit, and Webb has made luminous wine from it. But bottles must evolve for many years before what emerges can be judged. At this stage it is clear that Thelema and Gyles Webb are yielding some of the most promising wines ever seen in South Africa.

Almost across the road from Thelema is Delaire, the vineyard originally acquired by John Platter in the early 1980s and then sold to Storm and Ruth Quinan in 1988. It was Delaire which first drew everyone's attention to the vineyard potential of Helshoogte, and although Platter moved on to Clos du Ciel before his plantings yielded mature fruit, his decision to develop the vineyards there has been vindicated by the wines which have subsequently been produced.

The Quinans have brought a special quality to Delaire, the quality which comes from people who have invested a place with a commitment to make it a measure of their lives. The farm was originally purchased as a plaything: it has become a home, a very demanding responsibility, but also a way of life. Storm Quinan will stand with you at sunset on the very highest slopes of his vineyards, where even in midsummer the cool evening breezes bring a chill to the air, and say, 'I don't need more than this: a man can only eat three meals a day and those I can always buy. But I hope I never have to give this up because I know I shall never in my lifetime be lucky enough to own it again.'

The Quinans' first winemaker was Mike Dobrovic who has since moved on to set up Mulderbosch. They were fortunate to replace him with someone who has stepped so easily into the breach that there seems to have been no disruption at all to the farm's impressive range. Chris Keet has brought out of his first harvest at Delaire that same concentration of flavour and bouquet which characterised the best aspects of Dobrovic's winemaking. More to the point, he seems to have taken over the *élevage* of Dobrovic's wines and brought them in a very presentable condition to the market. The blended wines, and most especially those which have in the past been aged for some time in wood, have all emerged unscathed from the change in cellarmaster.

Among the white wines which have come from the new winemaker, the Weisser Riesling does just about as well as can be expected. The Chardonnay follows the direction of Dobrovic's highly successful vintages, well structured and not overburdened with wood. The reds have been well assembled: the Cuvée Rouge continues to provide good drinking value and the Barrique now has an even greater depth and intensity.

Delaire has the potential to produce full-flavoured wines

of great finesse. Grapes which have come off suitably mature vines and which have had the benefit of careful and unhurried vinification yield wines which compare with the best of the region's cool climate vineyards. The Helshoogte farms have their own microclimate, their own *terroir*. There is nothing quite like them anywhere else in the area of origin: their continued success is bound to bring more pioneers up the mountain.

At the foot of the Helshoogte pass is Ida's Valley, an enclave which has been declared a National Preservation Area in its entirety. In the midst of what is the most verdant and olde worlde part of Stellenbosch are two farms which together comprise the Rustenberg Estate. Owned by the Barlow family since the Second World War, Rustenberg and Schoongezicht are national monuments in their own right. The land grant dates back to 1692: the farms and their vineyards have enjoyed an international reputation since the 19th century. Cape Prime Minister John Merriman was a one-time owner. The rich and famous have made the valley a visiting place on their trips through the Cape, contributing, through their anecdotes and accounts, to the standing of the estate and its vines.

Rustenberg has had only three winemakers this century, the present incumbent, Etienne le Riche, having taken over from Reg Nicholson in the mid 1970s. The farm's general manager, Charles Withington, tells stories from his student days of how Nicholson managed the winery, beginning at dawn by writing all his own correspondence in copperplate longhand before setting out into the vineyards, or tending the prize Jersey herds.

I remember the Rustenberg and Schoongezicht wines from my childhood. My parents and their friends used to buy what seemed to be enormous quantities, arranging with Nicholson to rail them up to Johannesburg. At the time this was considered an unusual way to go about wine buying: in those days the Transvaal did not have much of a wine culture. It hardly seemed worth the effort to send for your wines from the Cape even though the choice of what was available in bottlestores was limited. When these consignments of wine arrived at the house, the delivery staff from the railways were clearly perplexed: who could possibly want to buy all this wine, and were we sure my father was not running an illicit shebeen, stocking it with liquor from the Cape? We provided whatever assurances we could and cellared the stocks. After several years of bottle maturation the old Rustenbergs gave us wines which were uncomplex but not simple, beautifully balanced and easy to drink.

In those days there were really only two wines to buy: the Schoongezicht White, a light and undemanding dry wine, and the Rustenberg Dry Red, a blend of two-thirds Cabernet and one-third Cinsaut, combined at the crush and fermented together. This rather simple method of vinification ensured a much greater harmony between the two varietals than a separate fermentation of each cultivar was likely to have yielded. Its disadvantage was the relative condition of ripeness and underripeness of two different grape types harvested at the same time. Occasionally this harmony in the bottle was short-lived, as the wine started breaking up with one varietal getting to the end of the road before the rest of the blend.

Reg Nicholson steadfastly refused to inoculate the must with commercially produced yeasts, believing instead that the natural yeasts on the grapes would perform an adequate and more natural function. His successor maintained the philosophy but also advanced it. Le Riche has changed much at Rustenberg since he has taken over from Nicholson, but never without due consideration, never in a hurry, and never to the detriment of the estate's wines.

The quiet, unassuming Le Riche is a graduate of Stellenbosch University's oenology and viticulture faculty. He is widely respected by his peers, and is probably one of the few

157

people in the Cape winelands who is universally admired. His successes at Rustenberg have been thorough and unspectacular, befitting his style. In the time that he has had charge of the cellar, the estate's range has widened considerably, new vineyards have been developed, new techniques judiciously employed. Rustenberg now offers a Cabernet as a regular wine within the range (Nicholson had only produced about three vintages of single varietal wine) as well as a Bordeaux blend. A Chardonnay is made annually, likewise a Pinot Noir, and there are the occasional releases of Port, and Méthode Champenoise. In addition, wines have been introduced and then culled, like a Blanc de Noir, a Sauvignon Blanc and a Rhine Riesling.

Etienne le Riche's best wines are his quietly understated reds. The Rustenberg Gold (the Médoc blend) has been on the market now since the mid 1980s and improves each year, allowing for obvious vintage variation. Often overly quiet in its youth, it is never so much unapproachable as slightly diffident until it has had a few years in bottle. The same is true, though even more markedly so, of the Cabernet: in its youth it seems structurally sound, but unexciting. It takes years to begin to open up, and when it does begin to yield its fruit and flavours, it is unrecognisably different from the shy, almost self-deprecating wine which was released perhaps ten years previously.

Rustenberg's Dry Red has also changed, not only because more recently the traditional Cabernet/Cinsaut blend has had the benefit of a little Merlot and Cabernet Franc, but also because with the widening up of the range, an earlier maturing wine has become a functional necessity. The older wines were a little bigger and perhaps more intense. The 1974, for example, is still going strong, one of the greatest wines of that remarkable vintage, and a Rustenberg blend that could perform happily in the company of fine claret.

Rustenberg's Pinot Noir is entirely Le Riche's achievement. He took over newly planted vineyards of the lightweight BK5 clone and, with careful viticulture and intuition in the cellar, has brought it into the front rank of South African Pinots. Not that this makes it a Burgundy look-alike. Despite the cooler summers and longer ripening season at Rustenberg, the wines which emerge lack the spice and intensity of even a Côte Chalonnaise. Just the same, the improvement in the past decade suggests that at Rustenberg, as well as at the other top Pinot establishments, a Côte d'Or-style product may not be impossible in the next few years.

Rustenberg's Chardonnay has its following among those who seek out the citrus-like austerity of a good Chablis: the wine is never too lean, and the light oaking gives it that extra dimension so often missing in all but Premier and Grand Crû Chablis. These Chardonnays age surprisingly well, following the pattern of the red wines in revealing least about themselves in their youth, and then flowering after several years in bottle.

Not far from Rustenberg, and almost as close to Stellenbosch though more to the east, is Rozendal, where restaurateur Kurt Amman surprised most of the country's wine fraternity by turning out a superb 1983 from his first ever vintage. That year, and again the following year, he had the undoubted benefit of really old vines, acquiring his grapes from the vineyards at Lanzerac.

Both the 1983 and 1984 Rozendals show some bottle variation. Those who have not had the pleasure of a top bottle of Amman's first vintage will be less inclined to marvel at how a Swiss-trained restaurant proprietor from Johannesburg arrived in Stellenbosch and turned out a wine which must rate as one of the best produced in the region that year. Later vintages vary inasmuch as the source of grapes has changed. By the late 1980s Merlot began to predominate in the blend; older vines have been replaced with younger, but healthier clonal material, and it will be some time before the wines of

Rozendal can settle down.

In the mean time Kurt Amman has finally succeeded in obtaining permission to run a guest house and restaurant on the property. With his culinary skills, and a European sense of what is expected of a country hotel, L'Auberge Rozendal could set new standards in South Africa.

Slightly beyond Rozendal, and therefore closer to the Jonkershoek Nature Reserve, is Oude Nektar. This is an estate in the midst of a transition. Its vineyards are being replanted, its cellar brought up to date. The wines from the earlier era were agreeable but unremarkable: the whites with enough flavour and structure to hold together; the reds, all vinified in one or another oak, showed varietal character through the wooding. The appointment of Neil Ellis as consultant winemaker and Eben Archer to establish the new vineyards suggests that this Jonkershoek estate is set to produce the kind of wine appropriate to the *terroir*.

Oude Nektar and Rustenberg are probably the two estates closest to the urban agglomeration of Stellenbosch. Within minutes of their front gates you find yourself driving through well-established suburbs. The growth of Stellenbosch has been achieved without the wholesale destruction of these vineyards which now form an integral part of the town. Farms such as these are also not threatened by the kind of encroachment which is creeping up on outlying estates like Jacobsdal through urban land hunger – the Cape Peninsula spreading towards Stellenbosch and not vice versa. However the town does have land pressures of its own, and this is nowhere made more clear than in the south, where the Helderberg mountains stretch down towards Somerset West and False Bay. Commercial, industrial and housing developments are taking land from agriculture. Individual vineyards have been absorbed in this southward movement of the town. Happily, most of the wineries lie beyond the golf course. This land loss nevertheless does have long-term costs for the region. The two cellars closest to the town are recent creations and were developed to handle grapes coming off vineyards that would most certainly have succumbed in time to urban spread. Both properties have revealed enormous potential and this will strengthen their chances to resist the incursions of the town. We do not know how much land of this quality has already been lost to townhouses and shopping centres. There is no shortage of wine in the Stellenbosch area of origin: the lament is not for a loss in volume, but in variety. Each of these zones has its own unique *terroir*. As you travel south from Stellenbosch to the sea and look at each of the wineries along the way, the pace of urban encroachment leaves this sobering thought: Rustenberg is the last wine estate left in Ida's Valley; Oude Nektar is the last wine estate left in the Jonkershoek. How long will it be before the economic logic of the town's spread towards the south leaves only a few survivors among the Helderberg wineries?

THE WINE CELLARS OF STELLENBOSCH
FROM FALSE BAY ALONG THE
HELDERBERG

The Stellenbosch area of origin extends as far south as the coast. While most of the major Helderberg properties are quite close to Stellenbosch itself, there has been an increase in wine farming activity right on the border of Somerset West.

In 1987 Anglo American acquired the historic Vergelegen property on the banks of the Lourens River. The corporation's wine farming interests already include Boschendal, the Cape's top-selling estate wine. It seemed logical that at least some of Vergelegen's 3000 hectares would be given over to wine production.

Vergelegen was established at the beginning of the 18th century by Willem Adriaan van der Stel, who succeeded his father Simon as Commander of the Dutch East India Company's settlement at the Cape. Inspired by his father's huge Constantia domain, it appears that Willem Adriaan determined to improve upon it. The Vergelegen location had advantages and disadvantages compared with Constantia. It was closer to the shipping lanes and provided early notice of vessels entering False Bay from the East. This meant that Van der Stel was better informed than many of the Stellenbosch farmers and could get his fresh produce to the harbour ahead of the competition, hardly the kind of conduct to make the Commander a popular figure among the farming community. The disadvantage of the proximity to the sea was the high risk of wind damage to crops. This could be minimised by selecting sites that were better protected.

Van der Stel's conduct as Commander led to considerable resentment among the Free Burghers, several of whom looked covetously at Vergelegen as they listed their complaints and grievances in a petition addressed to the Dutch East India's Council of Seventeen in Amsterdam. Their campaign was ultimately successful and led to Van der Stel's banishment and an instruction from the Company that the Vergelegen homestead was to be destroyed and the land divided. It is clear that these conditions were never fully complied with; what is certain is that the land was considered highly desirable. The property was ultimately partitioned and ended up with several owners. The manor house was burnt down, though this was probably at a later date and not as a result of the Company's instructions, and only the walled hexagonal garden survived Van der Stel's tenure by more than a few decades.

Vergelegen passed through several owners before being acquired by Sir Lionel and Lady Phillips early in the 20th century. Restoration and rebuilding work was undertaken on the main homestead and the farm was maintained at a level appropriate for a major agricultural enterprise. The estate passed into the hands of the Barlow family at about the time of the Second World War and continued to be farmed by them until the sale to Anglo American. By the 1980s, however, there were no longer any vines on the estate, and much of the farming activity revolved around the dairy.

As a result, the estate has been planned as though new. Extensive soil analysis tests as well as wind readings have been used to determine the suitable sites for viticulture. Plantings began in 1988 and the wine cellar was completed early in 1992. The first crush combines grapes from Vergelegen's new plantings with some bought-in material, in part to assess the winery's performance, in part to get a real feeling from the estate's new vineyards.

It is obviously too early to pronounce upon the Vergelegen project. Young vines will never show the full picture, and the first crush in a new winery also cannot tell everything. Winemaker Martin Meinert is an experienced and highly competent cellarmaster. Vergelegen's winery has been carefully planned to minimise grape handling and maximise flavour retention. The farm's cool climate should ensure that healthy, tasty fruit gets to the cellar. It is impossible to say at this stage whether all these flavour constituents will remain in the final wine: all that is known for certain is that one of the oldest and most important Cape farms is now back at last in the wine business.

That same part of Somerset West has two other properties which may, in time, have a role to play in the Stellenbosch area of origin. The Bergkelder's Fleur du Cap homestead is situated here and if the company is able to acquire any neighbouring land which may be up for sale it could extend its existing nursery and perhaps even vinify some wine.

Also nearby is Morgenster, yet another of the historic Somerset West farms. Now the property of Peter Bairnsfather-Cloete, whose family used to own Groot Constantia in its days of greatness, it too seems destined to return to quality wine production. The release of its wines is probably several years away. However, given the *terroir*, and the proprietor, there is little doubt that what will finally come to the market under the Morgenster name will have been worth the waiting.

From the sheltered land around the Lourens River until Avontuur, some 10 kilometres closer to Stellenbosch, there does not appear to be much viticultural activity. The area today is largely residential, a part of the sprawling town of Somerset West, without the same call to wine which characterises Stellenbosch.

Avontuur is considerably closer to the centre of wine farming activity, and more visibly part of Stellenbosch as a result. Although the farm is also a horse stud – with a considerable track record of success – its wines are now making a substantial contribution to the reputation of the property. Its reds are proof that it is possible to make accessible yet substantial Cabernet and Merlot in this part of the world.

Avontuur produces a highly creditable Chardonnay, though the style alters from one harvest to the next by an amount that is far greater than normal vintage variation. Later releases lack some of the richer, butterscotch tones of the very fine 1989. Of the red wines, the Merlot, with its rich and quite robust plummy style, is good drinking now and good for several years in the bottle. However, Avontuur's best value is the Avon Rouge, a Cabernet/Merlot blend which is full on the palate, soft and enormously chewy. It seems best in its youth and has acquired a substantial following in a very short period of time.

The story of why winemaker Jean-Luc Sweerts made Avon Rouge in the first place is already a little embellished with legend. One anecdote tells that it was produced to satisfy the drinking requirements of a fellow French winemaker who visits the Cape regularly. The story I know is that the proposal was put to the farm by Avontuur's Johannesburg agents, who pointed out that there was nothing quite like this sort of wine available in the country. Initial sales were not as strong as everyone had hoped: perhaps a little mythology was judiciously cultivated to add some cachet to the brand.

Up the road from Avontuur, facing the R44 as it winds its way towards Stellenbosch, is Eikendal, something of a rising star on the Helderberg side of the town. Winemaker Josef Krammer seems to have turned out enough good red wine for those who doubted whether this Swiss-owned winery would garner real attention. All the premium reds have a deep and very intense cassis colour, with berry flavours showing well on the Cabernets, and good taut acids and tannins to give

165

them the keeping time they need in order to evolve completely.

Two reds come to mind immediately, the regular Cabernet and the Cabernet Reserve du Patron. The former lacks the volume and length of the Reserve du Patron, though it does seem to age quite well, and should open up with fullness and flavour after about five years. The Reserve du Patron is bigger and richer in every sense: the tannins give the wine real grip on the palate and there is enough acidity to lift the fruit out of this dark and slightly unyielding wine.

Two white wines also recommend themselves, the Special Late Harvest, halfway to auslese style but beautifully balanced, and the latest Chardonnay. The 1990 Special Late Harvest had a lovely fruit/botrytis intensity which suggests that it, too, will repay the patience of those who cellar it. The 1991 Chardonnay has an almost smoky butterscotch nose, tinged with citrus and vanilla: a very good wine and one which confirms that Eikendal's premium wines, white or red, are being made with serious quality considerations in mind.

Behind Eikendal, nestling in the foothills of the Helderberg range, is John Platter's Clos du Ciel Vineyards. After Delaire, a farm of more manageable size was clearly on the cards for John and Erica Platter: their own winebook is an annual and enormously time consuming business. A property with 30 to 40 hectares under vines is not only labour intensive at the crush, but also a sales and marketing nightmare. It is evident as well that they did not wish to compromise their own position in the trade by entering the industry again with thousands of cases of their own wine to sell.

Clos du Ciel has the double advantage of satisfying the winemaking urge and keeping Platter abreast of vintage and cellar developments in a practical way. The yields will never be so great that the wine loses its capacity to provide pleasure in simply being there. Platter's own high integrity and his now considerable knowledge guarantee that it will deserve the market it obtains. Besides which, Clos du Ciel's elevated position against the mountain, cooled by the breezes blowing in off False Bay, does seem the kind of climate in which to grow fine wine.

Not much further along the R44, and at much the same altitude as Clos du Ciel, is Rust-en-Vrede. It is considered today to be one of the finest properties in Stellenbosch, a red wine estate in the front rank of the South African wine industry. This was not always the case: when ex-Springbok Jannie Engelbrecht bought the farm during the 1970s, it was run down, the buildings dilapidated, no cellar to speak of, and the farm in general disarray.

Engelbrecht has wrought miracles on his small, but perfectly positioned property. Where he could he used existing structures, though his bottle maturation cellar had to be added. The construction was handled so tastefully that nothing of the 18th-century feel of the farm has been lost. Vineyards were saved wherever possible, since nothing can replace the depth and substance which old vines give to a wine. Newer clonal material has also been planted, but circumspectly: winemaker Kevin Arnold constantly cautions against assuming that the virtues of the new outweigh the tried and tested benefits of the old.

Rust-en-Vrede's wines have been available since Engelbrecht released the 1979 vintage to a slightly incredulous wine fraternity. No one was ready to believe that a former rugby Springbok could walk into a grossly under-equipped cellar and produce anything substantial. I recall reviewing the winery very favourably in a magazine article at this time. The then chairman of the South African Society of Winetasters asked me, quite seriously, if perhaps my opinions had not been clouded by alcohol. I responded by asking him if he had actually been to the estate. Naturally he had not visited, nor had he tasted the wines. His view merely reflected the conventional wisdom of the time: how could an unknown estate, in the hands of an unknown cellarmaster, produce anything of note.

The truth was that Jannie Engelbrecht did know what he was doing, and was prepared to invest in quality red wine production. Within a few years he had culled the estate's Chenin Blanc, deciding instead to focus on red wines only. New barrels were standard equipment at Rust-en-Vrede before most other independent producers had even contemplated them. A bottle maturation facility was a logical necessity: you cannot sell wine that needs at least ten years to age without carrying a certain amount of stock yourself, if only as a visible act of faith.

When Kevin Arnold arrived at Rust-en-Vrede in time to vinify the 1987 vintage, the conventional wisdom had changed. Now the wine fraternity wanted to know what Jannie Engelbrecht was going to get up to if he no longer needed to be in his cellar at harvest time. Kevin Arnold was seen to be almost superfluous: why bring in one of the country's top red winemakers when the cellar is owned and managed by someone of unimpeachable reputation, so the argument ran.

In very little time Engelbrecht's decision to involve Kevin Arnold was vindicated by the results. A new kind of polish appeared on the wines, less hardness, more fruit, greater berry intensity, fewer bitter tannins.

This result was palpable on the estate blend. The 1986 harvest and crush had been Engelbrecht's, though Arnold inherited the wines in barrel and tank. Even at this relatively late stage he was able to fine-tune the wine, trimming off a little of the organic 'dustiness' and enhancing its richness and complexity. Two years later the estate's 'groupies' had an opportunity to see what Kevin Arnold could do, working from vineyard rather than fermented wine. The 1988 blend introduced Shiraz as a complement to the Cabernet and Merlot, maintaining the taut, almost European structure but adding a Barossa-like spice to it.

The same change is discernible in the Rust-en-Vrede Cabernet. The single varietal is still more austere than the blend, but it has gained in volume and shed a little of the meanness. Clearly Kevin Arnold does know how to coax extra fruit from the grapes, though not at the expense of the depth and staying power. The Shiraz has also been gently moulded, so that the leathery, mineral-like quality is there, especially on the nose, but not the robust coarseness which in the youth of earlier vintages came between the wine and its harmony.

All these changes since Kevin Arnold's arrival confirm Engelbrecht's self-effacing wisdom in bringing in the right man for the job. Little has changed in substance and what has altered has been more than mere cosmetics. Suddenly Rust-en-Vrede seems much better focused, one of the country's top red wine estates and definitely on an upward curve.

The Bergkelder's Alto Estate is part of the same stretch of the Helderberg, and home also to another former rugby Springbok, Hempies du Toit. The red wines of Alto have been part of the Stellenbosch wine culture for more than half a century.

Alto's Cabernet has always been marketed on rarity. I recall the 1965 and 1966 vintages fetching as much as R30 per bottle in the early 1970s, when a 1964 Pétrus would have struggled at a Johannesburg wine merchant to realise the same price. Deeply tannic, concentrated and full of hidden layers of fruit, these early Altos were hardly ever drunk: like the much quoted story of Abie's sardines, collectors thought of them as 'for selling, not for keeping' and the wines travelled around from one cellar of privilege to the next.

The demand for Alto Cabernet was clearly far greater than the supply. 1970 and 1971 were slightly more abundant, but then there was no more about until the general release of the 1976. This went some way to alleviate the shortage, as did the more plentiful supply from vintages in the late 1970s and early 1980s. On the way, the wine lost some of its cachet – an inevitable consequence of stock filling the vacuum – but it was still positioned at the top end of the premium wine market.

Then, for a variety of reasons, the wine started to fall behind the competition. New wood was not in evidence to the same extent as other Bergkelder estates and there was a curious lack of concentration in the fruit. While Alto was slipping behind, new players had moved forward. It took several excellent vintages before credibility was restored. A good 1984, a much better 1986, and some excellent pre-release samples all confirm that one of the Cape's legendary Cabernets has stopped trading off its past, and now comfortably exceeds the kind of quality on which its reputation was established.

Alto also produces a blended red wine which does sterling service for the estate in the midst of frequent Cabernet shortages. Alto Rouge is a wine which goes back to before the Second World War: it was exported to Britain in the 1930s and maintained a presence in the market on a more or less continuous basis right through to the present day.

In good vintages it combines an ease of access with a solid kind of keeping weight, a wine which could never be described as 'quaffable' and yet can be consumed in great quantity. 1972 was that sort of wine, so, to a greater extent, was 1974. In those days the blend comprised Cabernet, Shiraz and Tinta Barocca in varying percentages. I found that the best Altos of the 1970s were produced in those vintages which enjoyed a good reputation and yet, strangely, saw no release of single varietal Cabernet. Perhaps this is a coincidence, perhaps the Cabernet which might otherwise have been separately bottled was added to the Alto Rouge blend, thus upgrading the wine and decreasing the percentage of the Tinta.

This rule worked well until the replanting programme at

Alto changed the Cabernet clones and introduced Merlot for the Alto Rouge blend. Now the wine has altered its personality entirely: a Médoc blend with Shiraz thrown in for good measure, it has evolved to the point where its antecedents are no longer distinguishable.

Along the same stretch of the Helderberg is Stellenzicht, another property in the portfolio of erstwhile German banker, Hans Schreiber. The farm used to belong to the Bairnsfather-Cloete family of Alphen (in Constantia) fame and they named it after their Constantia base. Prior to its acquisition by Schreiber in the early 1980s (several years in fact before he bought Neethlingshof) it delivered grapes to Gilbeys and this arrangement continued for some years after the change of ownership.

When the contract with Gilbeys was not renewed, Hans Schreiber determined to bring the farm to full production with its own crushing cellar and in time its own bottling line. Yet again we see Stellenbosch vineyard land developed at great expense by foreign capital. Some of the locals acknowledge that the changes which have been wrought could not have come from South African investors; others complain about the colonisation, a cavil heard more and more in the vineyard areas of the New World. Those who claim to be in the know acknowledge the extent of what has been achieved but believe that a great deal of money could have been saved on the way if the vineyards, for example, had been properly cleared before replanting. Those who ridicule the conspicuous expenditure fail to grasp that it is exactly this which gives all Schreiber's projects the momentum to keep them moving. A tenor will sing to an empty auditorium only if he believes in the song.

Winemaker at Stellenzicht, Marinus Bredell, has a singular claim to fame: he produced the champion young wine at the national show in 1983 with a Zinfandel harvested at Gilbeys' Kleine Zalze farm. Not surprisingly, he harbours an

171

almost mystical reverence for the varietal and has ensured that Stellenzicht has been planted with a generous quota of Zinfandel vines. Hopefully he will find a way to incorporate their yield into Stellenzicht's production, if and when they come into bearing. No doubt his neighbours at Kleine Zalze await his solution with a generous measure of self-interest. Cape Zinfandel is about as easy to sell as a Lada, and works about as well.

Stellenzicht produces a curious Cabernet, underripe and yet surprisingly bold, a wine with texture but not enough fruit, likely to last some time, and on the way to smooth down some at least of the coarse edges. Among the white wines the Sauvignon Blanc has found a following among those who like the varietal with distinct grassy overtones. The Grand Vin Blanc has proved a great commercial success: well oaked and finely balanced, it drinks well in its youth and can certainly take a few years in the bottle.

The proprietary brand of Fragrance makes careful use of Erlihane table grapes to show a spicy muscat character on the nose without much body or alcohol. The blend has acquired something of a niche for itself. Unlike many of the Cape's wines which are overly demanding in relation to what they deliver, Fragrance delivers more than it could possibly demand.

Visitors to the cellars, maturation facility and bottling set-up at Stellenzicht are bound to be impressed with the sheer size and scale of the project, the state-of-the-art winery, and the level of automation that is built into the processing.

Back along the R44 towards Stellenbosch is Blaauwklippen, one of the Helderberg's best-known wine route establishments. In addition to the usual tourist attractions there is a fine collection of old carriages to add colour and mood to the farm.

Blaauwklippen continues to surprise the wine-drinking fraternity. Because of its popular marketing, and its wide

172

range of wines, it is often perceived to be a few levels below the rarefied slopes of the industry's top wineries. Yet it has twice won the coveted Diners Club Winemaker of the Year Award, it is a productive member of the Cape Independent Winemakers' Guild, its wines are sold on the Nederburg Auction and it frequently wins the blind tastings of panels such as the Alphen Wine-of-the-Month Club.

At the heart of this contradiction is the perennial problem of the limited size of the top end of the South African market, and the need to achieve economies of scale by widening the ambit of operations. Blaauwklippen, in other words, is really two establishments bound into one, though the difference is less a matter of cellar policy than of product positioning. The intrinsic quality is there, but there is no point in offering the whole range at the uppermost limit of its pretensions – not if you want to sell the wines and get on with dealing with the next vintage.

Jacques Kruger's wines show both the continuities and the changes since Walter Finlayson left the cellar in his hands at the end of the 1980s. He has focused the wines more, though he has taken many of them in the direction to which Finlayson was working. There have been some notable innovations: the Red Landau is now a Cabernet/Merlot blend with some Zinfandel added for good measure. This is a considerable change from some of the earlier blends, but may in fact reflect the availability of premium varietals.

The Cabernet is certainly filling out and gaining length and weight, though the wine which won the Diners Club Award was neither thin nor lightweight. What distinguishes the later vintages from this 1980 prize-winning wine is a greater fruit and soft tannin intensity, a depth which stays on the wine and won't fade after a few years. The Zinfandel is probably the best in the Cape, plenty of almost wild fruit reined in through a little oak maturation. Balance has been retained through real discipline in the cellar, the fruit is there, and the wine is much more than recently fermented grape juice.

Blaauwklippen produces a wide range of wine, with a considerable price variation between the premium cuvées, such as the Cabernet Reserve and the Barouche méthode champenoise, and the popular-priced Red and White Landaus. Most of the wines, irrespective of price, are good value. Some, like the Red Landau and the Cabernet, are great buys in absolute terms.

Less than one kilometre as the crow flies from Blaauwklippen are two properties which have acquired, in a short space of time, considerable recognition not only locally, but also among overseas buyers of Cape wines. Both cellars fall under the control of Jan 'Boland' Coetzee, formerly winemaker at Kanonkop, and now proprietor of Vriesenhof and cellarmaster at Talana Hill.

Jan Coetzee acquired Vriesenhof after he left Kanonkop in 1980. He worked a brief stint in the cellars of Joseph Drouhin in Beaune, during which time he obviously learnt a great deal about coaxing the subtleties out of a wine. Kanonkop is not the kind of estate where there would have been much call for these skills. The changes in his style of winemaking have come over a period of time, but all clearly since his arrival at the Helderberg side of Stellenbosch. The effect is most noticeable on his handling of white wines, but also in the finesse and distinction he seems to impose so effortlessly on the reds.

Vriesenhof produces one of the Cape's most reliable high quality Chardonnays, a wine of great breeding, with oak and fruit beautifully interleaved, enough early drinkability for those who like the butterscotch of the wood, and enough structure to permit real bottle ageing. The farm's Cabernet has improved immeasurably since the 1981: the earlier vintages reflected Coetzee's robust view of red wine making. The more current wines have been rounded off and softened, so that staying power is achieved with balance, and not at the expense of the fruit.

This same approach with the property's Médoc blend, the Vriesenhof Kallista, has yielded a wine that is now altogether more elegant and at the same time fuller than the first Cabernet/Merlots coming off the farm. Coetzee has managed to extract the maximum flavour from the grapes without compromising maturation potential. He has also optimised the wood ageing process, introducing firm yet gentle wood tannins through carefully selected oak, properly managed.

His second label, Paradyskloof, is the vehicle for one of the Cape's most easily approachable Pinotages and one of the best-value wines on any of the Stellenbosch farms; the Paradyskloof White, a Pinot Blanc/Sauvignon Blanc blend, would pass for a Chardonnay with a light, but definite wood dimension.

Not far from Vriesenhof is a small, triangular piece of land developed by Coetzee for a Johannesburg-based syndicate who have called the farm Talana Hill. The first Talana Hill wines were vinified at Vriesenhof, though more recently a beautifully compact cellar has been built. Jan Coetzee is still the winemaker, attending to the crush and then keeping a careful eye on the wood ageing and the bottling. Both the Royale (Médoc blend) and the Chardonnay bear his obvious stamp, though the wines are nevertheless noticeably different from those of Vriesenhof.

The Royale is even richer than the Kallista, but it does not have the same length or finish. This may be the result of younger vines, it may be a decision in the vinification. It is certainly approachable sooner and gives commensurate drinking pleasure. The Chardonnay has an almost honeyed lees nose and palate: a slight butterscotch combined with the smoky barrel fruit of the wood-fermented wine. As a young wine it has more fullness than the Vriesenhof. I prefer it for that extra plumpness, richer tropical fruit character.

Both Talana Hill and Vriesenhof are new wineries, ten years old or less. They are an integral part of the reputation of Stellenbosch yet the land they occupy is under constant threat of urban encroachment. For the time being the quality of their wines ensures the survival of the vineyards. Stellenbosch has not yet suffered the loss of vineyards to housing and industry that has been the fate of, for example, Durbanville. However, the next ten years could well see properties with the potential to become another Vriesenhof or Talana Hill irrevocably lost to viticulture. Each prime site that vanishes might have turned out to be a microclimate producing its own unique wines. Stellenbosch, with its many different pockets of land all capable of yielding superb wines, can least afford the vineyard loss with which it is threatened.

PAARL

ಎಳ ತಿ

The wineries which fall into the Paarl region lie mainly to the Stellenbosch side of the town. The approach towards Paarl from Cape Town on the N1 is not only the most direct route, but brings the majority of the cellars within striking distance.

The first estate encountered from the Cape Town side is Villiera. It is so close to several Stellenbosch properties, and so far from the next Paarl cellar, that the idea that it has been allocated to the incorrect region does cross the mind of many who visit the farm.

The Grier family has owned Villiera since 1983. The cellar is in the care of Jeff Grier, the first of the region's wine-makers to pass the Cape Wine Masters examination. His cousin Simon tends the vineyards. Between the two of them, soft-spoken, reflective but not unassertive, they have advanced the quality of Villiera's wines so that they are today unrecognisable compared with the very acceptable table wines they produced five years ago.

Villiera's first major brand success was the launch of Tra-dition de Charles de Fère 'Carte Rouge', a méthode champ-enoise sparkling wine made in association with Jean Louis Denois who produces Tradition in France. The decision to make their sparkling wine with French input and French branding was vindicated by its success. For several years Tradition was the top-selling méthode champenoise in South Africa, its classy packaging, its overall consistency and its very competitive pricing winning it an extensive following.

Initially the base wine contained neither Chardonnay nor Pinot Noir. Now the blend has both varietals, but also a little

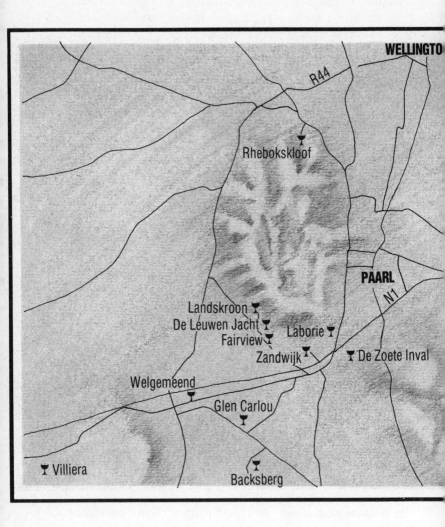

WELLINGTO

R44

Rhebokskloof

PAARL

N1

Landskroon
De Leuwen Jacht
Fairview   Laborie
          Zandwijk
                    De Zoete Inval

Welgemeend
        Glen Carlou

Villiera
        Backsberg

178

of the Pinotage and Chenin Blanc which made up the original Tradition. In recent years the méthode champenoise market in South Africa has seen an increase in consumption as well as a considerable proliferation in the number of brands present. No doubt this has reduced Tradition's share of the market: new products with new packaging acquire their own following but also erode existing trade.

Tradition has certainly developed as a brand: in many respects it is more Champagne-like now than previously, though it is by no means as close to French bubbly as several other of the Cape wines. However, it has found a following for its particularly steely style. The range has also been increased to include a Rosé, and a couple of prestige cuvées. These top wines are noticeably better, with a higher Pinot content, longer lees ageing and at least two years in bottle after *dégorgement*.

More importantly, the still wines of Villiera have advanced so that several are now very much front-rank products. The Bordeaux blend is wonderfully taut, packed with berry fruit and seemingly capable of great length. The Merlot – bottled as a varietal wine but also a 40 per cent component part of the Crû Monro – is one of the top five in the Cape, showing a concentration rarely seen outside Pomerol.

Among the white wines the Sauvignon Blanc (unwooded) and the Crû Monro Blanc Fumé (barrel-fermented) show that the Griers extract the full potential from the cultivar. In style the Sauvignon Blanc seems midway between the more fragrant Stellenbosch wines, and the smokier, almost mouth-gripping Franschhoek wines. The unwooded wine improves for several years in the bottle, and has a structure that will support even more substantial maturation, for those not in a hurry. The Crû Monro has been softened by the wood, so the Sauvignon fruit is rendered more complex by the underlying vanilla of the oak.

Villiera's Rhine Riesling is also one of the most interesting examples from the Cape. Free of the heavy, almost oily tones which come from bottle age, it keeps its fruit and balance long enough to win awards such as at the Paris Wine Olympiad.

There are other wines in the Villiera range, branded with proprietary names like Garonne, Gavotte and Sonnet. No doubt those who know what to expect from a wine thus labelled buy them: the quality is good, especially the Garonne, a Special Late Harvest with enough botrytis on the nose to add real complexity to the fragrantly sweet light dessert wine.

From Villiera eastwards towards Paarl there are no private producing cellars until Klapmuts, on the north-eastern corner of the Stellenbosch region. Here there are two small producers and one major estate whose achievements have advanced Paarl's claim to rival Stellenbosch as the country's champion wine region.

The Welgemeend Estate was South Africa's first Bordeaux blend producer and maintains a place in the vanguard even today. Land surveyor Billy Hofmeyr set about establishing the Welgemeend farm in the 1970s, convinced that the Cape could and should produce Cabernet/Merlot blends rather than rely so strongly on single varietal bottlings. Hofmeyr was a leading light in wine appreciation circles at the time, and treated the development of Welgemeend as a vindication of this view.

He has succeeded beyond most people's expectations. The Welgemeend Estate Wine is firm yet fine, elegant but not light, intense yet harmonious, never a big wine but one that develops splendidly in the bottle. Welgemeend has its followers who buy it every year from the estate, laying down their purchase for at least five years before even contemplating opening a bottle. Usually they are rewarded with a wine which resembles a Crû Bourgeois from the Médoc, never too woody, never evanescent, always well finished.

In some vintages Welgemeend does offer a single varietal bottling of Cabernet. When in the past it has been released, it provides an interesting foil by which to assess the merits of the blend. Usually more austere in its youth, it develops more slowly but finally yields a wine of strength and finesse.

There are two other wines – both blends – offered by Welgemeend: the Amadé, best consumed as an easy drinking wine, somewhat in the style of the Southern Rhône, and the Douelle, a light to medium-bodied Cabernet/Malbec combination.

For several years now the Welgemeend cellar has fallen increasingly under the control of Hofmeyr's wife Ursula and, more recently, daughter Louise. Illness now keeps him away from making the wines he pioneered in the Cape. However, continuity has been assured and the tradition that he established has passed in gradual transition to the next generation.

Not far from Welgemeend is another small boutique operation which in very little time has acquired an enviable reputation: Walter Finlayson's Glen Carlou has acquired a considerable following in somewhat less than four years for its Chardonnay and Cabernet blends.

Finlayson entered into the Glen Carlou venture with advertising executive Graham de Villiers as his partner, moving over gradually from Blaauwklippen in Stellenbosch. For a year or two he was still obliged to oversee matters at Blaauwklippen, at the same time plant vineyards at Glen Carlou and construct a very rudimentary cellar. Amazingly, from his first vintages, wines crushed from very young vines all showed colour, fruit and a fine drinking potential. The vines are not much older now, but already they reveal the kind of complexity and depth that can be expected from this Paarl property.

The Chardonnay is one of the fullest of the new generation wines in the Cape: Finlayson recognises that the slightly warmer climate of Paarl helps to fill out the wine, giving it muscle and structure and making that extra wooding all the more necessary. The Glen Carlou regular bottling is bigger and richer than most generic white Burgundies, though obviously only time will tell whether it will gain a comparable volume and depth as it matures in bottle. I would prefer to drink it now, buttery, laced with oak vanillas and with a slight lemony nose, than risk its flattening out for questionable gain. The Reserve Chardonnay has a richer, more butterscotch style, too heavy for some but likely at least to retain some of the fuller smokier lees style for a bit longer, with a better marriage in the bottle.

The farm also produces one of the Cape's best Pinot Noirs, from new clonal material, with better colour and fruit than the regular BK5 grapes seem capable of yielding. The climate and the clonal style, together with considerable use of oak in the vinification, makes it difficult to compare this wine with any Burgundy. In its youth it seems to have almost too much volume, but that may soften with age. As it stands, it is a promising, clearly too youthful, fine red wine, which will drink sooner than the other Glen Carlou reds and promises complexity and balance all the way to the end.

The farm produces two separate Bordeaux blends, the Classique (with new clone Cabernet) and Les Trois (old clone and a higher Petit Verdot content). The former is a textured rich red wine with plenty of fruit on the nose, and much of its tannin seemingly drawn from the oak; the latter in some years appears to be a lighter wine, but this may in part be the blend, since the old clone customarily yields a more solid sort of wine. Finlayson also bottles some Cabernet from his new clone vines: intense, with an almost minty quality to the berry fruit, it has better weight on the palate than many other bottlings of the new material in South Africa.

Up the road – literally – from Glen Carlou is Backsberg, the Cape's most successful and perhaps most versatile wine estate. Sydney Back is the doyen of the industry, a wine man who has more than fifty vintages behind him in the cellar. Pioneer of the estate wine business in the region, Back has lived and worked with wine since his youth. His world at Backsberg has been, in many ways, a microcosm of the wine industry at the Cape in the 20th century, and for this reason has been dealt with fully in the introduction to this book.

The farm itself has been an independent and self-sustaining operation since its first estate vintage in 1969. Its early vintages of Cabernet, Shiraz and Pinotage were of enviable quality at the time. They opened the way for the many thousands of private customers from all over South Africa who regard a visit to Backsberg in Paarl in the same light as a trip up Table Mountain or a drive around the peninsula: not simply because the farm is a tourist attraction (which it is) but because a visit to the Cape would be incomplete without calling on the tasting room and buying some of the best-value wine in the Cape.

Sydney Back's rules are so simple and so sound that it seems unnecessary to define them: know your clientele and respect their choice; maintain the best possible standards; price your wines accordingly. Over the years Backsberg has established a unique position for itself in the market, not only for the absolute quality of its wines, but also for their highly competitive pricing. When there was a Chardonnay shortage, Sydney Back set his Chardonnay price exactly as he would have had the wine been plentiful. He knew the shortage would end, and that the short-term gain of exploiting his customers could only have long-term deleterious consequences. His formula was simple: work out the cost of the grapes, work out the cellar cost of vinifying them, amortise the cost of the new wood, establish a fair mark-up and get on with selling the wine.

Backsberg's wines fall into two broad categories: the popular lines which have formed the backbone of its sales since the early seventies, and premium brands which are the result

of innovations in the 1980s. In the former group are Pinotage, Dry Red, Rosé, Chenin Blanc, Riesling (Crouchen
Blanc), Bouquet Blanc and Special Late Harvest. Most of
these wines represent excellent value, particularly the Chenin
Blanc which shows all the virtues of the varietal; the Cape
Riesling, which opens up well after several years in bottle;
and the Special Late Harvest, packed with fragrance, sweetish but well balanced.

It has been among the premium wines that Backsberg has
made the greatest strides. The estate's Chardonnay won the
Diners Club Award with the first release from new clonal
material. The earlier wines made with virus-infected vines
have held together remarkably well, carrying ten years of
bottle age with ease. The later style has much more fruit, the
result of healthier vines, and a finely balanced use of wood.
The Chardonnay provides a perfect example of the innovative nature of Sydney Back's enterprise. The fact that he had
vineyards planted to the only authorised clone (the virus-
infected material) ahead of the rest of the industry shows the
forward thinking which has always characterised the estate.
Similarly, once he was processing juice from virus-free
material, his was one of the first independent wineries to
have sufficient knowledge and experience of wood vinification to produce, from that first harvest, an award-winning
wine.

Wood-ageing has now been considerably developed upon
by Backsberg. The John Martin is the estate's barrel-matured
Sauvignon Blanc, a wine of elegance and complexity.
Maximising fruit and wood is a skill developed over years of
knowing your grapes, and also your cooper, and Backsberg's
success with these wines shows the thoroughness and care
which has gone into planning.

Among the premium reds, the Bordeaux blend sold under
the Klein Babylonstoren proprietary name, speaks eloquently
for itself. Much finer than the old-style Cabernets which the

estate produced in the 1970s, it is a consummate harmony of the best and most accessible characteristics of the cultivars and the wood. The Backsberg Shiraz is a useful complement to the Klein Babylonstoren. No heavier, yet often a little tannic on the palate, it too shows its fruit first.

It is a feature of Backsberg's wines that those who buy them from the farm itself, rather than through the retail trade, often undervalue them because of the price/quality relationship: they have difficulty believing that so much value is possible for what was paid. One of the consequences of this is that those producers who price their wines at the level of their pretensions obtain a temporary image benefit while buyers believe that the quality must be commensurate with the cost. One of the reasons that Backsberg has survived the fickle world of the top end of the wine market unscathed is that, in the end, the wines exceed even the expectations of those who think they know them.

On the short Suid-Agter Paarl road to the east of the town are three cellars, Landskroon, De Leuwen Jacht and Fairview. Landskroon has been something of a laid-back player, even in the context of the Paarl region. The farm is as old as any in the district, and the present cellar has been bottling wines for most of the certified estate wine era. Several of its wines have won trophies at regional or national shows and many of the old-timers confirm that this stretch of Paarl, with its unirrigated vineyards and bush vines, was always a source of premium wines.

Why Landskroon has never really capitalised on its position has never been entirely clear. In some respects the estate has been quite innovative: it offered for sale one of the first Pinot Noirs and Cabernet Francs. Its traditional varietals always performed creditably, especially the Cinsaut, the Cabernet Sauvignon and the Pinotage. Only recently have there been signs that the farm is looking to the future, with several wines worthy of attention.

These include the Premier Blanc, a wood-matured Pinot Blanc from young vines, rich and filling out, with that extra vanilla perfume that comes from Jupilles oak. The Pinotage continues to deliver excellent value, though in much the conventional style: good fruit, reasonable texture, robust yet accessible. The Shiraz is slightly unusual, smoky and saddle-leathery though not very heavy, and yet manifesting distinct minty, almost eucalyptus-like overtones.

Almost adjacent to Landskroon is the newly established De Leuwen Jacht, a farm so recently returned to making wine in its own cellars that there is little against which to measure the latest achievements. The brand name is memorable enough, for who would forget a wine whose meaty, fairly full flavoured red wines sold under the name of 'The Lion Hunt'?

These certainly look promising, good colours and some forward fruit. They are surprisingly accessible, not overwhelmingly big, the Cabernet with a noticeable eucalyptus character (a feature of several wines in this part of Paarl). This same aroma has also affected the Médoc blend, presumably from the Cabernet, though it is less immediately evident. The Chardonnay is big, buttery and good youthful drinking.

Despite upheavals and a recent change of ownership, the restoration of this old property is advancing to the point where it will clearly become a producer of some significance in the Paarl wine region.

Next door to De Leuwen Jacht is Fairview, unquestionably the most successful wine estate on this Suid-Agter Paarl road. The property of Cyril Back and his son Charles, it has quietly established itself as a treasure house of good-value table wines, with some excellent Reserve wines, especially the reds.

The Fairview wines from the 1970s were regarded at the time as being a little inaccessible, people often said 'too woody'. In fact, they were vinified in cement tanks and never passed within a metre of a stave of oak. Nevertheless, full-bodied tannic wines were very much the house style for most of this era. The 1974s were superb – all the virtues of that remarkable vintage, with an intensity and depth of colour that suggested that they might never quite open up. Certainly they were a little thick, too full of extract for early drinking, but when they did come round, more than ten years later, they were fine examples of an old style of Paarl wine.

With the decade of the 1980s Fairview went into a commercial mode, producing wines that were more accessible, but often lighter and less complex as a result. They acquired a considerable following, especially among those who drink wine – as opposed to the sniff-and-spit brigade. However, there was a cost to the estate's overall image. The wine buffs seemed unable to take the cellar seriously, because the wines appeared not to be sufficiently status-orientated.

The Reserve range has moved into this gap, providing limited-release quantities of premium varietal wines, chosen from select vineyard blocks for those who seek special occasion wines. These wines are obviously more expensive than the regular cuvées, though they are still superb value, compared with the ex-cellars prices of many competitor farms.

Among the regular range of Fairview wines, the Chardonnay has proved to be one of the region's best wines. Protracted lees contact ensures a rich, slightly smoky bouquet, and the vanilla of the oak combines with the tropical fruit nose to yield a gentle, almost butterscotch character. The estate's Chenin Blanc is remarkably full on the nose and palate, holding its flavours together well, dry, and made for a couple of years of bottle ageing. The Special Late Harvest continues to be excellent value. Always one of the farm's best wines, it combines just the right degree of richness, with enough acidity to support the bouquet and let the palate finish clean.

The Fairview Reserve wines justify their price premium

over the regular range. They are made for longer keeping, have a noticeably higher wood dimension and are altogether better integrated. The Pinotage Reserve has the wood and fruit in perfect harmony; the Cabernet Reserve shows varietal and wood fragrance; and the Merlot Reserve is big and full textured. The Fairview Shiraz Reserve has changed in style and is now a little like an Australian Cabernet/Shiraz blend: fruit with plenty of structure underneath.

Among the red proprietary wines, the Charles Gerard Reserve red is wonderful value, a fine Bordeaux-style wine that is forward enough for drinking now, but with maturation potential for those who prefer to wait. The wooded white Charles Gerard Reserve has much of the richness of a New World Chardonnay, but, confusingly, has been made instead from Sauvignon and Sémillon.

Visitors to Fairview can marvel at the peacocks if they are about, or cast an eye over the flocks of goats, whose milk is used to make the now famous Fairview range of cheeses.

A little closer to the town of Paarl itself, situated almost on the south side of the famous Paarl Rock mountain, is a small farm which fills a unique niche in the South African market: Zandwijk is the country's only Kosher winery and makes some of the only organoleptically acceptable Kosher wine found anywhere in the world. The operation complies with religious requirements of the Cape Town Beth Din, who not only supervise the proceedings from vintage to bottling, but also ensure that the grapes have been heat-treated (in terms of the Kosher regulations). All of the winemaking activities are actually performed by observant Jews. This in itself provides gentile winemaker Leon Mostert with a series of challenges enough to daunt even the most courageous. Not only has he flourished in this environment, but the wines coming out of his cellar are worthy of unqualified approval.

The two varietal wines which would appeal to any serious wine drinker are the Cabernet and the Chardonnay. Both have been heat-treated prior to fermentation and yet retain distinctive fruit and vinousity. The Cabernet is full and deeply textured, a wine which will develop a little finesse over time, but which will always be one of those plump, velvety reds. The Chardonnay is big and buttery, the result no doubt in part of the heat treatment. However, these varietal flavours have harmonised beautifully with the oak to offer a wine in the style of many of the Californian Chardonnays of the 1970s.

Not far from Zandwijk is De Zoete Inval, a property which seems to function happily outside the normal hurly-burly of the Cape wine trade. Adrian Frater's newsletters, which are often disarmingly honest, reflect his frank and not very fashion-orientated view of life and wine.

De Zoete Inval carries reasonable stocks of older vintage Cabernet and these are available for sale at prices which are surprisingly inexpensive. Wines from the late 1970s and early 1980s sell for less than current vintage Cabernet from most of the neighbouring farms. Several of these reserve vintages have aged quite well, developing an almost smoky bottle character. If the wines have an obvious shortcoming, it is that they lack depth and weight on the palate.

Even closer to Paarl, just below the Taal Monument, is the KWV's estate of Laborie, situated in what is now almost entirely residential land. The farm itself is something of a tourist attraction, with a restaurant serving traditional fare, several beautifully maintained Cape Dutch buildings, an old cellar, and now an estate brandy still located outside the restaurant building on the corner of the patio. The Laborie project raised temperatures around the winelands as the independent producers claimed – with some justification – that the KWV's estate was subsidised with their dues and was now trading in the same market in direct competition with themselves. The KWV's defence was simply that the restoration of Laborie had been undertaken with a view to preserving the property and establishing a model grape farm. Now that its vineyards are back in production, so the KWV claims, the bulk of the production is sold in export markets and hardly affects anyone else's domestic sales.

The truth in this particular debate resides with both parties, though the essence of the problem transcends matters of truth and locates itself instead in the realms of pure politics. The wine farmers contribute to the KWV and have every reason to object to their subventions funding a domestic competitor. The KWV's charter specifically prohibits the organisation from selling its wines in Africa south of the equator. The KWV maintains that this limitation does not extend to estate wines which have their own brand status. In arriving at this justification, the organisation is quibbling over niceties. If it were more concerned about its constituency, or rather, if the wine estate contingent represented a meaningful constituency to the KWV, the Laborie project would never have led to the sale of even one bottle of wine in the domestic market. The KWV can also not fall back on the 'small percentage of local sales' argument. When the organisation imposes a fine on an estate for producing wine in excess of its quota, even though that wine has been sold and has therefore not been a burden to the KWV, the official argument is that any excess production affects the saleability of all other wine in the crop. In other words, when it suits the KWV, the 'no winery is an island' argument is dredged up, but this is not to apply in the case of Laborie.

The debate in the first place is symptomatic of the level of dissatisfaction inside the wine industry. The actual sales of Laborie wines are meaningless. The KWV, no matter what is stated in its charter, should not be precluded from managing and operating a 40-hectare estate in downtown Paarl, producing good wines and providing an important tourism venue. Besides which, since the KWV has been a co-controlling shareholder in companies which together handle over

80 per cent of South Africa's wine and spirit sales at wholesale since 1979, the issue has been superseded by events.

As to the wines themselves, they are good, reliable, soundly made and unlikely to steal sales from anyone able to impose quality and personality on his wines. The premium cuvée Taillefert red and white are a noticeable improvement on the standard wines, showing balance, greater elegance and more roundness. The red is a Cabernet/Merlot blend with a little Shiraz which adds some spice, especially to the bouquet. The white is a Rhine Riesling/Sauvignon Blanc blend with a Chardonnay for the breeding. This unusual combination harmonises quite well, so that the terpenes of the Riesling are kept from overwhelming the more delicate fruit of the other varietals.

Laborie is the last estate on the south side of Paarl. To the north of the town there is only one private cellar of note, the recently renovated and newly consolidated Rhebokskloof Estate. The farm's history dates back to the 17th century, though the restored manor house is 18th-century and tells of an era of relative prosperity. The property now ranges over several valleys lying at the foot of the Paarl Nature Reserve, so that the buck which give the estate its name do in fact wander through the vineyards, much to the exasperation of the cellarmaster.

Rhebokskloof lies in the heart of the country's best table grape region and much of its production is sold as fruit. Export table grapes have been the major business of this side of Paarl for so long that wine farming was something of a neglected art. Many thought that the district's warm dry climate would make quality wine production impossible.

Mervyn and Michelle Key, who were responsible for bringing Rhebokskloof from near ruin to the status of a showpiece estate, have confounded the armchair critics. Many of the new vineyards are not yet in production, so it is difficult to pass a definitive comment on their achievement:

however, based on what has emerged from the winery so far, the premium varietals have produced premium wines.

Chief among the estate's quality wines is the Cabernet, a big rich muscular wine laced with tannin, colour, plenty of berry fruit and a round chewy texture. The old clone vines on Rhebokskloof get enough sunshine to reach full maturity, so the style of wine is more traditionally South African, that is, full and velvety, but not unduly hard.

The Chardonnay is a wine with the same feel, perfumed, almost buttery, with hints of butterscotch and vanilla from the oak. Like the Cabernet, it is on the soft, and rather too accessible side, likely to keep, but best drunk while the wood is still mingling with the fruit. Surprisingly for a supposedly warmer climate, the Rhine Riesling has plenty of spicy fragrance and very little of the terpene character that gives the varietal a doubtful name in most New World wine countries.

The Blanc Fumé is the Sauvignon equivalent of the Chardonnay, fruit and oak harmonising and the wine drinking well despite its youth. There is a slightly smoky bouquet which underlies the Sauvignon, and this aroma is also found on the Grand Vin Blanc, recently a much improved blend, gently wooded with a delicate lees nose.

Rhebokskloof is best approached from Cape Town off the R44 which goes to Wellington via Agter Paarl. It is not part of a major tourist route, and yet it is full throughout most of the year. Its restaurant, vineyard tours and winery visits are obviously major attractions. Ultimately, though, its reputation will stand or fall on its wines. What has been achieved in a few years gives grounds for optimism. What emerges from the cellar, now under the direction of American John Reagh, will tell the rest.

THE FRENCH CORNER: FRANSCHHOEK

The Revocation of the Edict of Nantes in 1685 ended nearly a century of religious tolerance between Catholics and Huguenots in France. It forced many Protestants to leave the land of their birth to find new homes in countries willing to accommodate the reformed religion. Holland provided an important refuge, sheltering many thousands of exiles either in Europe or in the colonies. By 1688 several hundred Huguenot families had arrived at the Cape, bringing with them a greater knowledge and expertise in wine than any of the Dutch Free Burghers who had settled there in the preceding three decades.

The Huguenots were granted land in a valley which lay to the north of Stellenbosch and the east of Paarl. Known as Franschhoek – meaning literally 'French Corner' – it offered an ideal agricultural environment much of which was eminently suited to viticulture. Clearing the land could not have been easy, for the undergrowth was probably quite thick and the wildlife extensive: elephants are recorded in the region for quite some time after the Huguenot settlement, adding their destructive ambles through the vineyards to all the other problems of 17th-century viticulture.

Most of the properties which today make up the Franschhoek wine producing region date back to the very early years of Huguenot settlement. Some of the land grants antedate the arrival of the main body of refugees. Many of the farms were subsequently consolidated and the Franschhoek district of today hardly resembles the neatly packaged parcels of land made over to the Huguenots in the early years

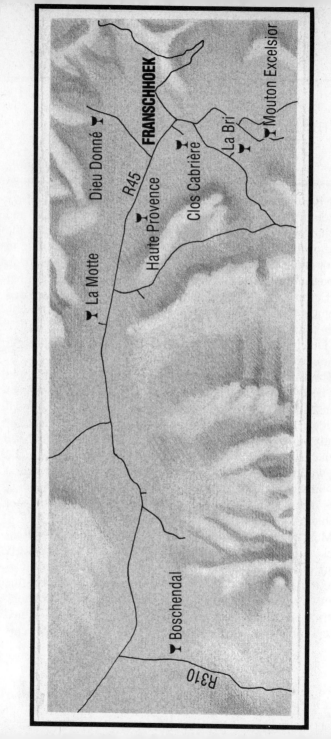

of Van der Stel's rule.

Boschendal Estate, for example, which stands at the entrance to the valley, is made up of several holdings which together comprised Cecil John Rhodes' farming project in Paarl at the end of the 19th century. Some of these farms date back to the original Huguenot land grants, and many of the vineyards and homesteads on the property have Huguenot names – La Rhône and Pierre Simond being obvious examples.

The Anglo American Corporation now controls Rhodes Fruit Farms and the Boschendal Estate. Since the late 1970s when estate wine production again became a priority, the operation has become South Africa's most successful de luxe wine venture. Boschendal markets more estate wine than any other farm in the country, achieving higher average prices than any of the other major estates. The wines have an extensive presence domestically and internationally, and are highly reputed for their quality, consistency and, in several cases, originality.

Boschendal's launch pad into the wine trade was partly a matter of happy coincidence. In about 1980 the estate determined to launch a méthode champenoise sparkling wine and sought to obtain a first pressing 'white wine' from some of its red grapes, in much the same way as Champagne usually has a sizeable percentage of Pinot Noir or Pinot Meunier in its base wine. Such a wine would correctly be called a Blanc des Noirs, a white wine from red grapes, and would add some body and dimension to the final blend.

The first attempts at producing a totally white blanc des noirs proved unsuccessful: the burst skins of the red grapes imparted more than a little pigment to the otherwise white grape juice, leaving the wine with a delicate 'onion-skin' apricot pink hue. This obviously would not have precluded the production of a pink bubbly, though its market would have been restricted.

An alternative use had to be found for the off-white wine. A still rosé was also out of the question: pink wines were generally ill thought of, subject to the damning observations once levelled at one of the world's most successful rosés: 'Neither red nor white, neither sweet nor dry, neither wine nor water'. Boschendal was left with attempting to filter out the pigment at the expense of the flavour constituents, or creating an altogether new kind of wine whose positioning could carry a slightly pink colour without compromising status.

The launch of the Boschendal Blanc de Noir proved to be the turning point of the estate's history. The wine was an unanticipated and resounding success: the sleight of hand by which the farm had disposed of its pink wine problem created an altogether new difficulty – how to meet the seemingly limitless demand.

Over the next few years Blanc de Noir became something of a conditional sell, a wine offered as long as the rest of the product range was also listed. Blanc de Noir was allocated in proportion to total volume of Boschendal wine purchased. Licensees soon provided the estate with an enviable platform for the sale of its more marginal wines. By the mid 1980s almost every item on the Boschendal price list was sold out before the next vintage became available.

Commercial results preceded oenological success. It was only by the latter part of the 1980s that the wines of Boschendal reflected in their quality the esteem in which they were generally held. Not that the earlier wines were in any way flawed: merely that the more recent Boschendal wines are infinitely more complex and tasty, with better balance and structure, than the wines on which the estate founded its reputation.

Boschendal has never really produced extraordinary red wines. In general its vineyards are too cool for the older Cabernet vines to achieve full ripeness. New plantings of

196

virus-free clonal material, as well as varietals like Pinot Noir (also from decent, recently imported material) may change this. In the past the demand for Blanc de Noir helped alleviate the red wine problem: free-run juice from the red grapes could be used for the Blanc de Noir while the remaining must would extract a higher proportion of colour and flavour for the estate's red wines. These vinification techniques ensured that some of the Boschendal red varietal wines often collected prizes and medals despite the difficulties of climate.

The 1978 Cabernet and Shiraz – both from the pre-Blanc de Noir days – became collectors' items, developing an elegance and finesse which belied their ageing potential. Later vintages, particularly from warm, dry years often surprised critics of the farm's red wines. When the cultivar wines were discontinued in the early 1980s – to make way for new plantings and an increased demand for blends – their passing was widely lamented.

At present the farm offers two red wines, both available in reasonably limited quantities, the Grand Vin (Cabernet/Merlot) and Lanoy (Cabernet/Shiraz/Merlot). The former has acquired something of a following for its lighter, elegant style of claret. The Cabernet has enough structure to give the wine length and ageing potential; the Merlot does soften an intrinsic leanness and flesh out the mid-palate. Lacking the alcohols and tannins of many of the Cape's Médoc blends, the Grand Vin is often disregarded at blind tastings. However, its delicacy and finesse give it great value as a drinking wine, forward enough to appreciate within a few years of the harvest.

The Lanoy is a fuller, slightly more savoury wine, the result no doubt of the generous dollop of Shiraz which goes into the blend. In its youth the signs of oak ageing are more obvious on the nose and mid-palate, though the wine rounds off after a few years to become quite complex, yet accessible.

The Blanc de Noir continues to enjoy the popularity with

which it launched the estate's name in the early 1980s: it is quite the most commercially successful wine in a category it has come to dominate as its own. Over the years its style has changed, so that the more recent vintages are obviously softer and even more approachable than the earlier wines. Although wine fashions have changed, the Blanc de Noir is probably one of South Africa's most popular, premium priced restaurant wines.

Among the whites firmly grounded in the earlier era of Boschendal are the Chenin Blanc, a fine, full-flavoured delicately fragrant wine, and the Le Bouquet, a highly perfumed off-dry white of great versatility. The Chenin Blanc has improved in line with all the estate's wines so that it is now easier on the palate and still eminently fruity. The Le Bouquet is one of the finest wines of its kind made in the Cape, a blend of perfumed varietals like Gewürztraminer and Muscat with an almost Alsace-like nose and a beautifully balanced finish.

The varietal wines from single vineyard sites include the Jean Gardé Gewürztraminer, the Rachelsfontein Rhine Riesling and the Pierre Simond Sauvignon Blanc. Of these the Sauvignon Blanc and the Gewürztraminer are perhaps the more noteworthy, the former because of the fruit intensity achieved without compromising its dryness; the latter because of its particularly earthy fragrance. The Rhine Riesling has precise varietal characteristics, though it sometimes seems to lack dimension. All three wines are only released as single vineyard products in those vintages where the quality of the crop justifies the extra claims of provenance.

Boschendal's Chardonnay has also acquired a front-rank position among the Cape's estate examples of this varietal. It is full without being overblown or clumsy, elegant, slightly citrussy with a good lees character and just enough oak on the nose and palate. I think it drinks well when young: wood vanilla combines with the smoky lees bouquet to produce an additional butterscotch layer. Since the first vintage in 1986 the Boschendal Chardonnay has supported bottle age quite well and current vintages will certainly repay cellaring.

Among Boschendal's new generation of blended white wines is the Grand Vin Blanc, sold in a trade mark bottle which looks dangerously like De Ladoucette's Baron de L. Sauvignon Blanc with a little Rhine Riesling to add dimension, the Grand Vin Blanc has passed through enough oak to have added wood to the medley of flavours. It is an excellent restaurant wine, opening up easily and promising great reliability.

The Pavillon Blanc, so far only offered for sale at the annual auction of the Cape Independent Winemakers' Guild, is a very promising Sémillon. Perhaps in time it may take on some Sauvignon Blanc to add lightness to its distinctively oaky character. The Vin d'Or, only available in select vintages, is one of the Cape's most complex noble late harvests.

Finally, Boschendal has been one of the country's méthode champenoise pioneers: the regular Boschendal Brut enjoys a premium status even in this de luxe market, and ages well, showing a yeasty, almost nutty bouquet after about seven years. More recently, Boschendal launched a less expensive méthode champenoise under the brand name of Le Grand Pavillon. Beautifully packaged, it seems capable of developing a very champagne-like nose to go with its typically French, very upmarket presentation.

Boschendal's success has been the result of a series of good marketing decisions, an early commitment to run its own sales force in the trade, two winemakers (initially the high profile, somewhat outspoken Achim von Arnim, and since the late 1980s the quieter, more subtle Hilko Hegewisch) who played a key role in producing quality wines, and a few happy coincidences. The net effect is that South Africa's most powerful and most successful wine estate is located not in Stellenbosch or Paarl, where most of the country's private producers have their cellars, but in Franschhoek, home to fewer than half a dozen estates.

Closer to the village itself from Boschendal, the next major property is L'Ormarins, which has belonged to the Rupert family for just over two decades. Anthonij Rupert, son of the founder of The Bergkelder, has lived here for much of this time. Under his direction the vineyards have been extensively replanted, more recently with an enviable dedication to soil preparation. It goes without saying that the winemaking facilities are state-of-the-art, though never with wasted investment. Every feature is functional; the actual crushing cellar may lack the olde worlde charm which characterises the rest of the property, but winemaker Nico Vermeulen turns out an impressive array of wines.

The L'Ormarins Chardonnay is one of the most successful estate Chardonnays, a fine balance between wood and fruit, quite citrussy on the palate, though not unduly harsh. Part of the reason for the following it has acquired is the estate's very sensible pricing policy. Even before South Africa's Chardonnay production began to exceed demand, L'Ormarins positioned its wine at an affordable level. Consumers are therefore able to buy a highly regarded estate product, of good quality, well wooded and typical of the cultivar, for no more than ordinary branded wines.

The Blanc Fumé was the first wooded Sauvignon Blanc to obtain a real following in the South African market. At one stage the food and beverage director of the country's most upmarket hotel chain showed me that it was the dominant dry white wine at the group's two most prestigious establishments. At a time when most of the Cape's Sauvignon Blancs were harsh, acidic, unattractive and indigestible, L'Ormarins used the softening effect of wood to round off and balance out the varietal. Initially over-oaked and almost too vanilla on the nose and palate, the Blanc Fumé in more recent vintages has let the varietal fruit show through. Unlike any Loire or Bordeaux Sauvignon, the big, slightly smoky wine with its rich wood overtones sometimes fools fairly proficient palates into believing it is a heavily wooded Chardonnay.

In recent years, however, much of L'Ormarins' reputation has come to rest on its red wines. Replanted vineyards, the best clonal material and a rigorous selection of the grapes have all contributed to some superb Cabernets and Cabernet blends. The estate's proprietary wine is sold as L'Ormarins Optima. The Cabernet Sauvignon, Cabernet Franc and Merlot harmonise into a typically Médoc style. The 1984 showed excellent balance, with a fullness and richness of fruit that was surprising in its youth, and which has lasted well, mingling with the now emerging bottle-aged character. More recent vintages seem slightly more accessible, though this change in style has not been achieved at the expense of overall balance.

The regular Cabernet Sauvignon is more powerful and seemingly more austere. Packed with blackcurrant fruit, well integrated with the oak, its essentially vertical style complements the greater breadth and dimension of the Optima. The concentration and intensity suggest a greater need to age in bottle; some vintages will certainly improve for between ten and twenty years before levelling off.

L'Ormarins produces a limited-release Noble Late Harvest, easily one of the most luscious and most intense wines of its kind from the Cape. Earlier vintages seemed particularly rich, though current releases balance out the fruit, botrytis and acidity to more approachable levels. The Sauvignon Blanc presents itself with surprisingly pungent fruit, something midway between a Bordeaux and a Rhine style; the Gewürztraminer-Bukettraube is more reminiscent of the Moselle.

L'Ormarins' other wines include the Guldenpfennig Guldenlese, a beautifully drinkable late harvest; an unwooded Sauvignon Blanc which I find too harsh and inaccessible;

a Pinot Gris and a Rhine Riesling which have their followers; and a Franschhoek (that is, Cape) Riesling. The estate will also shortly release a méthode champenoise sparkling wine and a trio of ports, the reputation of which already precedes them.

Still further up the road towards Franschhoek lies another estate in the front rank of South African producers: La Motte is the home of Anton Rupert's daughter and son-in-law, Hanneli and Paul Neethling. Beautifully restored over the past twenty years, La Motte's rise to prominence has been recent and meteoric.

Paul Neethling and his winemaker Jacques Borman are deeply committed to the individuality of the estate and its wines. Each varietal is treated according to its merits, and the wines which have emerged bear a stamp of authenticity often lost in the larger, more commercial cellars.

The estate's Sauvignon Blanc is crisp, dry, quite alcoholic, smoky on the nose, not aggressive on the palate. It has an almost Bordeaux Sauvignon style, the herbaceousness having advanced from underripe 'grassiness' to a fuller, rounder character. The Blanc Fumé, by comparison, has a little of that early gooseberry fruit, though well layered with wood, and not over-oaked.

The Merlot has plenty of structure and colour, less of a quaffing wine and more like a St Emilion. The same leaner, more controlled style characterises the Cabernet Sauvignon: taut, well held together, dry, but with the fruit built right into the heart of the wine. The recently released Cabernet/Merlot blend, sold under the proprietary name of Millennium is surprisingly accessible, especially given the estate's more austere style of varietal wine. Here the fruit tannins and some judicious wooding give the Millennium blend an approachability which belies the wine's maturation potential.

La Motte also offers a small quantity of Shiraz: intense, slightly smoky, elegant, never clumsy. I also recall some experimental Pinot Noir which seemed quite promising, though so far this wine has never been released.

La Motte was the first of The Bergkelder estates to insist that its wines are bottled on the property. Paul Neethling's views on the subject are sometimes forcefully expressed. In the end, he maintains, it has little to do with the quality of the technology at some central bottling facility: bulk wines should not be moved more than is necessary and the wine-maker should work with his harvest all the way to the bottle. The Bergkelder handles sales and distribution; the wine, however, is still the exclusive domain of the cellarmaster.

Further into the town itself, the Dieu Donné vineyards remain one of the few Franschhoek properties making the wine on the farm. Most of the other regional growers deliver their grapes to the local co-op for individual vinification, and then take over the marketing of the bottled wine. Dieu Donné, formerly known as De Lucque and Dieu Donné, has had something of a chequered history since the mid 1980s when former owner John Smeddle first launched its wines on something of a mail order basis. Presently owned by the Maingard family, who have spent considerable sums replant-ing vineyards and upgrading the winery, it seems to be mov-ing forward into a happier era.

New Chardonnay and Cabernet Sauvignon vineyards are now yielding a crop, so that varietal wines are beginning to replace the rather obscurely named Grand Saint-Marc, Sainte-Jo, Chiara de Lucque and Fait de Foi. Early signs are that the Cabernet will make an easy-drinking, well-balanced wine, and the Chardonnay a well-rounded, citrus-with-wood-overtones muscular kind of wine.

Through to the other side of the town is Clos Cabrière, a property which has acquired a special reputation for its méth-ode champenoise sparkling wines. Owned by Achim von Arnim, former winemaker at Boschendal, Clos Cabrière is the home of the Pierre Jourdan brand of bubbly. This was the first commercially available Champagne method Cape sparkling wine to work with only the traditional French varietals of Chardonnay and Pinot Noir.

Von Arnim is something of a maverick, rigorous and unrelenting in whatever he chooses to do, entertaining in his philosophy of life and wine, and dedicated to producing a world-beater at Clos Cabrière. Years ago, a woman at a wine-tasting asked him why winemakers don't put wood chips in their wine, instead of putting the wine into expensive barrels. His reply has achieved something of an immortality in wine circles: 'Madam,' he is reputed to have said, 'do you know about artificial insemination?' 'Yes,' she replied. 'Aha!' he said. 'But do you prefer it?'

Clos Cabrière is dedicated solely to the production of bubbly, though a more recent vineyard development on the slopes above the town includes Pinot Noir plantings destined for a Burgundy-style red wine. At present, however, all the Clos Cabrière wines are sold under the Pierre Jourdan label. These include the standard estate sparkling wine, the Pierre Jourdan Brut, 60 per cent Chardonnay and 40 per cent Pinot Noir, dry, elegant, a little lacking in complexity but capable of useful bottle ageing.

There is also a Blanc de Blancs, made from Chardonnay in select vintages, some oakiness coming through and extra yeastiness, compared with the standard Brut. The Brut Sauvage has a zero sugar dosage giving it a taut, lean, flinty quality, beloved by purists and worthy of considerable bottle ageing. Finally there is the Cuvée Belle Rose, all Pinot Noir, unusually forward, with a fine fragrance, a perfumed dryness offering extra accessibility without compromising the estate's naturally austere style.

Achim von Arnim has been making méthode champenoise in South Africa almost longer than anyone else. Clos Cabrière has now passed through the early stages of finding its style, getting to know its grapes and how they will perform. Vineyards are moving towards maturity and there is every indication that in the next five years the estate will start producing world-class wines on a regular basis.

Another of the Franschhoek producers working in his own winery is Mike Stander who, with partner Glennie van Hoogstraten, produces the La Couronne range of wines. A recent venture, with 1989 as its first vintage, La Couronne has swiftly acquired something of a reputation for its Sauvignon Blanc and its Blanc Fumé. The former, available as a regular or a Reserve wine, is fragrant, slightly herbaceous, a hint of fig and gooseberry. The Reserve is altogether bigger than the standard wine, plenty of flavour and length on the palate; the regular is more grassy, more intense, with acidity which makes it an easy choice to go with food.

The Blanc Fumé has plenty of oak, though the Sauvignon character still manages to show through quite well. Alongside the first vintage of Chardonnay from the farm, the Blanc Fumé performs admirably, smokier and quite alcoholic, while the Chardonnay offers finesse, and a slight butterscotch lees character. La Couronne also produces a white Bordeaux blend of Sémillon and Sauvignon Blanc, sold under the proprietary name of Richesse: easy drinking though quite complex.

Mouton-Excelsior is another of the district's maverick producers, with proprietor Ben Mouton combining some bought-in production with his own yield. A newly released Merlot seems quite promising, as does a recent Chardonnay. New vineyards will still take a few years before yielding a reasonable production, though the farm at least seems poised to do more than trade in wine purchased from other growers.

The remaining Franschhoek properties all arrange to have their wines vinified for them at the local cooperative. The moving force behind this concept, and the later launch of the Vignerons de Franschhoek, was Mike Trull, owner of La Bri and marketing man *par excellence*. Trull recognised the enormous potential of the Franschhoek area, both because of its soils and milder climate, and also because of the direct link to the Huguenot heritage.

From the early 1980s Mike and Cheryl Trull set out to focus attention on the viticultural and historical significance of Franschhoek. At the time the region was dominated by fruit farming though many of the properties had vines and delivered grapes to the local co-op. La Bri, for example, had very old Sémillon vineyards whose commercial value was directly proportionate to the very low yield. Trull consulted the experts and discovered that by the simple expedient of planting Sauvignon Blanc, and blending the fruitier, earlier maturing Sauvignon with the longer lasting Sémillon, he could create a classic Bordeaux white blend. This would enhance the value of the Sémillon, and give the farm a wine with a unique point of difference.

One thing, as usual, leads to another: there was obviously a useful economy in avoiding the cost of winery construction if the local co-op had the capacity to take up this production. On the other hand, it did not have the space to age the wines, so Trull built a maturation facility. The idea, and the region, desperately needed a little marketing and what better vehicle than an initiative involving the whole district – so the Vignerons de Franschhoek was born.

La Bri is now clearly the front runner among the properties producing and bottling wines through the Franschhoek Co-op. In addition to the original Blanc de la Bri (Sauvignon/Sémillon and barrel-aged) there is an excellent Sauvignon Blanc, marketed under the name of Sauvage de la Bri. The property also produces a creditable Rhine Riesling, sold in a Liebfraumilch look-alike pack as Weisser la Bri; and a fruit salad of all the farm's varietals, La Briette.

Michael Trull is now also involved in the Denbies winery project in Surrey, United Kingdom, as a shareholder and executive. He divides his time between the northern and southern hemispheres effectively enough to maintain the quality on which La Bri established not only its own credibility, but also the 20th-century reputation of the Franschhoek district.

There are several other properties delivering grapes to the co-op for vinification under the individual farm's name: La Provence, one of the region's best known homesteads, brands several white wines and one non-vintage Cabernet. The Cuvée Blanche is mainly Sauvignon and Sémillon, a little too oaky to be mistaken for white Bordeaux; the Blanc Fumé can be quite grassy, often with plenty of flavour, and the Sauvignon Blanc is fragrant though sometimes a little too crisp.

A little further along is Haute Provence which now offers several good-value white wines to its ever-increasing clientele. The Chardonnay, though a little light and evanescent, has a distinct Mâcon character, the Blanc Royale (Sauvignon/Sémillon) is an easy-to-drink Graves style, and the Blanc Fumé shows good fruit and wood harmonising well together. There is also an excellent semi-sweet Muscat/Chenin Blanc blend sold under the proprietary name of Larmes des Anges (Tears of the Angels).

Franschhoek has several other properties which have, or which may in the future yield, wines under the farm's name. Of these, Les Chênes, which used to produce an excellent Chenin Blanc, and Chamonix, which yielded a creditable Cabernet, come to mind. The former seems intent on upgrading its vineyards and new releases are planned shortly. The latter offers a Cabernet and a Blanc de Noir, with a Chardonnay destined for release shortly. The farm also sells two different carbonated bubblies in the Courchevel range.

The Atlantic Seaboard: Durbanville

The Durbanville district is as close to Cape Town as Constantia, and in many ways can claim the same precedence over Stellenbosch and Paarl as Van der Stel's original property. It is remarkably close to the cool Atlantic, lying as it does just off the national road that runs through to Paarl. The Tygerberg Hills protect the vineyards from the breezes gusting in off Table Bay less than 20 kilometres away. Urban encroachment has deprived wine drinkers of many of the district's best sites. Most of the area is now residential, part really of greater Cape Town.

The remaining properties surround the outskirts of the town, lying to the west and north. Altydgedacht is one of the best known: it has been in the Parker family for several generations. Until it began bottling its wines in the mid 1980s it delivered all its grapes to Nederburg in Paarl. When the wine of origin legislation was introduced in 1973 the law condoned all existing contractual arrangements, freeing Altydgedacht to continue its business across viticultural districts. This means in effect that those Nederburg wines which contain Altydgedacht grapes can still be certified for Paarl area of origin, notwithstanding the presence of Durbanville production in the cuvée. Probably in most cases the percentages were not significant, though Nederburg's Gamay must have contained a high proportion of grapes from the Parkers' vineyards.

Now that Altydgedacht bottles some of its production, it

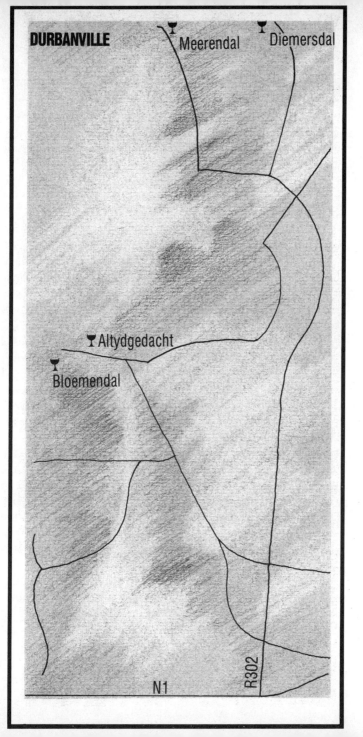

DURBANVILLE

Meerendal

Diemersdal

Altydgedacht

Bloemendal

R302

N1

has contributed to the renaissance of the district as a whole. Firstly, it is an important and well-established estate; secondly, John Parker actively promotes the region through his role as chairman of the regional wine trust; finally, Altydgedacht was the first Durbanville estate to receive visitors, thus putting the area back on to the wine route.

Altydgedacht is not a run-of-the-mill wine farm. The Parker brothers are not conformists, even by the very broad standards of the wine industry. Their wines are often individualistic, powerful, never overly big, but well structured and with plenty of flavour. The Tygerberg Wood-Aged Dry White, for example, began life as a mistake: Chenin Blanc left too long in a newly skimmed wooden vat. Young Sauvignon redeemed the fruit, and the current blend is wood-fermented, but not wood-matured, and gets a fruit fillip from Bukettraube.

The estate's Sauvignon Blanc has plenty of herbaceous fruit, without the harsh acidities normally associated with this style of wine. The farm's Bukettraube has balance and spice, rare enough in this otherwise bland, slightly muscatty varietal. Altydgedacht also produces a fine Gewürztraminer, layered with rose petal aromas, dry and slightly earthy, never cloying, never too lean.

The early Chardonnays were adequate, but lacked balance and personality. A certification problem led to one vintage being marked under the trade mark name of Charade, an irony which hopefully was lost on the Wine and Spirit Board. The latest release shows that the Parkers are working on the varietal: given the region's climate, it can only be a matter of time before Durbanville produces a really striking Chardonnay.

The farm's red wines include a Barbera/Shiraz blend marketed under the name of Tintoretto, a Pinotage and a Cabernet. The Tintoretto is an excellent pasta wine, good grip on the palate, slightly smoky on the nose, easy to drink but not simple or lacking dimension. It is not an obvious sort of wine, earthy, a little like the Mediterranean country reds implicit in its name, but one well worth seeking out to accompany Italian food.

The Pinotage is packed with berry fruit, layered with vanilla and oak, easy-drinking though not light, a wine of flavour without unnecessary punch. The Cabernet is old clone, intense, concentrated, deep coloured, sometimes a little eucalyptus-like on the nose, and well wooded. In top vintages the Altydgedacht Cabernet is surprisingly resilient, opening up slowly, showing excellent structure. In the lighter vintages it is no less impressive though it presents earlier, as if to give encouragement to those holding on to their 1986s.

Near-neighbour Jackie Coetzee at Bloemendal has already shown, in the few years since he began bottling his estate's wines, that Durbanville's quality wine claims are not a matter of chance: the newly released Bloemendal Cabernet embodies the same combination of fruit and balance, and the same elegance.

The Bloemendal Chardonnay has also developed its own style since the first bottlings came to the market. Originally a little lean and insubstantial, current releases show good harmony between wood and fruit, as well as a little richness creeping into the mid-palate. The Sauvignon Blanc has gooseberry, almost smoky aromas, and lots of flavour, before the dry though not harsh finish.

Almost due north of these two properties is Meerendal, an estate marketing through The Bergkelder, while still maintaining a personality and individuality which centralised maturation and bottling facilities have been unable to supersede. The late Kosie Starke, who brought the estate into its recent prominence, was a lion of a man, courageous, free of the vanity of fashion, honest and warm-hearted.

Until Meerendal entered The Bergkelder arrangement with its 1974 vintage, the estate's wines were sold through

211

the KWV. Even today, the best KWV bottlings are bench-mark wines. Shortly before Kosie Starke died I drank a few of his older Pinotages with him. Twenty to twenty-five years old, they had kept remarkably well. A lot of the rough ace-tone character of young Pinotage had left the wine and had instead been replaced by a gentle berry bouquet reminiscent of the Southern Rhône. Kosie was pleased with how the wines had turned out, but in a direct, almost self-deprecating way, as if this were all the work of nature, and not of man. His Shiraz bottlings from the same era have also matured as elegantly and as gracefully and even today the 1969, 1970 and 1972 Meerendals are worth seeking out at auction sales.

In many ways Meerendal epitomises the virtues of the Durbanville area: close to the Atlantic, its vineyards are kept cool throughout the summer by the westerly breezes. The high clay content soils retain moisture, making irrigation unnecessary, and summer dews keep the dry land vineyards stress free. While the estate only markets two red wines, it is also planted to varietals like Chardonnay which are delivered direct to The Bergkelder. Wines made from these grapes have the elegance, freshness and intensity which are the hall-marks of the district.

The estate's reds are equally true to the Durbanville style. The Pinotage combines a berry richness with just the right amount of French oak to enhance complexity. The Shiraz can be one of the Cape's best: smoky, full but never unduly heavy, in its finest vintages it is a wine to rival a good Cor-nas.

Slightly to the east of Meerendal is Diemersdal, an estate whose reputation has so preceded it that virtually no market-ing was necessary when its wines were launched on the domestic trade for the first time. The KWV had taken up all of Diemersdal's production for so many years that every assurance that the farm would also sell a little of its wines in the South African market was treated with scepticism. John

Platter's wine guide despaired of fulfilling its annual prediction that the wines would shortly be made available to locals. When the Louw family finally announced their first domestic sales, only the black market dealers in KWV stocks had any cause to lament.

The wines are not robust, though they are not insubstantial. The Dry Red, a Cabernet-dominated Bordeaux blend, is elegant, slightly spicy on the nose, not very big, but with quite forward tannins at present. Perhaps the wood tannins have edged out the fruit tannins, perhaps the finesse has been achieved at the expense of the mid-palate.

The regular Cabernet is certainly fuller, with a bigger colour, more fruit, and the wood better integrated with the cassis-like nose and finish. Diemersdal will also be releasing a Pinotage and a Shiraz, a sign perhaps that aficionados of the estate's wines will no longer have to engage in covert and unconventional trading arrangements to get the stocks they seek. Diemersdal and Bloemendal have sold their wines on a commercial basis in the domestic market only in the past five years. Altydgedacht can claim an earlier presence in the trade, but only by a few vintages. Meerendal has been available in general distribution since the late 1970s. In other words, Durbanville had all but vanished from the wine drinker's vocabulary before being brought back from the brink of extinction. Once its estates develop their vineyards and cellars to the point where a clear regional style is discernible, where new clonal material has reached some maturity in properly prepared soils, the measure of what has been lost to urban encroachment will be known. Happily the district is swiftly regaining its viticultural reputation, ensuring, in a way, its own survival.

The Allesverloren Estate, in the Swartland area of origin, is a lone private producer north of Durbanville, west of Paarl, south of the Olifants River. For convenience sake, I have included it at the end of the Durbanville section, though neither climate nor soil would seem to justify this decision. In the Western Cape a distance of 50 kilometres as the crow flies can produce changes in *terroir* so extreme that the wines which emerge are as different from each other as Châteauneuf-du-Pape from Santenay.

Allesverloren dates back to 1704, though its history of wine production begins in the early 19th century. The Malan family acquired the farm in 1872 and have been making wine here ever since. The estate's unique position accounts for its survival as a quality wine producer in the heart of wheat country. Its vineyards lie along the Kasteelberg and range in altitude from 170 to 370 metres, with a difference in annual rainfall of 200 millimetres between the lower and upper sites. The summers are warmer than nearby Paarl and Stellenbosch, though the westerly breezes from the Atlantic ocean – some 60 kilometres away, cool the ripening grapes in the late afternoon.

Allesverloren is red wine country, and its wines reflect best the robust features of the varietals to which the estate has been planted. Allesverloren's Cabernet is never delicate and subtly perfumed: the blackcurrant character is there, but layered with tannins, strong alcohols and mineral/earthy overtones. The vineyards are unirrigated and the roots of the vines extend for several metres below the pebbly Malmesbury shale in search of summer moisture. Careful vinification and good *élevage* at The Bergkelder ensure that in most vintages the muscularity of the wine is softened by oaking into a more gentle breeding.

The farm's Shiraz won international recognition at the 1989 Vinexpo. Full-bodied, smoky, rich, and with enough tannin to see it all the way through to the finish, it is, in George Saintsbury's much-quoted phrase, the manliest of wines, better to savour on a winter's night than at a summer lunch. The same is true of the Tinta Barocca, though it is

214

never likely to age with anything like the balance or range of flavours.

Allesverloren is not a new era South African producer. Its wines are full and demanding: they need time in the bottle and are not intended for the faint of heart. However, they reward patient cellaring in much the same way as a good Barolo.

WELLINGTON AND TULBAGH

The Wellington district, adjacent really to Agter-Paarl, has started to earn a reputation for its wines. Probably the first producer to focus attention on Wellington was Trevor Harris, who bought the Onverwacht Estate almost by default, and then decided to make a success of it, at all costs.

Things have not been easy for Harris, an accountant by training, and an optimist by inclination. The farm was planted to cultivars appropriate to the climate of the district, though not necessarily to the taste of the fine wine market. Several very acceptable wines, made from Tinta Barocca, Chenin Blanc, Pinotage and Weisser Riesling, have had a slow passage through the trade. A restaurant aimed at promoting the estate was opened, and then closed down. As far as tourists from Cape Town are concerned, Wellington is just a town too far. The business continues, however, and the wines are obtaining something of a franchise in the market, since they represent good value for money.

The Bouquet Blanc is something of a fruit salad wine, semi-sweet, fragrant, good easy-drinking value. The Weisser Riesling is surprisingly good, coming as it does from the warm Wellington region. Dry or off-dry, the wine has a spicy, almost perfumed bouquet and plenty of flavour on the palate.

Among the red wines, the Tinta Barocca is obviously the estate's flagship. This is a well-structured, complex Tinta, almost plummy on the nose, a combination of hard and soft tannins on the palate, softened by six months in new French barrels, and tautly balanced on the finish. The Cape offers surprisingly few good Tinta Baroccas, mainly because those

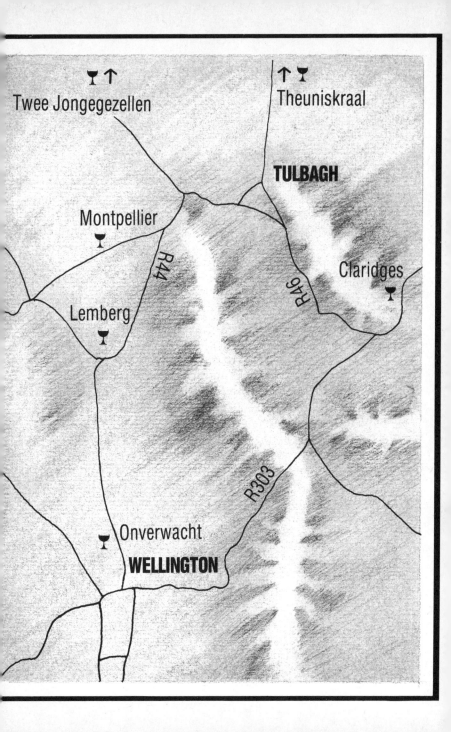

who have quality plantings hardly find it worth their while to invest in the varietal. Trevor Harris and his winemaker Mark Ravenscroft have little choice, given the vineyards at Onverwacht. They have certainly shown what is possible with a little commitment.

Onverwacht also produces a carbonated bubbly sold under the proprietary name of Savoire Brut. It is widely distributed, an easy-drinking, well put together sparkling wine suitable for festive occasions.

Another Wellington property likely to make a name for itself in the next few years is Claridges, where Roger and Maria Jorgensen have started making wines from vines growing on the Rustenburg Farm just outside the town. With a Chardonnay and a Cabernet blend in the pipeline, Claridges will obviously focus even more attention on the district and its fine wine potential. Perhaps in time tourists will be more inclined to make an excursion through the area, and also take in Tulbagh, another of the country's lesser known wine regions, no more than an hour's drive from Paarl.

Tulbagh is one of the quaintest and most beautiful villages in South Africa. Set in the amphitheatre of the surrounding mountains, it is part of the wheat basket of the Cape. Many of the buildings in the town are historic monuments: their whitewashed walls and thatched roofs give an almost time-less feel to Tulbagh. It is difficult to believe that most of the town was destroyed by an earthquake in 1969, and that much of what remains today is the result of painstaking restoration.

The area can be approached from Paarl on the main road, or, for those given to more scenic routes, via the spectacular Bain's Kloof pass. Here the road has literally been hewn out of the rock face, a 19th-century feat of construction worthy of the detour. Tulbagh is home to several wine estates, including the newly launched Kloofzicht farm of Roger Fehlmann. The first wine from this property is a well reputed blend of Merlot and Cabernet, one of the few red wines presently produced in the region. Tulbagh has always enjoyed a following for its whites, with several of the country's best-known white wine producers located in the district.

Chief among these is Twee Jongegezellen, one of the Cape's pioneering quality wine cellars. The estate has been in the Krone family for centuries. The property was granted to two bachelors (as the name implies) more than two hundred years ago, though its status as one of the Cape's foremost white wine farms dates back to the middle of this century. N.C. Krone, father of the present proprietor and winemaker at TJ, is credited with introducing cold fermentation in the 1950s, a distinction shared with the Graues at Nederburg. From then onwards the estate's reputation flourished. By the 1970s the brand had grown like Topsy, a vast and unwieldy range selling under the Twee Jongegezellen banner. At a time when most South African farms offered at best a choice of Cape Riesling, Chenin Blanc and Late Harvest, TJ's selection covered nearly a dozen wines, including Gewürztraminer, Rhine Riesling and several blends, of which the 39 Grand Prix comprised as many as seventeen different varietals. For a brief moment the Krones even sold a light red wine, the TJ La Marque, a delicate and undistinguished assemblage of Cabernet, Shiraz, Tinta Barocca and Pinotage.

In the mid 1980s the historic estate needed a marketing injection. Its wines lacked precision and thrust in the trade and the range was too large for distributors Gilbeys to handle with real punch. The result of a major brand rethink was a consolidation of what was available into four wines, all blends made up from the vast variety of cultivars planted on the estate. There have since been a couple of additions to this basic range, but TJ's continued commercial success seems to be the direct result of replanning and repackaging the wines at this crucial time in the farm's history.

The TJ 39 Grand Prix still enjoys a substantial following. Among the blending components are Chenin Blanc, Sémillon, Muller-Thurgau, Chardonnay, Sylvaner and Cape Riesling. The result is a wine that is dry but delicately fragrant. The more commercial-looking bottle which came with the new-look TJ may frighten off purists, but on its taste qualities alone, the TJ 39 deserves real attention as a quality table wine.

The TJ Schanderl is Nicky Krone's homage to his former professor and mentor. A spicy, off-dry, pungently perfumed wine, it is a blend of Gewürztraminer, various Muscats and Rhine Riesling. It has the same virtues as fresh Alsace wine, and can be drunk young, though it does knit together well after a few years in the bottle.

Two other Twee Jongegezellen wines of note are the TJ Light, a delicate low-alcohol lunchtime wine, and the TJ Night Harvest, a perfumed wine whose fruit is sweeter than its palate. The estate also produces the occasional Noble Late Harvest, botrytised rather than sweet, packed with an array of tropical fruit scents. Sold as Engeltjiepipi (Angel's Piss), the only dubious taste feature is its name.

The latest release from Twee Jongegezellen is the estate's méthode champenoise, marketed under the proprietary name of Krone Borealis. The base wine comprised Chardonnay, Pinot Blanc and Pinot Noir. Made without the addition of sulphur dioxide, it is one of the finest and most delicate of the Cape's Champagne method bubblies. With its depth, complexity and balance, the premium pricing seems more than justified.

The Krones have played a pioneering role in the region's viticulture and their farm is undoubtedly Tulbagh's most successful estate.

Near-neighbour Theuniskraal has enjoyed prestige status in the Cape wine industry for much of this century. The wines have been marketed by The Bergkelder since the 1970s, but the estate's reputation antedates this distribution arrangement by many years. In the days when the best dry white wines of the Cape were produced from Cape Riesling (Crouchen Blanc), the Theuniskraal wine was in such great demand that it was only supplied on allocation, and only to select outlets. Nowadays it has been somewhat superseded by the Chardonnays and Sauvignon Blancs, and by more sophisticated vinification techniques, though it still has a considerable following.

Theuniskraal also occasionally markets a Gewürztraminer, sweetish, with a typically perfumed rose petal bouquet, though often a little cloying. It ages well, drying out slightly on the way and developing an interesting bottle character.

Just south of Theuniskraal is the Montpellier Estate where the Theron family has farmed for many years. De Wet Theron, late father of Jan and Hendrik who now run the operation, was something of a doyen of the Cape wine industry in his day, a director of the KWV and an experimental and successful winemaker. Montpellier was the first Cape estate to obtain a Superior rating from the Wine and Spirit Board and many of its wines from the vintages of the 1970s seem to have aged remarkably well.

The early 1980s were difficult years for the Theron brothers, as their winemaking methods and their singular attitude to bureaucracy led to a stand-off situation with the authorities. The Wine and Spirit Board withheld certification of whole vintages of Montpellier's wine, leaving the Therons with no alternative but to take the matter to the Supreme Court. They won, but it turned out to be something of a pyrrhic victory. The court ruled that the Board had exceeded its authority. South African bureaucracy, however, is not a sporting loser: within a year the Act was changed giving the Board absolute discretion, and for many years it exacted punitive retaliation, seemingly harassing the Therons at every possible opportunity.

Fortunately these events are now history, and although it will take the estate many years to claw back the market share that it lost, it is on course to do so. Its first Pinot Noir, under the Gleno proprietary brand label, is perhaps too light and too easy, but it does show that Montpellier is looking to a place in the vanguard. Previously the estate offered only white wines, mainly blends around Chenin Blanc and Rhine Riesling.

The Tuinwingerd is the Rhine Riesling on which the farm's reputation in the 1970s was based. Variable in the past few years, it is capable in good vintages of showing a lovely balance between fruit and mid-palate. The Suzanne Gardé Sauvignon/Pinot Gris blend is an easy-drinking, off-dry wine with gentle Sauvignon fruit, not crisp or cloying. The Blanc de Blanc brings Sauvignon and Sémillon together in a fruity, white Bordeaux style while the Special Late Harvest is rich, quite botrytised, with a complex range of varietal flavours on the palate and finish.

Finally, Tulbagh boasts the country's smallest wine estate, the Lemberg farm of Janey Muller, one of the country's most individualistic and courageous winemakers. Since the early 1980s she has been making full-bodied white wines, more French than German in style, vinous, robust, not for the faint of heart. Both the Aimée (a Sauvignon Blanc named after her daughter) and the Lemberg (Hárslevelü) bear the unmistakable stamp of the winemaker.

The estate's cellar is small, free entirely of smart gadgets, and the winemaking is still very much a matter of handcrafting. There can be significant variation vintage to vintage. Janey Muller's refusal to overhandle the wines spares them cold stabilisation and destructive filtration, but it does mean that the bottles tend to have a harmless deposit of tartrate crystals.

Lemberg keeps its contact with the country's wine bureaucracy down to an absolute minimum. Wine and Spirit Board certification is not a priority to Janey Muller, though this should not discourage wine drinkers seeking authentic and artisanal wines.

OVERLOOKING THE INDIAN OCEAN: HERMANUS

♨ ℰⅇ

The coastal village of Hermanus is just over an hour's drive from Cape Town. The national road follows a more or less easterly course through the spectacular Sir Lowry's Pass and the apple basket of Elgin and Grabouw before dipping southwards down towards the sea. Hermanus is a good two degrees further south than Stellenbosch or Paarl. This is much the same difference in latitude that divides Chambertin from the Mâcon.

Before phylloxera decimated the Cape wine industry in the last two decades of the 19th century, many of the farms around Hermanus managed a little wine production. By all accounts it was not a particularly successful crop, suitable for domestic consumption but not really marketable. The climate of the region was simply too cool, partly on account of latitude, partly because of the moderating effect of the ocean.

Not all the land around the town is appropriate for viticulture. However there are portions of the Hemel-en-Aarde Valley situated directly behind the cliffs which overlook the village where the soils are eminently suitable.

After the phylloxera catastrophe farmers in the area abandoned viticulture. There seemed little point in replanting vineyards if the likely value of the crop was much less than could be earned from other, less status-imbued, agriculture. Relative to many of the regions of the Western Cape, Hermanus is simply too close to the outermost climatic limits of the vine. At the end of the 19th century, when much less was

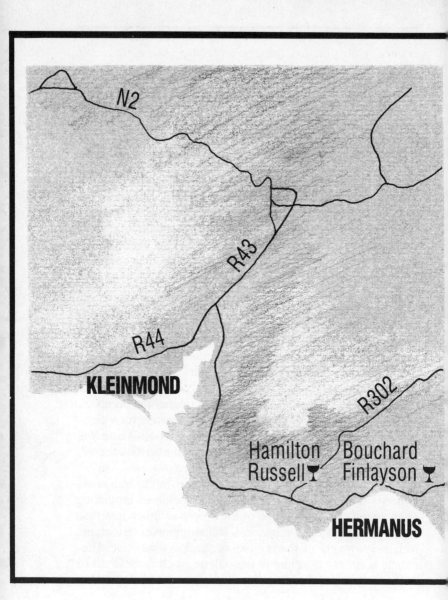

known about grafted rootstocks and clonal selection, it was not really possible to capitalise on the benefits of the cooler climate. All potential advantages were liabilities. Each year there was a very real risk that the grapes would not achieve full ripeness. In a market which traded almost exclusively in bulk wine, where the producer was rewarded for the alcoholic strength rather than the delicacy of his yield, Hermanus would always be at a disadvantage to the warmer regions, many of which lay closer to the main market of Cape Town.

Many factors contributed to the renaissance of viticulture in the Hemel-en-Aarde Valley some three-quarters of a century later. The development of a fine wine market in the years after the Second World War provided a real incentive to producers willing to exchange quality for quantity. Initially this was a slow process, affecting growers in the Paarl and Stellenbosch regions. The country's wholesale merchants, many of whom were situated in Stellenbosch itself, began developing brands with a premium positioning. The market responded to this by acquiring a palate for wines with greater complexity and finesse. Cellar technology also changed, so that vinification methods took account of the demand for balance and elegance. There was a gradual move towards estate wine production, with its emphasis on provenance. Legislation in its turn focused attention on the smaller production units with their boutique wines of greater rarity.

The single most important boost to the creation of a premium wine market was the launch in 1975 of the Nederburg Auction in Paarl (see page 42). Despite a slow start, within a few years the Auction showed a strong enough purchasing pattern for quality wine producers to anticipate that there would be suitable financial rewards for those who invested in quality. This was the era which saw the beginnings of vineyard improvement programmes in much of the Western Cape. Since cooler climate is a central aspect of premium wine production, it was inevitable that those who aimed to lead the new generation of Cape winemakers into a world of international competition would look to those regions with slightly less generous ripening conditions. Everyone seems to know the old adage of 'making the vine struggle a little'.

There were plenty of cooler pockets within the established viticultural areas. The Constantia region, for example, gets considerably fewer degree hours during the ripening season and benefits from the moderating effects of its proximity to the sea; Durbanville and parts of Stellenbosch closest to False Bay can be positively cool; so is much of Somerset West. Ida's Valley, the Helshoogte side of Stellenbosch, the Franschhoek side of Paarl, and Franschhoek itself are all markedly less sunny or simply more temperate than the rest of the Western Cape.

The 1970s was an era of change and innovation in many of the wine-producing regions of the New World. Investment in California was already showing what dividend in quality might be expected through proper soil preparation and careful selection of microclimate. In the United States and Australia wood vinification was producing gratifying results. The famous Bicentenary tasting in Paris, in which Californian wines usurped the claims of leading French contenders and took top honours, encouraged the more innovative wine people in the Cape to re-examine the potential of South African viticulture.

For a start, many of the internationally accepted premium varietals were entirely absent from the Cape. There was also a frightening paucity of clonal material, little or no experience of wood vinification and a tradition of training winemakers in the German rather than the French schools. The leading lights of the Cape wine industry were smugly complacent about their wines, confusing the commercial success of their large industrial wineries with the quality achievements of producers setting new benchmarks in Europe and the United States. Comparative tastings with European or

New World wines were rare, and they were usually set up to make a carefully orchestrated statement about Cape wine. The cellarmaster at the Cape's most successful quality winery publicly denied the significance of comparing what was being produced in South Africa with the wines of Europe or America. 'South Africa,' he said pompously, 'produces the best South African wines in the world.'

For the small band of innovators who led the vanguard of change in the Cape, the decade from the mid 1970s to the mid 1980s was not an easy period. The Government departments responsible for controlling and quarantining plant and seed material were bluntly uncooperative: an over-meticulous application of the rules could block the entry of new varietals and clones for up to twenty years. South African wine styles also counted against those who hoped to latch on to the international trends. Traditionally the Cape's red wines were heavy and full, lowish in acidity, clumsy and sometimes even slightly porty. There was no certainty that the market would react positively to wines which would, of necessity, be lighter, more refined, perhaps even delicate in comparison. The red wine market of the Cape's producers was a veritable temple of machismo: there was a very real risk that a wine style which bucked this system would be a social and financial failure.

Several producers, often working in ignorance of one another's innovations, single-handedly laid the foundations for the changes in the quality wine industry which became evident in the 1980s. Of these, one whose role as an innovator as much as publicist of the changes is unparalleled, is Tim Hamilton Russell. His Hermanus venture in the Hemel-en-Aarde Valley behind the sleepy coastal hamlet not only caught the imagination of the avant-garde of the wine-drinking fraternity; in order to set it up and make it work he had to bend so many rules and break so many regulations that he had no alternative but to become the *enfant terrible* of an industry unaccustomed to political mavericks.

In many ways, there was no less likely candidate for the job. Hamilton Russell was the son of the founder of the J Walter Thompson advertising agency in South Africa. He was brought up in the élite circles of English colonial society in the Cape. Educated at a suitably smart school, he went on to Oxford where he read geography. In manner, dress and background he epitomised the conventional and orderly world which disapproves of rebellion and rule breaking. Stints in various J Walter Thompson offices around the world no doubt widened his wine-drinking perspective, and access to the family homes – in Constantia and Hermanus – enhanced his love of life in the Western Cape. By the 1970s he was chairman, chief executive and majority shareholder in the advertising agency, heading its operations from the Johannesburg office. A member of all the socially important clubs in the city, he rode to hounds, entertained lavishly, and was an undisputed prince of the blood in what passes for aristocracy in English-speaking South African circles.

He was also a consummate wine buff, an active member of the prestige wine societies in the city, clearly a businessman destined to become a vineyard proprietor, a candidate for the viticultural landowning syndrome which has claimed innumerable victims in California. En route to establishing his Western Cape venture, Tim Hamilton Russell planted a few hundred vines on his Johannesburg/Sandton property. The microclimate of Little Fillan was never expected to produce South Africa's answer to Romanée-Conti and its yields were as unsurprising as they were unmeritorious. But they did show that Tim Hamilton Russell was a man of great determination, committed to familiarising himself with all the aspects of viticulture and oenology necessary to ensure that when he began his Cape vineyard project in earnest, he would not lack for elementary experience.

Over this time he utilised his many international trips to

228

establish contacts and visit wineries in the New World. He also benefited from this extensive network by obtaining samples of the leading Pinot Noirs and Chardonnays of Europe, California and Australia. By the time he had wooed his winemaker, Peter Finlayson, from Boschendal in 1979 he was unquestionably one of South Africa's best-informed New World wine authorities.

His acquisition of two farms in the Hemel-en-Aarde Valley behind Hermanus raised a few eyebrows in even the most esoteric wine circles. The district's history of wine production had long been forgotten by all but a few of the locals. The small plantings still present on a few of the farms were thought of as contemptuously as a chicken run on a cattle ranch. More importantly, only one of the farms he bought enjoyed a KWV production quota, authorising the farmer to plant vines with a view to harvesting the grapes for wine. Since the farm which did have the right to enter the wine business was some distance away from the other property – on which Hamilton Russell chose to site his cellar – the logic of his thinking defied all except perhaps the most devious. By the time he started to plant vineyards on the farm without quota, his intentions had plumbed the depths of obscurity.

When Hamilton Russell began his Hermanus project he had not refined his thinking to the level of coherence suggested by his subsequent marketing efforts. While he intended emulating the success of the French in Burgundy, he had not abandoned an interest in Bordeaux, nor a lingering desire to see what he could do with Sauvignon Blanc, Gewürztraminer and Rhine Riesling. His first plantings were therefore something of a fruit salad, a situation exacerbated by the paucity of choice in the clonal selections of Cabernet, Pinot Noir and Chardonnay.

At that time the only Cabernet and Chardonnay material was virus-infected: in the warmer parts of Stellenbosch and Paarl this problem – which ultimately affected the vine's ability to photosynthesise and produce sugar – was considered unimportant for the Cabernet. South Africa had been a successful Cabernet producer for generations and delayed ripening at the end of the season was only a problem in cool, wet summers. There had, however, been no real attempts to cultivate Chardonnay in South Africa for perhaps half a century prior to the 1970s renaissance. The virus-infected clone available to growers like Hamilton Russell was clearly unsuitable, and inappropriate for innovators wishing to bring South African viticulture in line with the rest of the New World. The Pinot Noir material was also unsatisfactory, though for reasons that seemed less obvious at the time. The approved BK5 clone had been genetically selected in Switzerland to yield wine destined for méthode champenoise production and was surprisingly prolific. However, its juice lacked concentration and its colour was plainly insipid.

Hamilton Russell assumed that the shortcomings of the Pinot Noir could be compensated for in the vineyard and in the cellar. Proper canopy management and rigorous pruning could, he thought, concentrate the sugars and the fruit. The success of Cabernet elsewhere in the Cape concealed the shortcomings of the planting material in the cooler Hemel-en-Aarde region until the vineyards were fully established. When it came to the Chardonnay, however, the clone was clearly irredeemable. With the rigorous and unsympathetic approach of the officials from the Department of Plant and Seed Control, Hamilton Russell's vineyard development programme obviously necessitated the establishment of unconventional avenues of supply.

As things turned out, he was not alone in this view. During the period 1978 to 1985, nearly every winery committed to upgrading its vineyards and to introducing the internationally accepted premium varietals, engaged in smuggling operations which were sometimes mind-boggling in their vastness of scale. In comparison with what became the norm, Hamilton Russell's carefully sourced Chardonnay (advertising material freighted to Swaziland and brought by road via Johannesburg to the Cape) was positively low key.

In the ordinary course of planning extraordinary schemes, such circumspection would have been justified. The penalties for smuggled vines can be severe: a grower, operating in isolation, can expect the full wrath of the law to descend upon him. Contraband plant material undoubtedly caused the appearance of downy mildew in the Cape in the last twenty years. The industry's spraying programme to combat this potentially disastrous vine disease runs to millions of rands annually.

As things turned out, Hamilton Russell need not have operated so carefully, nor on so small a scale. With many of the major players in the winelands engaged in moving substantial numbers of contraband vines into the Cape, his low-key exercise cost him unnecessary time delays. From a countable number of 15-centimetre cuttings he had to develop his own nursery, grafting roots on to the sticks and planting them in greenhouse conditions. A year later the new shoots were cut to the length of a single 'eye' and grafted on to more rootstock to begin the process again. Cloning a whole vineyard this way is a painstaking and time consuming business. After a few years there are obviously so many shoots for grafting that a nurseryman lands up with more vines than he can ever hope to use. But the delay in getting to this point is a consequence of the small opening stock from which to work. Had Hamilton Russell been able to begin his little nursery with thousands rather than, at the most, hundreds of sticks, he might have had vineyards of Chardonnay in production at the same time as his Pinot Noir – in 1981.

Nevertheless he was one of the first growers able to work with Chardonnay in his cellar, but even here he was unable to maximise his advantage. He owned two farms in the Hemel-en-Aarde Valley: one was destined for the quality wine business and this was the farm on which Chardonnay and Pinot Noir had been planted as soon as he was able to establish vineyards. The other had been acquired for its KWV quota. Hamilton Russell used it to maintain the fiction that all the wine going into his bottles derived from grapes grown on land approved for this purpose by the KWV.

By the early 1980s the farm without quota was clearly being planted to vines. The KWV inspectors were told that it was all experimental and that the grapes were simply cut from the vines to rot on the ground. In order to lend a little credibility to this story, bunches of grapes were left lying around the vineyards. Wherever possible the premium vari-etals from this farm were 'incorporated' into the authorised production of the other farm. Unfortunately, by 1983 when the Chardonnay was yielding a crop, there were no Chardon-nay vineyards on the farm which had KWV quota. Conse-quently Hamilton Russell could not apply to certify his Chardonnay as Chardonnay: the same inspectors who check that there are Chardonnay vineyards wherever a producer applies for a Chardonnay certification are the ones who had been told that the vines on the farm without quota had been planted for 'experimental' purposes. So, for the first few Chardonnay vintages from Hamilton Russell, the wine was sold under the proprietary name of Premier Vin Blanc, deprived of the legal right to lay claim to the name of the varietal from which it had been produced.

In fact, for several years the Hamilton Russell wines were sold under the most curious assortment of names. The Pinot Noir – legally in much the same position as the Chardonnay – was put into the market as Grand Vin Noir. The Caber-net/Merlot blend, confusingly enough, was called Grand Crû Noir. The first vintage of Hamilton Russell Sauvignon Blanc was sold as Grand Vin Blanc.

With the second label Hemel-en-Aarde range the situation was also not entirely lucid. The white Hemel-en-Aarde wine went through three name changes in as many vintages: from Hemel-en-Aarde Blanc de Blanc to Hamilton Russell Hemel-en-Aarde Vin Blanc to Hamilton Russell Grand Vin Blanc. While all these apparently different wines were sending unclear messages to their loyal consumers, the rest of the Hamilton Russell range did little to clarify up the chaos. Only on its fifth vintage was the Pinot Noir certified for vintage and it took a further year before the Grand Vin Noir name became Pinot Noir. The red Hemel-en-Aarde blend also used the proprietary name of Grand Crû Noir, while the Cabernet/Merlot blend under the Hamilton Russell name moved on from this name to Premier Reserve, in the few vintages in which it was released. Somewhere in the middle of all the name changing and brand bungling one of South Africa's wittier and more erudite wine judges quoted *Macbeth* when he looked at the branding of the latest Hamilton Russell releases and observed: 'Confusion now hath made his masterpiece.'

In part, this chaos over names derived from the curious legal status of the Hamilton Russell operation. Nevertheless Tim Hamilton Russell himself must carry a share of the responsibility, if only because he went from one brand name to the next with a cavalier disregard for the commercial consequences. The branding situation only really normalised once both farms had obtained sufficient quota to enjoy legal status in the industry for which they were flagship production units.

Even in this, Hamilton Russell was obliged to take on the establishment. Prior to the abolition of the system, the KWV had the sole discretion to issue production quota, though its grants were theoretically subject to Ministerial approval. New quota was only made available when there was evidence of need, and this in turn would require that there should be something of a wine shortage. The purpose of quota, after all, was to limit the amount of surplus wine which, in terms of its charter, the KWV was obliged to take up and dispose of.

The quota system was only really established in the 1950s. By the 1980s the industry was faced with surpluses of up to 50 per cent of the distilling wine crop. This was hardly the kind of environment in which to expect the KWV's support for a new quota application. Hamilton Russell ran a campaign which lasted several years, inviting journalists to examine the shortcomings of the KWV and its management of the wine industry. He made a special point of revealing the impact on the quality wine consumer of the minimum wine price. He detailed the inadequacies of a production control mechanism as broad as the quota system.

His strategy aimed at finding a chink in the KWV monolith. He realised that as a publicist with access to a sympathetic press, he could make himself sufficiently irritating to the authorities that they would help to find a mutually face-saving solution to the problem. It was quite clear that the uncertified wines emerging from Hamilton Russell Vineyards were fast becoming industry benchmarks. Like Sassacaia and Tignanello in Italy, the Hamilton Russell wines enjoyed an international reputation while the wine control system forced the proprietor to sell them as mere table wines. In the mean while, they outperformed long-established competitors in blind tasting after blind tasting. It was hardly surprising that the highly publicised stand-off between Hamilton Russell and the Wine and Spirit Board was beginning to embarrass the KWV – an organisation which ordinarily seemed impervious to criticism and change. It is difficult to assert that your regulations are there in the interests of quality wine production, and then find yourself pilloried for failing to make provision for an innovator with vineyards in Hermanus.

The final arrangement was a face-saving measure for both sides: the KWV amended the quota regulations to permit wine farmers with an excess of quota to sell some – or all – of their surplus to another producer in the same or an adjacent viticultural region. Hamilton Russell could acquire the right to produce wine on the vineyards he had already established, enriching an inefficient (or perhaps over-graciously endowed by the KWV) wine farmer in an area like Worcester. The KWV could be seen to be making a necessary concession without increasing the total amount of quota in the winelands, and therefore without authorising a potential increase in the country's surplus. Everyone was surprised that any concession had been wrung from the industry's managers: the KWV has never been seen as a flexible and market-responsive organisation. Everyone knew that the new quota arrangements were really an interim measure. However, as long as the country's distilling wine farmers were going to enjoy the protection of a minimum wine price, it seemed only reasonable that the KWV could impose a ceiling on the quantity of wine produced.

The quota deal meant that from the 1986 vintage onwards all of the Hamilton Russell wines could be sold with full certification as to vintage, varietal and origin. Single varietal wines like the Pinot Noir did not need to fall back on proprietary names like Grand Vin Noir in order to come to the market. Hamilton Russell could retain these, and the opportunity to continue confusing his consumers, for his blends. By the end of its first decade in operation, the Hamilton Russell winery in Hermanus offered two ranges of wine – the lower-priced Hemel-en-Aarde wines and those bearing the full Hamilton Russell pedigree.

The Hamilton Russell wines have all, in their time, been industry benchmarks. The Sauvignon Blanc, for example, was one of the first Cape Sauvignon Blancs to achieve that balance between accessibility and herbaceousness. The original vintages made by Peter Finlayson had an almost Loire-like intensity, never as extreme in flavour as some of the New

Zealand wines, but a perfect compromise between showy fruit and drinkability. For some years – mainly after the winery concentrated more on Chardonnay and Pinot Noir – the Sauvignon Blanc never got the attention it deserved, and this showed on the wines. They became leaner and less complex. However, after Peter Finlayson left to begin his own Hemel-en-Aarde Valley winery (called Bouchard Finlayson) the new winemaker Storm Kreusch-Dau showed with her first vintage that the Loire style could be recaptured. Her 1991 Sauvignon Blanc has fruit, length and balance and is one of the best unwooded Sauvignons in the Cape.

The Chardonnay was initially offered as a full-bodied wine with sufficient wooding to justify the premium price at which it came to the market. It was one of the Cape's first Chardonnays, and probably the first to have been produced from high-quality clonal material. It was destined to be the wine on which the winery's reputation would be established and no expense was spared in its vinification. Hamilton Russell recognised that the South African de luxe wine drinker was more interested in the Chardonnays emerging from the boutique wineries than in their Pinot Noirs. His investment in new wood for the early vintages derived in part from this realisation, and in part from the fact that new cellars acquire new barrels, so first vintages tend to show a greater presence of oak in the wines. The Hamilton Russell Premier Vin Blancs and Chardonnays sold out almost before the vintage was released – a measure of the success of the marketing as much as of the quality of the wines.

In the last few years the Chardonnay has slipped a little from its pedestal. The more recent plantings in the vineyards of various competitors show a greater clonal variety which gives them an edge when it comes to complexity. Hamilton Russell has also used less wood and fewer new barrels in the past couple of years. By the end of the eighties he began offering the Chardonnay either as a Reserve wine, with a reasonable amount of wood maturation, or a regular Cuvée, 'lightly wooded in the Chablis style'.

The Reserve wine is certainly bigger and fuller, and rates with the top ten Cape Chardonnays. The regular Cuvée is well made, with some complexity and enough wood on the younger wines to give them appeal in their youth. The vineyards are now relatively mature, and are among the oldest in the Cape. It is difficult to predict how the wines will position against competitors over the next few years. The early advantage of good planting material and some experience with the varietal has been lost. The cool Hermanus climate seems less important for Chardonnay than for Pinot Noir. It is unlikely that the Hamilton Russell Chardonnays will disgrace the brand, and much more likely that the Pinot Noir will be the flagship varietal.

The Hamilton Russell Pinot Noirs won the undivided attention of the Cape wine industry from the moment of their release. The first vintage was the 1981, marketed as Grand Vin Noir and sold with a round neck label. The 1982 Grand Vin Noir had a square neck label and a small '82' after the printer's mark at the bottom margin of the label. The 1983 followed this pattern except with the imprint changed to '83'. The 1984 carried the letters 'P4' in a half tone on the neck label. The 1985 was vintaged but could not be certified for varietal and from 1986 onwards the labels bore all the relevant information. While this deprived the more competitive wine drinkers of the pleasure of trying to unravel Hamilton Russell's secret codes, it certainly simplified the communication of essential details.

The change in the winery's relationship with the KWV could not have come at a more opportune time. The annual Diners Club Winemaker of the Year Award selected Pinot Noir as the category in which the presentation would be made in 1989. In order to qualify as an entrant, a producer must submit certified wines which comply with the competition's criteria. Hamilton Russell was able to enter Pinot Noirs which had at last been certified by the Wine and Spirit Board. The 1986 won the prize for winemaker Peter Finlayson, and the 1987 came in second, fractions of a point behind the winning wine. The outcome surprised no one except those cynics who claimed that Hamilton Russell's wines were all hype and no substance. Year after year the industry's own blind tastings had put the Pinot Noirs from the Hemel-en-Aarde Valley well ahead of anything produced in Paarl or Stellenbosch.

Despite the shortcomings of the BK5 clone – a problem in those days shared by all the Pinot Noir producers – Hamilton Russell consistently yielded wines which were delicately reminiscent of Burgundy. They may have lacked 'bigness', concentration and colour, but they were unmistakably 'farmyard-like' on the nose with a fine, raspberry, spicy fruit on the palate running all the way through to the aftertaste. Auberon Waugh, writing for the *Spectator* wine club, challenged any producer of Burgundy to match their value. Undoubtedly, through careful management of the vineyards, and a vinification aimed at concentrating the structure (including some stalk contact), Peter Finlayson had obtained the best from the clone and dovetailed it with the benefits of the Hermanus climate.

The Premier Reserve is produced mainly from grapes grown on the Attaquaskloof vineyard, originally acquired because this farm had some KWV production quota. Now that quota is not a problem for the other vineyard adjacent to the cellar, Hamilton Russell means to dispose of this property. Its plantings also no longer coincide with the long-term goals of the brand. Cabernet and Merlot simply do not fit in with the Burgundy image of the Hermanus climate and the emphasis on Chardonnay and Pinot Noir.

There is also another, more material reason for moving away from these Bordelais plantings. The Cabernet vineyard was established with the old clonal material irremediably virus-afflicted. Ripening is a problem even in a warm vintage and is out of the question in all other years. On average this means that the Premier Reserve is offered only every second harvest, a rate of return made all the more unacceptable by the South African regulations which forbid chaptalisation. Newer clonal material could conceivably address this problem: certainly the area produces good Merlot which might form the bulk on any blend. However, given Hamilton Russell's marketing stance, the Bordeaux blend is sufficiently out of place to justify the sale of the Attaquaskloof farm.

Whoever buys the vineyard would certainly have to address the present state of its plantings. Just the same, the few vintages of Premier Reserve to come to the market should provide real encouragement. The wine has always been beautifully structured, accessible but with good ageing potential. It seems to gain in complexity and length for at least five years after the harvest. More subtle than many of the Stellenbosch Bordeaux blends, it performs well with experienced blind tasters and does no disservice to the other wines in the Hamilton Russell range.

The same cannot be said for the winery's Grand Vin Blanc and for its second label Hemel-en-Aarde range. The wines are all respectable enough, flawless and well turned out. The Hamilton Russell Grand Vin Blanc is a much improved version of the fruit salad table wine which gave the operation its cash cow in the early days. However acceptable it may be as a Chardonnay/Sauvignon blend, it is overpriced and it undermines the image of the premium wines in the range. The Hemel-en-Aarde wines are less directly connected to the main range, though the circles of wine *cognoscenti* are incestuous enough for there to be no secret of their provenance. The Vin Rouge is the best of the three, drinkable but not a candidate for the wine bargain-of-the-year.

Tim Hamilton Russell has made an enormous contribution

to South African viticulture. In opening up the Hemel-en-Aarde Valley, he invoked the prospect of premium wine production from vineyards outside the traditional areas. Projects like the Nel family's Ruiterbosch venture near Mossel Bay flow directly from his courage and innovation. Nearer to home, he set an example which encouraged his winemaker Peter Finlayson, and the Hamilton Russell farm manager Michael Clark, to go it alone and set up their own winery a kilometre or so up the road from the cellar at which they both worked until 1990.

In the late 1980s Peter Finlayson and Michael Clark bought the Klein Hemel-en-Aarde farm adjacent to the property on which they worked for Tim Hamilton Russell and announced their intention of developing their own vineyards. Hamilton Russell indicated that they were free to continue working with him until they were ready to go into production. Perhaps he planned on having them around for many years: the project they had in mind far exceeded their own supplies of capital and the economic downturn would limit their access to banking funds.

As things turned out, however, they were able to launch their own winery with surprising speed. A syndicate of investors comprising various business and professional people took up the stock options. Suddenly there was enough gearing to build a winery, plant vineyards and buy in grapes. Peter Finlayson processed the first crush on his own Hermanus farm in the first quarter of 1991.

Finlayson and Clark moved into action so quickly that this harvest had already been completed before they came to a name for their brand. As it turns out, this delay gave them the opportunity of attracting to their syndicate Paul Bouchard, scion of the long-established Burgundy shippers Bouchard Aine & Fils. Bouchard's announcement – in April 1991 – that he would become part of the project gave them their opportunity to follow the Californian precedent.

240

Hermanus' second winery was launched with the release of some of the 1991 wines in November of that year. The name, in true New World style, was Bouchard Finlayson, and the project was the first joint Franco-South African wine venture. Bouchard's involvement only weeks after the completion of the vintage means that more or less from the outset he was able to make a contribution to the venture. Finlayson handled the harvest itself, as well as the fermentation of the wines, without Bouchard's French influence. But the *élevage*, the maturation and final blending where necessary, reflect the suggestions of the investor from Burgundy.

Bouchard's interest in the project does not appear to be a distant, arm's-length arrangement. He travelled to South Africa for the launch of the wines and spent some time getting to know the vineyards from which the first crop was produced. He seems to have familiarised himself with local viticulture, and will no doubt add French experience to the local knowledge of Finlayson and Clark. Finlayson – who has already visited Burgundy on several occasions – will work some vintages in the Côte d'Or. It may take several years for the full impact of the partnership to be felt in the wines, but there is no doubt that the project will benefit from Finlayson's knowledge of local conditions and Bouchard's extensive experience of Chardonnay and Pinot Noir.

Even from the first vintage, this much has been evident in the wines. Both the Chardonnay and the Pinot Noir are more intensely 'French' than their average South African counterpart. The former is not over-wooded or buttery, but has instead a slightly steely austerity which reflects the Burgundian approach to wood vinification, as well as the region's cooler climate. The Pinot Noir, from new clonal material, is much deeper, fuller and more complex than other examples of the varietal. The vineyard supplying the grapes is situated in Elgin, about a 40-minute drive from the winery. Over the past five or so years more and more of the country's viticulturists have come to regard Elgin as South Africa's premium cool climate region. The Pinot block was planted on an experimental basis in the early 1980s. This means that Finlayson was able to make his first Bouchard Finlayson Pinot Noir from well-established vines of the best clonal material, planted in an area whose climate more closely approximates Burgundy than most other vineyards in the Western Cape. This wine is yet to be released: the barrel sample shows an intensity of colour, fruit and flavour never before seen in South African Pinot Noir. No doubt this is the first of several such wines, all made from better material than the watery BK5 which became the South African benchmark. Enthusiasm for its obvious depth and complexity should perhaps be tempered with the knowledge that the grapes which make such wines possible will be more readily available over the next few years. Notwithstanding Finlayson's achievement in producing a wine that has redefined Pinot Noir in South Africa, it is important to realise that he benefited immeasurably from the quality of the vineyards from which he purchased his grapes. Only once his own vines have come into production will a more complete appraisal be possible.

Finally, there is the Bouchard Finlayson Blanc de Mer: this is a blended wine, the heir to the Hamilton Russell Hemel-en-Aarde Blanc de Blanc, both in terms of style and purpose. It gives the winery a certain amount of volume by which to amortise its operating costs, and provides it with something of a cash cow from which to milk extra income until the Bouchard Finlayson vineyards are in full production. It is a well-made wine, with intense fruit flavours and a crisp, almost steely structure. Its virtue – from a wine drinker's point of view – is versatility: it complements most summer menus, and satisfies most palates. It has a useful place in the short-term planning of the winery though it ought to be phased out as the authenticity of Hermanus vineyard grapes supersedes the bought-in production.

The Hemel-en-Aarde Valley has produced enough exciting wine in the first decade of its modern production to justify its inclusion on any short list of quality wine regions of the Cape. Hamilton Russell's decision to go wine farming there in the mid 1970s has certainly been vindicated. Finlayson's past experience of the area leaves one in little doubt as to the long-term prospects of his quality wine cellar. What comes between the district and its long-term viticultural security remains the simple issue of financial momentum. It is not worth producing wine grapes in Hermanus unless they can recoup investment costs at the middle to top end of the premium wine market. A protracted recession can easily decimate the sector into which these wines must trade. Without real proximity to cellars which buy in the best premium material, Hermanus is an appellation too far for its own good. Tim Hamilton Russell brought it back from the wilderness phylloxera had made of it. There are other kinds of viticultural catastrophes which could still claim it for their own.

OVER THE MOUNTAIN

❧ ❧

Until quite recently the wine production regions which lay 'over the mountain' were regarded with some disdain by the Western Cape wine fraternity. Considered fine for fortified wine and brandy, these districts have had to wage a considerable campaign to earn the credibility they justly deserve for their quality white wines. Only in the past two decades have they come to be seen as more than a cheap source for white table wine. The introduction of premium varietals has consolidated the claims of Robertson and Bonnievale. It is now generally acknowledged that the Breede River Valley is home to some of South Africa's best white wines.

The climate of this region is much drier than Stellenbosch and Paarl, with a mean annual rainfall of 200-250 millimetres – much less than is ordinarily associated with quality viticulture. However, the soils are mainly calcareous and this lime-rich alkalinity makes them infinitely more suited to viticulture than many sites in the better climatic districts of the Coastal Region.

Many of the estates in these districts are still not fully committed to bottling and marketing their wines. Farms tend to be larger than in the Coastal Region and this imposes a greater discipline on relations with the wholesale merchants. The distance from Cape Town also pushes the estates beyond the day-tripper retail market. Some of the properties enjoy a local following, some even an adequate national distribution, and a few do a little international trade. However, on average there is a less developed boutique business and consequently less recognition from the more rarefied wine circles.

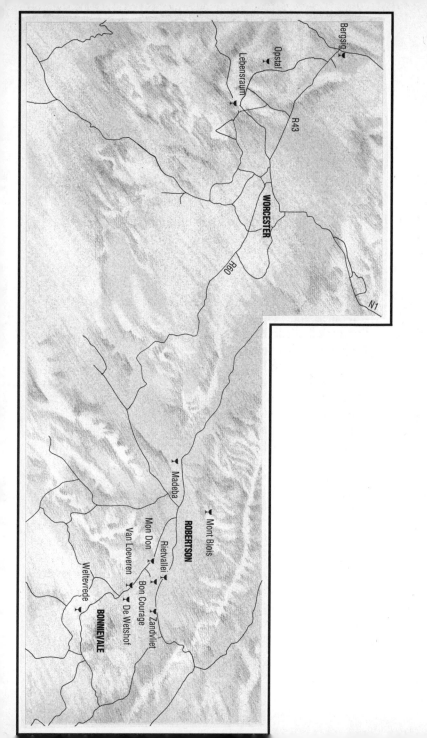

The town of Worcester is now about two hours' drive from Cape Town: the tunnel through Du Toit's Kloof shaves at least half an hour each way off the trip, and makes all the adjacent regions much more accessible to Western Cape visitors. The Breede River area is dominated by cooperatives, many of which sell their wines in bulk to the national wholesalers and do not seek to jeopardise this trade by chasing retail custom.

The Bergsig Estate has been bottling its wines since the 1970s and has, over the years, acquired a reputation for its value-for-money wines. The production is dominated by white wines, as befits the district, though easy-drinking Cabernet and Pinotage form part of the range. The Cape Riesling (Crouchen Blanc) is delicately balanced, with more fragrance and personality than is usually encountered with this varietal. The Fernão Pires is well put together, the fruit supported on enough acidity to conceal the sweetness. Bergsig also markets a Furmint, the varietal from which Hungary's great Tokays are produced. Here along the Breede River the Lategan family have chosen to make it 'aboccato', softly aromatic and eminently drinkable.

Bergsig's Gewürztraminer is also on the soft side: as a late harvest, the fruit and sweetness manage to stay in balance; the drier version can be a little too evanescent. Among the sweeter wines have been two very successful Noble Late Harvests, both offered with reasonable bottle age. Rich and luscious, they are more German in style than French and do not come Weight-Watcher approved. However, those who like their botrytised wines aromatically sweet and full will not be disappointed by Bergsig's achievement.

There are other estates in the Breede River/Worcester area: Opstal near Slanghoek produces creditable whites, notably Colombard and dry Steen. Lebensraum delivers its production to the wholesalers. It seems as if the first impression a visitor from Paarl or Stellenbosch might have of the 'over the

246

mountain' region could well confirm the long-standing prejudices about co-op wines and Muscadels. It is only once the
traveller has passed through Worcester and continued
towards Robertson that a broad commitment to quality wine
production again becomes evident.

The first property along the road, well before Robertson
itself, more than forces a revision of earlier views: Graham
Beck's Madeba vineyards and cellar is a state-of-the-art
winery equipped in the most modern taste, and with the most
advanced equipment. Even before the release of its first vintage, Madeba was destined to be a significant player in the
South African wine scene.

Proprietor Graham Beck is a larger-than-life coal miner
cum racehorse breeder whose Kentucky stud is said to be the
envy of those who have seen it, and whose colourful, though
curiously private, personality has already enriched the Cape
wine industry. In the few years since he began turning a portion of his Robertson stud into a wine farm, he acquired joint
control of wholesaler Douglas Green Bellingham, stole the
limelight at the charity section of the annual Nederburg Auction, and has sent out clear signals that he will be a force to
reckon with in the Cape.

Consultant to the operation has been Jan 'Boland' Coetzee
of Vriesenhof, one of the country's most knowledgeable
oenologists/viticulturists. Winemaker Pieter Ferreira joined
Beck from Achim von Arnim's Clos Cabrière, bringing with
him expertise in bubbly production and a dedication to produce a real Champagne look-alike on the lime-rich Robertson soils.

There are now some 160 hectares under vine, including
the usual fruit salad of Colombard, Chenin Blanc, Cape Riesling and Muscat. More importantly, there are substantial
plantings of Chardonnay and Pinot Noir, and the first base
wines for the méthode champenoise have earned critical
approval. The 1991 still Chardonnay has already set the

pace: it is crisp, citrussy, lean but not mean, well layered with fruit and oak and picking up generous butterscotch nuances in the bottle.

It is of course too early to predict the performance of the farm's bubblies. The regular Brut will be released shortly, though the Blanc de Blanc will rest on its lees for several years. The goal posts for South African méthodes champenoises have moved considerably in the past five years: it is no longer sufficient to ensure that the bubble gets into the bottle by the time-honoured French method of bottle fermentation. The quality of the base wine, the yeastiness which develops on the bouquet, the fineness of the mousse and the balance and length have all become as important in the Cape as they are in Reims and Epernay. Any one going into this kind of wine production today knows that he must be prepared to take on the French, since Champagne remains the only indisputable benchmark. Graham Beck's decision to commit Madeba unequivocally to bubbly represents something of a gauntlet challenge to France. In as many words, he has indicated where he is going, and he is not likely to be satisfied until he has taken a winning position on the field of play.

Before the town of Robertson, and slightly to the north, is Mont Blois, one of the Cape's foremost Muscadel producers. Recent success with dry white wines more than justifies its inclusion in this section of the text. The family has owned the property since 1884, naming it after Blois in France, the home of the Bruwers who first set out to settle in the Cape.

Estelle, the young widow of winemaker Pieter Bruwer, took over running the estate in 1991. A cold fermentation cellar was built in the 1980s for the farm's dry white wine production. The estate lies along the De Hoop Valley at the foot of the Langeberg. The dry summers necessitate the installation of computer-controlled drip irrigation, the cool south-easterly breezes ensure that the grapes enjoy a relatively long ripening season, and rigorous pruning limits the size of the harvest.

Mont Blois markets its wines through The Bergkelder. The Blanc Fumé is a beautifully balanced, delicately fashioned dry white wine. The Sauvignon fruit is well rounded, gooseberry/fig rather than grassy, and the light wooding has added an extra dimension to the nose and palate. While not an obvious sort of wine, the Mont Blois Blanc Fumé has an elegance and dimension which makes it very easy to drink.

The estate's Chardonnay also reveals the extent to which this champion Muscadel producer has adapted to unfortified wine production. Citrus/butterscotch flavours layer the vanilla and oak, giving the impression of volume, rather than weight. Mont Blois is another property whose shift into quality white wine marketing is already contributing to the overall reputation of the region.

Just beyond Robertson in the direction of Bonnievale is Bon Courage, home of Andre Bruwer, three times South African champion wine estate and winner of the coveted Diners Club Award for its Gewürztraminer Special Late Harvest. It is perhaps a measure of how little attention the wine-drinking fraternity invests in the Robertson/Bonnievale area that achievements such as these do little to alter the underlying prejudices about the region. Those who know the Bon Courage wines continue to marvel at their value-for-money qualities. Show successes have had little impact on price: the estate's whites sell for about 20 per cent less than similar varietal wines in Stellenbosch.

Over the years the estate has acquired a reputation for its sweeter wines. Earlier vintages of the Kerner Special Late Harvest have been as good as any wine made from the varietal in the Cape. More recent wines have shown less of the cultivar character which gave such distinction to the 1986 vintage. The Gewürztraminer Special Late Harvest has taken over, however: the Diners Club award-winning wine has wonderful balance, a whole range of fruit flavours, and plenty of spice on the palate and aftertaste. The estate's Noble Late Harvest is a high acid/high sugar botrytised Rhine Riesling, rich and taut, and altogether better structured than the earlier vintages.

Among the dry whites, the Cape Riesling reveals what is possible with this otherwise bland, much abused varietal. The Bon Courage wine performs well in its youth, an altogether different style from some of the Stellenbosch classics. The Chardonnay looks promising, though the first vintages have softened out, perhaps becoming too buttery too soon.

Not much further along the road towards Bonnievale is Pierre Marais' Mon Don Estate. Most of the production is sold in bulk, and only a few of the wines find their way into the retail trade. The Chenin Blanc and Colombard, both of which looked good in their youth, lots of fruit on the nose and gently off-dry on the palate, appear to have been discontinued. The Blanc de Blanc combines some of their virtues, and is good value sold off the farm.

Closer to Ashton is Johnny Burger's Rietvallei Estate. He is another of the region's Muscadel producers to have shown a real feel for dry white wines. The farm has been in the Burger family since 1864, and it has always been associated with superb red Muscadel. The decline in demand for fortified wines must have prompted the shift to Chardonnay and Rhine Riesling. The vineyards are now quite well established, and the past few vintages of Chardonnay have been excellent, though underrated by many of the country's wine writers.

The Chardonnay is new oak fermented, and then matures for about nine months in wood. The result is a wine that is rich, alcoholic, still lemony, but also with hints of butter, vanilla and butterscotch. A lees-like smokiness is also evident, adding further richness and complexity. The Rietvallei Chardonnay is not lean, austere or Chablis-like in its structure, and perhaps for this reason has not attracted the attention of those who seek European look-alikes from South African vineyards. It is however a big, full-bodied, rich, New World style of wine, one of the best examples of its kind.

Lying a few kilometres to the east of Rietvallei, and somewhat to the south, is Wynand Retief's cellar, Van Loveren. Its wines are among the best value, high quality production in the Cape. The selection is considerable, even before red wines are added to the range. But, notwithstanding the difficulties of managing so varied a production, Wynand Retief seems to maintain a quality and consistency that would be the envy of a more highly staffed cellar.

His Blanc de Noir from Muscat grapes is one of only two such wines in the Cape. Spicy, even a little immodest, it makes an easy lunchtime wine and a lovely complement to charcuterie. The Chardonnay is one of the most muscular from the region: high alcohols, usually well wooded (though one vintage seemed to lose its oakiness rather too soon), citrus fruit, vanilla and butterscotch. This is not an elegant, cool climate wine, but it does deliver what it promises on the nose.

Far more extraordinary is the Pinot Blanc, at least to judge from the first vintage: the Chardonnay which forms a minor portion of the blend has fattened out the wine, and the small oak vinification has layered the fruit with toasted wood aromas. Young, it might have fooled most experts at a blind tasting for its Chardonnay-like balance and depth. Launched at under R10 per bottle, it was one of the wine buys of the year.

Van Loveren's Blanc de Blanc and Premier Grand Crû land up in innumerable house wines. Both are crisp, delicately fragrant, undemanding and attractively inexpensive. The cellar's young Colombard occupies a similar taste slot: lots of fruit, finely balanced acidity, easy and immediate drinkability.

Danie de Wet of De Wetshof is a near neighbour, and

251

something of a kindred spirit. One of the Cape's Chardonnay pioneers, and one of the key personalities in the Chardonnay/Auxerrois scandal of the mid 1980s, De Wet is a great bear of a man, warm, generous, thoughtful and very self-possessed.

The De Wetshof Estate distributes through The Bergkelder. This arrangement does not appear to have constrained the winemaker's individuality, though earlier vintages of Sauvignon Blanc and Rhine Riesling finished off harsher and more acidic than Danie had expected. Lately the Mountain Cellar and the Robertson estate have been more in kilter.

Danie de Wet's 1985 Chardonnay won the top award at the 1987 Vinexpo tasting. More recent vintages have improved immeasurably, the result of better vineyards, greater age and wider clonal selection among the vines, greater familiarity with the varietal and with the effects of wood vinification, and automatic malolactic fermentation.

De Wetshof, like many of the Robertson estates, uses computer-controlled drip irrigation to ease the vines through the rigours of the long dry summer. Purists may argue that the vineyards should be left to struggle; proof of the virtues of controlling the moisture content of the soil is to be found at Danie de Wet's estate. The drip irrigation is not intended to swell the crop, but rather to ensure that the vines can continue to photosynthesise and keep on feeding the grapes.

Certainly, none of the De Wetshof wines are watery, evanescent, elusive in flavour. The Chardonnay Reserve is big, intense, smoky and complex. The Chardonnay Finesse is much more lightly wooded, and shows more varietal fruit. The regular Rhine Riesling is dry and quite lean. There is no shortage of cultivar character though, as with most Cape Rhine Rieslings, and therefore not much incentive to get excited about it either.

However, Danie de Wet's innovative, tangy, perfumed, seemingly off-dry Rhine Riesling launched in 1991 is easily the best wine produced from this varietal in the Cape. High natural sugars (90 g/l) and intense fruit acids lift the grape fragrance to extraordinary heights. Perfumed, rich and demanding on the palate, yet seemingly dry on the finish, this wine has all the complexity of a good Moselle and none of the sweet paraffin character of most of the Cape's production.

Danie's cousin and neighbour Paul de Wet is the region's only serious red wine producer. The Zandvliet Estate is one of the country's major horse studs, and has been the property of this branch of the De Wet family since 1860. Zandvliet also makes use of a high-tech drip irrigation system, and low-tech vineyard feeding, using stable and cellar waste to produce a compost for the young vines.

Zandvliet's Shiraz has been famous almost since the release of the 1975, its first vintage. Not nearly as big as some of the Paarl and Stellenbosch blockbusters, it offers easy drinkability, an excellent balance between wood, fruit and tannin, and an elegance too often absent from this varietal. Recent vintages are certainly more complex than the wines of the 1970s. Wood maturation adds an extra dimension to these medium-bodied, early-drinking reds.

Zandvliet has also taken to producing Cabernet, though not yet with anything like the success of its Shiraz. The first vintage – a 1984 – was altogether too taut, mean and unrelenting. More recent wines offer a little extra flesh. No doubt as the vines age, their fruit will improve and Zandvliet may yet prove (as it did with Shiraz) that the region is capable of producing a serious Cabernet.

In the town of Bonnievale itself is Weltevrede, the Jonker family estate since the turn of the century. Proprietor Lourens Jonker is one of the leading figures in the Cape wine industry, the regional (elected) director of the KWV, and a broadminded force for reform in winelands' politics.

Weltevrede has consistently led the way in producing quality, often innovative, wines in the region, and then getting them to consumers at prices which make it possible for good wine to be an everyday drink. The estate's Colombards from the 1970s have aged remarkably well. I have tasted several bottles ten or more years old and found them wonderfully mature, still holding up, intensely flavoured and very easy on the finish. The current vintages are from the same mould: plenty of youthful fruit makes them attractive to drink young, though their structure will keep them for several years.

The estate's Rhine Riesling is also excellent: spicy and quite dry, it is one of the few wines made from the variety in the Cape deserving of more than a sidelong glance. Weltevrede's Gewürztraminer is also consistently good: plenty of the litchi/rose petal fruit, sweeter than many on the palate, yet dry enough on the finish to serve as a perfect aperitif wine.

The first few vintages of Weltevrede's Chardonnay confirm the estate's single-minded dedication to quality winemaking: wooding is generous but not excessive, and the citrus-lime fruit sustains itself amid the oak and lees aromas. The wood-matured Privé du Bois continues to offer vinous qualities, well integrated with its cask character, to those who are not slaves of varietal names on the label. The Blanc de Noir, Lourens Jonker's own creation, is packed with personality, flavour and dry Muscat fruit.

The farm also produces an important range of fortified dessert wines, which will be dealt with in the appropriate chapter. Among the unfortified sweet wines, the occasional Noble Late Harvest, high in sugar and botrytised fruit, has been something of a regional benchmark. Balance, a feature of all the Weltevrede wines, ensures that richness and lusciousness harmonise with enough fruit acidity to leave the palate clean. The first release, from the 1981 year of the flood, lasted long enough for those who contemplate laying down this sort of wine to feel confident of the ageing potential of the current vintage.

VINEYARDS OF THE SOUTHERN CAPE: THE KAROO

♨ ♨

Hundreds of kilometres to the east of Robertson and Bonnievale lie the vineyards of the Klein (Little) Karoo. Much of what is produced in these near-desert conditions goes to the once-booming fortified wine trade. Changing tastes and the swing away from the heavier, more alcoholic beverages have forced the more adventurous growers into the table wine business. Several have become so proficient at making unfortified wines that they are investing the district with the beginnings of a reputation for quality wine.

Chief among these is Boplaas, in the quaint Karoo village of Calitzdorp. The estate has belonged to the Nel family for several generations. Current winemaker is Danie Nel's son Carel, a graduate of Stellenbosch University and also a Cape Wine Master. Boplaas, through Carel Nel, gained entry into the Cape Independent Winemakers' Guild, focusing the wine-drinking fraternity for the first time on the quality wine potential of the Southern Cape.

The Nels have two farms, one in Calitzdorp itself, and one just over an hour's drive to the south, adjacent to the State forest of Ruiterbosch. Boplaas has a warm Karoo climate, ideally suited to port and red wine production; Ruiterbosch is protected by the moderating breezes blowing in from nearby Mossel Bay. It is one of the coolest vineyards in the country, and it has been planted exclusively to delicate varietals like Rhine Riesling, Chardonnay, Sauvignon Blanc and Pinot Noir.

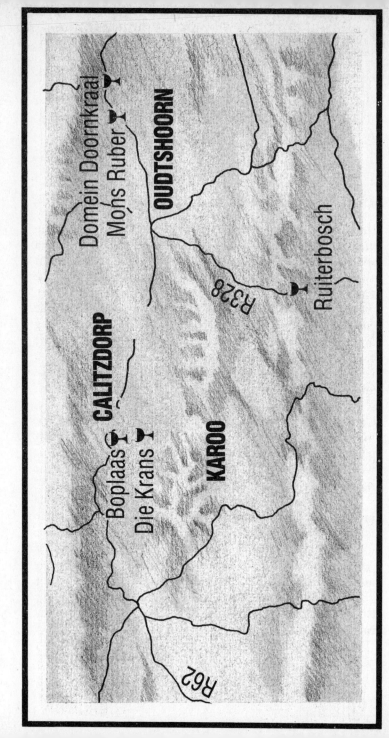

Boplaas' fortified wines will be dealt with in detail in the appropriate chapter. Its natural wines of distinction include a Médoc blend called Grand Vin Rouge, a creditable Cabernet, a Merlot and a respectable Special Late Harvest.

The Grand Vin Rouge is a Cabernet/Merlot blend, the percentages of each cultivar varying depending on the vintage. As befits the warmer climate, it is full, dry, somewhat tannic, not short of fruit and well-oaked. Its component wines are good in their own right: the estate's Cabernet combines varietal character with an evenly stated dryness that leaves the wine slightly austere, but not brittle. The Merlot is usually an undemanding wine, though some vintages have shown enough fruit and soft tannins to present themselves from the outset as rather plummy, fragrant wines.

The Boplaas Special Late Harvest is a well-composed fruit salad of Muscat and Rhine Riesling, plenty of easy sweetness on the palate and enough botrytis on the nose to satisfy all but the most demanding of olfactory senses. It is the kind of white wine which does credit to the cellar, given the climatic conditions of the Karoo.

It seems extraordinary that less than 100 kilometres away, the Nels' Ruiterbosch venture should flourish in quite the opposite environment. The Sauvignon Blanc is a taut, asparagus/gooseberry flavoured wine, the fruit balanced out by an almost Loire-like acidity. Earlier vintages have held together well but, probably on account of the young vines, have not improved with age. Current releases will profit from the increasing maturity of the vineyard.

The Chardonnay, also from young vines, has an austere, though well-structured finesse, the oak in proportion to the fruit, and nothing in excess anywhere. The Rhine Riesling has a fine, dryish fruit character moving swiftly into that style of bottle age which has its followers.

The Ruiterbosch wines have had an easy passage into the trade. Carel Nel is an indefatigable promoter of himself and his wines, and the unique location of the Ruiterbosch site has helped to open many doors. The long-term future for Mossel Bay wine depends on how the Ruiterbosch vineyards establish themselves over time. The first signs are sufficiently encouraging, however, for the Nels to feel that their faith in the project has been vindicated.

Boets and Stroebel Nel, cousins of Carel and his father Danie Nel of Boplaas, own the other Calitzdorp estate of Die Krans. They, too, have acquired a reputation for their unfortified wines in recent years. Some, like the Shiraz, have benefited from robust grapes and intelligent wood vinification; others, like the Grand Vin Blanc, profit from vineyards planted to varietals which can at least perform in the sometimes inhospitable climatic conditions of the Klein Karoo. Others, like the very spicy, slightly sweet and extraordinarily well-priced Gewürztraminer, simply defy explanation.

Much of the estate's production is still fortified, and together with the Boplaas Nels, the Die Krans Nels have focused on Port and Jerepigo. Still, for those who prefer their sweet wines free of the adulteration of brandy, the Die Krans Noble Late Harvest and the somewhat less luscious Special Late Harvest justify their following.

Further eastwards still, beyond Oudtshoorn and almost on the longitude of George, are the two Cape estates which lie furthest from Cape Town. I have visited neither of them, and know only slightly the Blanc de Noir from the one, Swepie le Roux's Domein Doornkraal. I was saddened to learn of the recent death of Raadus Meyer, the proprietor and winemaker of the other farm, the Mons Ruber Estate.

Both these properties survive, and even perhaps flourish, in conditions that are alien to the vast majority of the Cape's winemakers. Their achievements are usually in the area of fortified wines. However, they sustain themselves many hundreds of kilometres away from the technical heart of the Cape's wine industry. If in time the viticulture of the Klein

Karoo develops its own momentum, so that the district advances from satellite status to something that outsiders recognise for its own virtues, their resilience will have been rewarded. The frontiers of the Cape wine industry are not only to be encountered in clonal selection, or techniques of wood ageing. Sometimes they are really a matter of geography, and the Klein Karoo represents one of the outermost limits.

COOPERATIVE WINE CELLARS
☙ ❧

No account of the South African wine industry would be complete without some remarks about the cooperative wine cellars. In a country where only 2 per cent of all wine grapes are processed on the farms where they are grown, it is clear that cooperative production units are the norm, rather than the exception.

It may even be argued that since various central processing facilities handle the harvests of 98 per cent of the country's farms, the allocation of text in this book has been vastly out of proportion: probably 98 per cent of this text is about 2 per cent of the wine growing properties in the Western Cape.

The cooperative wine movement in South Africa is a 20th-century phenomenon, and it reflects both the nature of the industry, and the demand for its products. If South Africa had developed like many of the Western European countries, with a solid middle class comprising a significant percentage of the population, and wine consumption as part of the national culture, there would have been a greater demand for artisanal, farm-produced wines.

Instead the country is characterised by extremes of wealth and poverty, a small bourgeoisie and a vast proletariat; wine never really formed part of the cultural heritage of the inland areas, and black prohibition until the 1960s was hardly designed to encourage responsible drinking habits. The majority of the population prefers beer, except in the wine growing regions of the Western Cape. Cheap fortified wines, local wine spirits and even beer, are the most economical sources of drinking alcohol. Under circumstances such as these, South Africa was never going to develop a fine wine culture in which a substantial proportion of the population could participate.

Cooperative production facilities provide the logical alternative for the grape growers. Their harvests can be processed efficiently in terms of the market's needs: either for inexpensive branded wines handled by the national wholesale merchants, or as part of the alcohol chain, the raw material for the local brandy, gin and vodka market.

Just the same, even with blended or distilled products (the destination of nearly everything they produce), the co-ops have shown themselves to be capable of high quality wine production. True, their yields can be variable, since the cellars are the victims of the grapes grown by their members. Obviously some co-ops have organised themselves in such a way that better quality grapes bring the grower a suitable reward. These same cellars tend to be most consistent in producing good wines. The winemaker is clearly limited by the grapes at his disposal, and his average quality here will be better than at those processing facilities which provide no incentive for low yields, or rot-free bunches.

All good wine production is about the right grapes, in the right condition, handled by a competent and experienced cellarmaster in a winery that is at least adequately equipped. When these circumstances come together, the odds favour the end result. This is as much true of pocket-size estates as it is of the mammoth cooperative cellars processing tens of thousands of tons of grapes each year.

In assembling this section on the country's wine cooperatives, mainly those willing or able to supply bottled wine to private consumers, the observations carry the caveat of statistical probability. Some of the country's cooperatives have dominated regional show results for years, a sure sign that the region and its quality incentive system favour good wine. But it is possible that variation will occur, vintage to vintage

– and sometimes even tank to tank – to a greater extent than in private cellars. This is not a reservation which should frighten off the adventurous consumer, since there is a palpable cost benefit. Co-op wines are priced in the bottom 20 per cent of the industry. Those who seek them out, having adjusted their selection on the basis of the average chance of finding good wine at a particular cellar, will not be disappointed: there is no more cost-efficient way to buy quality wine.

It goes without saying that this co-op wine selection is even more idiosyncratic than the estate wine choice. Those offended by exclusion will have to accept as excuses the constraint of space, the fact that this book is not a laundry list of South African wine, and that the private producer is the focus of my attention.

There are several co-ops of note in the so-called Coastal Region around Stellenbosch and Paarl. Bottelary, situated on the Bottelary hills (naturally) to the north-west of Stellenbosch, has a place in this listing. Notable on its lengthy product list is the Gewürztraminer, a sometime inclusion for the New World Wine Auction. Often typically rose petal on the nose, more recent vintages seem to have lost a little of that beautifully balanced fruit.

The co-op's Weisser Riesling and Bukettraube are also worth a flutter; so is its Noble Late Harvest, only made in select vintages, and always worth buying at the price.

To the south of Stellenbosch, the Eersterivier Co-op in the capable hands of Manie Rossouw produces its fair share of quality wines. Winner of the Diners Club Award for his 1984 Sauvignon Blanc, Rossouw continues to make fine wines from this varietal.

His Chardonnay (heavily wooded) may not please those who set finesse above flavour, but it has its following and Rossouw is still experimenting with the style. Cabernet and

Pinotage here are also usually good buys. The former gets the full wood treatment and looks all the better for it; the latter is a juicy, easier drinking style.

Further to the south and east is the Helderberg Co-op, where Inus Muller puts on a good show with his red wines. The Cabernet is always a safe bet, well-knit, sometimes quite big, and almost always capable of bottle maturation. The Shiraz can also be worth seeking out, lighter, fragrant in a smoky/saddle kind of way, good for a stretch in the bottle. The Vin Rouge is a little clumsy, maybe even a little blowsy, but it drinks easily enough and needs no further maturation. The cellar's Blanc de Noir is also a little special; more pungent than many, it fills the slot vacated by the decline in the Rosé market.

Vlottenburg, just between Eersterivier Co-op and the town of Stellenbosch, regularly produces a fine array of wines. The Gewürztraminer is certainly worth hunting down, litchi/rose petal fruit all in excellent balance. The first Chardonnay has also been impressive, suggesting that winemaker Kowie du Toit has a good intuitive grasp of the varietal. The Chenin Blanc continues to prove itself superb drinking value; so does the Sauvignon Blanc and the Special Late Harvest.

Among the reds, the Cabernet is nearly always a good buy and neither the Pinotage nor the Merlot is likely to disappoint. On its present track record, Vlottenburg is proving to be one of the Cape's best quality co-op producers.

Finally, there is the Welmoed Co-op where Nicky Versveld makes several fine wines including a very good Cabernet Sauvignon, fairly full in colour and on the palate, and capable of considerable bottle maturation. His Shiraz is also an excellent buy, almost spicy and carefully wooded.

The Sauvignon Blanc can often be surprisingly good: there was a time when grapes were delivered to Welmoed from the Steenberg farm in Tokai near Constantia. These

Sauvignons were absolutely packed with flavour and style. The same varietal 'tastiness' seems to describe the Welmoed Chenin Blanc, off-dry but held in check with a generous dollop of fruit acid.

Across to Paarl, where there are several co-ops which consistently yield high-quality wines. Boland, for example, has produced striking examples of good-drinking Cabernet for as long as I can remember: bottles from the 1970s still taste sound, and have knitted together remarkably well. More recent vintages have all had a stint in oak, sometimes perhaps too obviously so, but the basic fruit, and the care which goes into vinification, justifies keeping this wine on your regular co-op shopping list.

Boland's Pinotage enjoys a similar reputation, ageing well in bottle for several years. The youthful fruit is sometimes a little overpowering, but for those who prefer their wine toned down a little, maturation will work miracles. The co-op also produces an eminently drinkable Cape Riesling and a very creditable Chenin Blanc.

Also in the Paarl region is the Perdeberg Co-op, a major supplier to the country's national wholesalers. I recall some very good Pinotage in the 1970s, though more recent bottlings have disappointed. The Cinsaut can also be quite good, though the co-op's reputation rests more on its white wines.

Here the Chenin Blanc (available as a dry and also as a semi-sweet) is worthy – in Michelin terms – of a pilgrimage rather than a detour. The dry Chenin has been SA champion wine in its time and the semi-sweet acquires an almost Savennieres-like complexity.

Simonsvlei Co-op on the Stellenbosch side of Paarl has also been a quality leader for many years. Several of its wines from the 1970s have found their way on to the annual Nederburg Auction, and I recall an excellent 1974 Cabernet which was the equal of the best estate Cabernets of the time.

Current Cabernet vintages are a little evanescent, a criticism which could apply equally to the Pinotage. The Shiraz is better value at the moment, but all three reds need to be judged on the merits of a particular year. Among the white wines, the fruity off-dry varietals – like Bukettraube and Rhine Riesling – are performing better at the moment than the dry whites. Simonsvlei's wines seem to have lost a little of their concentration lately, though the co-op must still be counted among the best of the Cape.

Adjacent to the vineyards of Paarl is the Huguenot settlement of Franschhoek, where the local co-op vinifies wines for its members, and also, on a separate contract basis, for the individual growers who take back their production to market it themselves under their farms' names.

The Franschhoek Co-op offers two ranges of its own wine, the first sold under the La Cotte label, the second under the regular co-op name. Among the La Cotte wines the Sémillon is one of the industry's best: Franschhoek is the heartland of old, well-established Sémillon vines and the co-op vinifies this yield beautifully. Sauvignon Blanc is also worth seeking out from the cellar: the fruit is never harsh, and the nose and taste reveal a satisfying harmony. Recently the La Cotte Cabernet has been particularly good, and its pricing reflects this more elevated status.

Over to the west of Paarl, almost against the Atlantic coastline, is the Swartland, home more to wheat farmers than to wine producers. The Swartland Co-op, however, crushes over 15 000 tons of grapes and collects more medals, prizes and trophies than cellars which can afford to handle their harvests in a more leisurely manner.

Much of the credit for Swartland's success is attributable to Neil Schnoor, who, though he has now left, spent a couple of years introducing systems into the production process, and method into the members' viticulture. In the past Swartland was regarded as an excellent source of Pinotage and Tinta Barocca: KWV Pinotage bottlings from the 1970s are sometimes still remarkably good. More recently, however, Cabernet and Cinsaut seem to be stealing the red wine limelight.

It is the white wines which now reflect the greatest progress: recent vintages of Sauvignon Blanc match the best in the Cape, and sell for a fraction of the price of competitor wines. The Colombard, especially in the year of production, is also superb value: jam-packed with fruit and beautifully balanced, it is also one of the country's finest. The co-op's Steen (Chenin Blanc) is in the same league: more easy fruit and drinking pleasure than many wines selling for double the price.

Swartland is one of a few co-ops which has actively chosen to market its wines outside the network of the wholesale producing merchants. A consequence of this decision is that the winemaker cannot feel assured of a ready market for bland wines which are easy to blend. This imposes a real discipline on the cellar to capture the fruit and flavour of the grapes in the bottled wines. So far, it seems, Swartland understands the formula.

North of Swartland, in the Olifants River region, is Citrusdal Co-op. Several good Tinta Baroccas warrant its inclusion on this list; likewise, a good Blanc de Blanc, an easy and uncomplicated Bukettraube, and a Pinotage Jerepigo – about which more in the section on fortified wines.

Even further north, and closer to the Atlantic ocean, is Vredendal, where the eponymously named co-op consistently surprises the wine fraternity. This is partly because Gielie Swiegers, the co-op's general manager, cannot resist publicity; but it is also because, in refusing to fit into the known industry stereotypes, he is innovative in a truly creative way.

Vredendal produced the first co-op Chardonnay, and its current production reflects the competence and familiarity which it now enjoys with the varietal. This north-western Cape winery (crushing over 50 000 tons of grapes annually) makes a typical New World style of wine, full, alcoholic, buttery and rich. Surprisingly, despite the warm climate, Vredendal also sells a creditable Sauvignon Blanc.

Over the mountain are several co-ops which have earned a deserved reputation for their wines. Du Toitskloof near Worcester, for example, offers an impressive selection of inexpensive good drinking whites, including a Chardonnay, a Cape Riesling, a Colombard and a Special Late Harvest.

Beyond Worcester off the Robertson road is Nuy, a co-op with only 21 members, and a very much hands-on approach to quality winemaking. Willem Linde, who has run the cellar for the past two decades, has collected a couple of Diners Club Winemaker of the Year Awards on the way.

Among the co-op's excellent value wines is the very popular Chant de Nuit blend of Colombard, Steen and Ferdinand de Lesseps. Also worth looking out for are the cellar's two Colombards (dry and semi-sweet), the award-winning Cape Riesling, and the Late Harvest Steen (Chenin Blanc). Nuy is also held in high regard for the quality of its fortified wines.

Further along the Worcester road towards Robertson is a trio of quality wine producers. Robertson Co-op makes an excellent Cabernet, light, very oaky, sweet vanilla mixed with berry fruit, and immediately accessible. It also sells a creditable Chardonnay and a very good Special Late Harvest.

The Roodezandt Co-op, under the guiding hand of Robbie Roberts, has also moved into deserved prominence. The Cabernet can sometimes repay a little cellaring, while the Red Housewine is good drinking value.

Rooiberg Co-op has long enjoyed a reputation for its white wines. Over the years Dassie Smith has made some of the Cape's most memorable Colombards, as well as good drinking Chenin Blanc, well-blended Blanc de Blanc and good-value Premier Grand Crû. Special releases worth seeking out include Chardonnay (wooded and unwooded), Noble Late Harvest, and a dry Chardonnay bubbly which is surprisingly inexpensive.

No note on co-op wines would be complete without a remark on the Barrydale Chardonnay. This Klein Karoo cellar, literally hundreds of kilometres east of the traditional quality wine areas, has produced several successive vintages of fine Chardonnay. The wine has concentration, balance, fruit, and a good layering of oak. The co-op may be too far off the beaten track for the casual cellar purchase, but on the strength of this performance alone, it is worth the annual flutter of a few cases sent by rail.

It is not always easy to pick up co-op wines for cellaring. Since most of the wineries are dependent on the custom of the wholesale merchants for their bulk sales, they are the victims of a Mafia-like pressure not to market their wines to the public through the retail trade. Understandably the big wholesalers do not want their suppliers running a parallel trade directly to their customers.

Threats of outright boycott have kept most of the co-ops in the wholesaler fold. Those who chose to break rank, however, have done very well: the market polarised along a line which left those willing to deal with retailers more than enough custom for their stocks.

The co-ops still committed to supplying the wholesale merchants only bottle a small percentage of their harvest. Their wines are generally not available in bottlestores. Many are willing to rail case lots to private homes, although transport can become a significant cost factor. One of the ways of controlling this is to consolidate orders so that the minimum dispatch from each cellar is five cases. Ten cases and more become quite economical. Up-country wine drinkers who want to keep their co-op purchases cheap enough to qualify as their daily tipple must add bulk buying and bulk transportation arrangements to all their other wine buying attributes.

FORTIFIED WINES
✍ ❧

Although the Cape's fine wine industry is today associated with natural wines like Cabernet and Chardonnay, earlier this century fortified wine formed the backbone of the trade. In part this was a result of an excise structure inherited from Britain: the impost demanded by the state for the higher-alcohol fortified wines was proportionately less onerous to the consumer seeking out the most efficient source of inebriation. More importantly, however, fortified wines require less cellar technology, and flourish in warmer climates. It was therefore easier to make Muscadels and Jerepigos in the days before cold fermentation, and consumers were more likely to get a quality fortified from any of the many producers, than a good dry white wine.

Circumstances affect tastes and fashions, and also alter them. The trend to drier, lighter wines is fairly recent, and would not have been possible (at least not to the same extent) had cold fermentation, cold stabilisation and sterile bottling not become the norm.

The decline of the fortified wine market over the past two decades is a matter of record. The number of people who now drink Brown Sherry or Jerepigo as their daily tipple is vastly less than in the 1960s. Since the bulk of the market resided with this kind of consumer, any increase in quality Port or Muscadel consumption is likely to be off-set by the losses at the lower end of the spectrum.

The dedication which went into fortified wine production in the earlier part of this century has ensured that the residual knowledge now harnessed to make Sherry, Port and Jerepigo is considerable. There are also reserve stocks of older wines in the major producers' cellars. This means that the promotion of quality fortifieds can proceed in the presence of mature wines, justifying, in the mind of a new convert, the investment in laying down the wine.

Broadly speaking, the quality fortified wine industry today divides into three categories: Sherry (or Sherry-type wines); Port (or Port-type wines); and Jerepigos made by fortifying one or more of a number of varietals soon after the fermentation has begun.

EC regulations have now made it increasingly difficult for South African producers of Port and Sherry to label their wines as such. Port, so it is argued, is an appellation specific to the Douro Valley in Portugal, and Sherry to the town of Jerez de la Frontera in Spain. Nevertheless these generic terms best describe much of South Africa's quality production.

The Cape is one of the few wine growing regions in the world where the sherry yeast, or flor, occurs naturally. However, as with most other producers, the casks are now 'seeded' with flor produced under laboratory conditions. The best Cape Sherries compare favourably with those of Spain. These wines are sold as branded lines, from cellars such as the KWV, Drostdy, Bertrams and Monis.

Ports, on the other hand, are much more artisanal. The country's best production comes from the estates and private wineries. Much of what is sold as Port is really red dessert wine, a Jerepigo made from Tinta Barocca, Cinsaut and even Red Muscadel. These are often too sweet, and would not pass for Douro wine even to an amateur taster.

Allesverloren in the Swartland was one of the first estates to acquire a reputation for the quality of its vintage Port. Made from Tinta Barocca blended with a little Souzão (which also enhances the richness of its colour), the Allesverloren has rich, mineral flavours, and ages in bottle, gaining in nutty intensity over the years. Blaauwklippen in Stellenbosch has also produced several good Port-type wines, though the varietals used give the wine more of a New World flavour.

Boplaas, in the Klein Karoo, has acquired almost legendary status for its vintage-style wines. Since the remarkable 1986 vintage (the Reserve wine is sold at the annual auction of the Cape Independent Winemakers' Guild) Boplaas has laid claim to the front slot in the local Port industry. The estate sells a percentage of the crop forward on to a futures/options market, underwriting the buy-back price and hence guaranteeing a minimum return. Part of the promotion includes a remark made by one of the Symingtons of Grahams (with whom Boplaas has reciprocal arrangements) to the effect that this Klein Karoo estate makes the best of the New World Ports.

There is no doubt that Boplaas is right in the front rank of the local producers. Its best wines compare in style with the drier, more intense character of Portuguese vintage Port. The regular estate production is passably good, slightly plummy, fortified and red. It is as good as an aperitif, or after dinner, as many such wines, but it travels on the reputation of the farm's top reserves. Neighbouring Die Krans is not quite in the same league, though current vintages show that the Portuguese style is infectious, at least in Calitzdorp.

Landskroon Estate in Paarl has always made creditable Ports, and the latest vintages are fuller, deeper and nuttier than the wines from earlier in the 1980s. I recall that the De Villiers family used to fortify their Port with mature brandy, and not with harsh wine eau-de-vie. Landskroon Port is dryish and contains only classical Portuguese varieties.

L'Ormarins Estate is also acquiring a striking reputation for its young Ports. To my knowledge none has been released, and I have not had the opportunity of tasting the wines still maturing in the cellars. By all accounts, these are tasty and full-flavoured and will be worth laying down.

Mooiuitsig, a small Bonnievale wholesaler, consistently produces a good, well-aged Port, sometimes a little raisiny on the nose but well-integrated and not overly sweet. Muratie in Stellenbosch also makes a creditable wine, richly coloured and quite fragrant.

Overgaauw Estate, also in Stellenbosch, has been a leading producer for most of the last two decades. Its vineyard of classic Port varietals goes back to the 1950s and the wines which have been allowed to age develop that delicate 'deadleaf' character reminiscent of the vintage wines from the Douro.

Finally, among the estate and private producers, Rustenberg stands out. Its wine is deep, rich and intense, often slightly 'dumb' in its youth, but opening up well after about six years. Not always available from the farm, it is sold at the annual auction of the Cape Independent Winemakers' Guild.

The Cape's Jerepigos, Muscadels and Hanepoots could easily fill a section of their own. There are literally hundreds of them and they form part of a forgotten tradition of great fortified wines. The world speaks of Madeiras and Malagas with reverence, but consumes less and less of them. The same fate has befallen the Cape's great dessert wines. Everyone says how good they are, but very few serious wine drinkers keep stocks of them in their cellars.

This may in part be the result of the shift to lighter wine drinking: less sugar and less alcohol have become more than a fashion, almost a way of life. The result is that people no longer think about how to use these often great wines, and instead dispense with them entirely. In doing so they deprive themselves of access to world-class products, many of which sell at bargain prices. The KWV, for example, offers twenty and thirty year old Jerepigos for about the same price as a good young Cabernet blend.

These fortified wines can be used as aperitifs, they can

accompany the starter, they are frequently the ideal complement to cheese, they do sterling service alongside most
desserts and can be taken after dinner as digestives. They are
made with a wide choice of varietals, including red and white
Muscadel, Muscat de Frontignan, Muscat d'Alexandrie,
Muscat de Hambourg, even Pinotage and Chenin Blanc.
Often they are blended together and sold under the generic
name of Jerepigo or Jerepiko. They age indefinitely on
account of the sugar and the alcohol. Those that are well balanced, with enough acidity to support the fruit, improve for
many years in the bottle, and frequently only show at their
best after thirty or forty years. Nowhere in the world of wine
is this kind of product made with such expertise and sold for
so little.

A quick review of the best production of the industry may
read a little like a shopping list to dozens of the Cape's cellars. The simple truth is that it is difficult to buy these wines
badly. So much of what is available is good that all it takes is
a little adventurous spending for the virtues of Jerepigo to
lead to addiction.

Ashton Co-op in Robertson is a reliable producer, particularly of Red Muscadel; Badsberg Co-op does a superb
Hanepoot. Bon Courage Estate consistently produces champion quality wines and the Boplaas non-Port fortifieds are
wines deservedly in the same league – especially the Bona-
parte Red (sold usually at the Guild auction). Citrusdal has
made a splendid Jerepigo from Pinotage – a wine of such
intensity and cassis-like character that it defies description.
De Leuwen Jacht's Red Muscadels are both completely different and excellent.

Die Krans Estate keeps turning out superb white Jerepigos, as does another Klein Karoo producer, Domein Doornkraal. Du Toitskloof Co-op is another quality Jerepigo cellar,
as is Goudini Co-op, a frequent trophy winner at the national
wineshow.

Helderberg Co-op does a very good Jerepigo from Chenin Blanc (and often an excellent Port). Jonkheer's dessert wines are good, and inexpensive, and so are the Muscadels and Jerepigos at the Kango Co-op in the Klein Karoo.

The KWV's range deserves special mention. My first choice is the 1953 Jerepigo which was available well into the 1980s and cost a fraction of the price of a comparable Madeira. All the older Muscadels and Hanepoots released by the KWV are worth tracking down: I cannot recall ever being disappointed.

Mons Ruber in the Klein Karoo is another producer of quality fortifieds, while the Mont Blois estate in Robertson turns out a spectacular White Muscadel. Mooiuitsig's Jerepigos are consistently good; Nuy's Muscadels have brought the Diners Club Award to the cellar (the co-op recorded first and second positions at the taste-off for the best Muscadel in the country).

The Rietvallei Red Muscadel is one of the Cape's most complex and intense fortified wines, easy to find and well worth cellaring. Robertson Co-op's Muscadel is another front-ranker, while neighbour Roodezandt regularly yields wines in the same league. Up the road at the Rooiberg Co-op there is an equally impressive array of fortifieds, with both the Red and White Muscadels real benchmark wines. Simonsvlei Co-op collects medals for its fortifieds, so does Spruitdrift Co-op, whose Hanepoot is one of the Cape's best.

Vredendal in the Olifants River region has produced enough good Jerepigo to qualify for inclusion on this list, so has the Waboomsrivier Co-op. The Weltevrede Estate in Bonnievale bottles so much good Muscadel that it is difficult to single out any (though I have a special regard for the 1986 Oupa se Wingerd, produced from a vineyard that was planted in the 1920s and has since been grubbed out).

This list is certainly not complete, nor are all the wines readily available from the local off-licence. Average quality, however, is impressive. More than any other style of wine, Jerepigo/Muscadel is a real achievement of the Cape, and the good wines are worth seeking out.

THE FUTURE OF THE
CAPE WINE INDUSTRY

🙠 🙢

The changing face of the Cape winelands during the 20th century makes any attempt to chart the future a matter of educated guesswork. During the lifetime of some of the country's great wine personalities production has changed from fortified wine to sweet wine, from high yielding German-style whites to premium French-style reds. In the last thirty years open concrete fermenters have been replaced with stainless steel. Now in the boutique establishments small oak barrels have begun to usurp these tanks. Outside the bulk grape growing areas Cabernet, Sauvignon Blanc, Chardonnay and Merlot have made real inroads into the plantings of Cinsaut and Clairette Blanche. Within the premium production regions independent growers and private estates selling wine under their own labels have doubled in number since the estate wine law was introduced less than twenty years ago.

Over the same period of time the KWV has shifted in focus: initially the united front of the grape growers in their collective bargaining with the country's wholesale producing merchants, it has become instead a bridgehead in both camps with a sometimes tenuous superstructure linking the two sides. The big brand owners dominate the cashflow of the entire industry, setting the prices and payment terms to the producers from whom they buy their raw material, as well as to the licensees who purchase from them. Legally imposed limitations on the ownership of retail chains has emasculated this sector of the industry, undermining consumer impact on price negotiations. The result is that wine prices have risen ahead of competing alcoholic beverages like beer, leading to stagnation in the domestic market. In the process of attrition which has ensued, smaller wine farms, several co-ops, regional wholesalers and retail licensees have closed shop, amalgamated, sold out to the bigger players or simply gone to the wall. Those of the small operators who survive have sharpened their skills; those who have gained strength through consolidations and mergers now have the critical mass necessary to trade in this environment.

The Cape's international presence declined over the course of this century. As a member of the Commonwealth, South Africa traded through London until the Republic was declared in 1961. From then onwards the imposition of apartheid policies and the increasing isolation sought by both the Nationalist government and its international opposition reduced the exportability of Cape wines, culminating in the real sanctions era of 1986 to 1990. The winds of change which have blown along the corridors of power in South Africa have been felt as a fresh breeze in the vineyards, bringing the prospect of new export markets just as the decline in local demand occasions a great deal of concern.

What does the immediate future hold for an industry so buffeted by change that what is real today seemed inconceivable years rather than decades ago? Will the recent abolition of the quota system undermine or entrench the KWV? Will an export boom strengthen the primary producers, will freer licensing laws breed greater diversity of product? Who will bear the cost of the upgrading programme that has changed the face of the Cape's vineyards and modernised so many cellars? How can wine producers deal with the country's endemic problem of inflation and how can this be built into the price of mature wine without alienating potential buyers?

Grape growers (rather than estate wine producers) will

become increasingly dependent on those few remaining organisations able to process and dispose of their crop. Those who have the *terroir* and the courage to build cellars and vinify their harvests will be obliged to sell wine in a local market unlikely to show real growth for many years, or in an export market where price sensitivities will militate against the quality of their income. Those who remain in the grape business will have to encourage their cooperative either to trade in competition with the wholesale merchants (either via exports or directly to domestic consumers) or to establish more secure contracts with their bulk customers. Some of those who break rank and offer their wines directly to the market will certainly succeed. Price rather than branding seems to be an increasingly important issue on the local and the international markets and primary producers with quality production facilities will be able to operate an effective parallel trade against the wholesale merchants. This in turn will undermine the volume trade of the national wholesalers, increasing their cost per case handled and loading a further premium to their medium and de luxe wine ranges. Those who go it alone and fail will be forced to deal on the best terms possible with their erstwhile customers: as long as the KWV can export grape juice concentrate profitably and in increasing volumes they may survive, but they will not flourish.

Those who obtain reasonable supply contracts with the wholesale merchants will have postponed for a time their day of reckoning. However, the inevitable decline of merchants' low-priced brands will force a rethink of this whole sector of the market: wines will either have to satisfy a price critical category (which can never be very profitable to the growers) or there will have to be a significant upgrade in quality. This change in focus will certainly polarise the growers who remain with the merchants. The wholesalers will respond to declining low-priced wine sales by making their wines more price competitive and by following the KWV's export example at the lower end of the market. Only the super-efficient growers will continue to trade with them under these circumstances. The remainder may have to consider grubbing up their vines and planting fruit trees.

The estate cellars will have to cope with an influx of competitors as growers who previously supplied co-ops and wholesale merchants abandon the roller-coaster before the ride produces a crop of casualties. Those whose planting programme best reads the needs of the market will flourish, providing they can achieve international levels of productivity. South Africa's estate wines will ultimately have to face calibration in export markets. Those who are seen to be delivering value in this context will obviously succeed in terms of sales; whether they are profitable will depend more than ever on cost control.

Some will supply the vacuum left by the decline of the brand market. They will be the beneficiaries of the 'drink less but drink better' trend. While some of their custom may come from those who read the image rather than appreciate the taste, increasing wine knowledge and serious long-term economic constraints will limit the prospects of those who mean to survive on puffery. The days of limitless discretionary income among South Africa's wine-drinking bourgeoisie are limited, at least in the immediate future.

The estate wine producers will try to recover margin from cutting out the middlemen of the distribution and retail trade. This in turn will thin out both these sectors, the former much more than the latter. Retailers will still have a full cabinet of liquor to sell, but the wholesale distributors will feel the loss of product from an already limited range. The survivors will band together, fixing the price for the service they offer. This in turn will reduce the producers' freedom of choice. The delicate balance which will ensue may satisfy a few, and tolerate many, but in the end it will breed casualties, estates which will have become victims of the tendency to monopoly in the South African economy.

The retail trade may survive the changes in the production and wholesale sectors, but it is likely to have problems enough of its own. The policy of limiting the number of stores in a retail chain has ensured that the politically dominant wholesale merchants control the high ground of the industry. Unlike the grocery business where the supermarket chains are able to offer a counterveiling negotiating power in dealing with the major producers, the liquor industry has been stripped of the right to fight against wholesaler domination. To compound matters, the government has taken to granting retail licences on so liberal a basis that the sector has already become over-traded. On its own, there is no real harm in this, except for the breach of the undertaking of exclusivity implicit in the original grant of the licences.

However, it is only a matter of time before food outlets will be authorised to sell beer, thus eliminating many retailers for whom the country's biggest-selling alcoholic beverage is more than a matter of bread-and-butter. Faced with a crisis of these proportions, the retail sector will polarise: high volume traders will survive on low margins and the widest possible range of goods. Specialist outlets will seek niche positioning and wine is likely to be an important product in their survival strategy, if only because it takes some expertise in stocking and some skill in selling. It is also likely to survive the depredations of the anti-alcohol lobby for longer, given its low-alcohol, civilised-beverage status.

With all these changes, what is likely to happen to the KWV? Will it retain all the powers it enjoyed in the heyday of its alliance with the Nationalist government? Politically adept as its managers may be, they are unlikely to acquire an equivalent relationship with the rulers of the so-called new South Africa. Their willingness to throw out the quota system ahead of an interim government suggests that they know that the organisation must acquire a less protectionist image. Giving up the right to control where and what tonnage of grapes may be grown is a highly visible concession, albeit one which still leaves the KWV's real powers intact.

The organisation's diminishing access to government is likely to leave wine relatively less protected, compared with other beverages. Excise will become a cost factor as wine's privileged status *vis-à-vis* beer comes to an end. The KWV's partners in the wholesale producing sector will probably also see their 'connections' reduced in this process and their absolute domination of the industry is bound to acquire limitations.

Any new government will probably see the virtue in keeping the KWV in some industry-managerial capacity: disposal of surplus, distillation and brandy ageing, the production and export of grape juice concentrate, all require the aptitudes and experience of the organisation's present management. However, some separation between the KWV's commercial and administrative roles could be imposed. In this event, the quality of performance of both functions might improve: without the current conflict of interest the KWV would do a better job across the full range of its activities.

What sort of wines await the quality wine drinker over the next decade? Undoubtedly better and certainly, on average, less expensive. Whatever the attrition in the farming sector, there will be more than enough grapes, mostly from properly established vineyards which were renewed from the mid 1980s onwards. Quality varietals, healthy clonal material, thorough soil preparation all mean better grapes in the cellars. Greater experience in techniques such as barrel fermentation and wood ageing will yield further improvements in the wines. The pressures of an open, internationally calibrated trading environment will encourage efficiency and discipline prices. The extremists may still enjoy a following, but the centre of gravity of the fine wine trade will reveal better quality at better prices.

What can go wrong? Quite a lot if the country's new rulers decide to rebuke the industry for the undue privilege it has enjoyed until now: excessive taxation, or an unrealistic method of assessing the value of unsold stocks, will discourage farsighted planning and chase away businessmen who see wine as a profitable industry, rather than as a hobby. Great wine will only be produced by those who can anticipate a worthwhile return on a very long term investment. Given the achievement of the last decade, it would be a great sadness if the dark ages descended again on the quality wine industry of the Cape.

SELECTED INDEX